05/07

Linguistic Conflict and Language Laws

Linguistic Conflict and Language Laws

Understanding the Quebec Question

Edited by

Pierre Larrivée

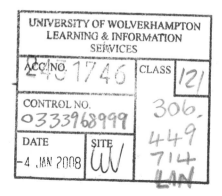

macmillan

Published by
PALGRAVE MACMILLAN
Houndmills, Basingstoke, Hampshire RG21 6XS and
175 Fifth Avenue, New York, N. Y. 10010
Companies and representatives throughout the world

PALGRAVE MACMILLAN is the global academic imprint of the Palgrave Macmillan division of St. Martin's Press, LLC and of Palgrave Macmillan Ltd. Macmillan® is a registered trademark in the United States, United Kingdom and other countries. Palgrave is a registered trademark in the European Union and other countries.

ISBN-13: 978–0–333–96899–4 hardback
ISBN-10: 0–333–96899–9 hardback

This book is printed on paper suitable for recycling and made from fully managed and sustained forest sources.

A catalogue record for this book is available from the British Library.

Library of Congress Catalog Card Number: 2002026757

Printed and bound in Great Britain by
Antony Rowe Ltd, Eastbourne

Contents

Acknowledgements

We are grateful to the following for permission to reproduce the tables in Chapter 1: Oxford University Press, for Table 8, from *Linguistic Imperialism*, © R. L. H. Phillipson 1992.

Multilingual Matters, for Tables 3 and 4, reproduced from Kaplan and Baldauf, *Language Planning: Theory and Practice* (1997); and Table 5, from *The Other Languages of Europe*, © G. Extra and D. Gorter (eds) 2001; and for Tables 6 and 7, reproduced from *Foundations of Bilingual Education and Bilingualism*, © Colin Baker 1996.

Every effort has been made to contact copyright holders but in the event that any have been inadvertently overlooked, the author and publisher will be pleased to make the necessary arrangements at the earliest opportunity.

Notes on the Contributors

Marc Chevrier is Assistant Professor of Political Science at Université du Québec at Montreal. He is also the editor of the journal and encyclopedia *L'Agora*. As a jurist and political scientist specialising in the philosophical foundations of constitutional systems, he has published many articles and essays on the politics, law and culture of Quebec and of Canada.

Pierre Larrivée is Lecturer in French Linguistics at Aston University, Birmingham. Specialising in the construction of meaning through language, he has published one monograph (*L'interprétation des séquences négatives*, 2001), several collective works and nearly fifty papers in linguistic semantics.

C. Michael MacMillan is Professor of Political Studies at Mount Saint Vincent University, Halifax, and a specialist in the Canadian politics of language. He has published a number of articles on human rights, language rights and language policy, and his book *The Practice of Language Rights in Canada* (1998) was short-listed for the Donner Prize for the best book on Canadian public policy.

Jean-Philippe Warren is Assistant Professor of Sociology at Concordia University in Montreal. His research concerns the organisation of North American Francophone groups: he has written a major study of the prominent Quebec sociologist Fernand Dumont (*Un supplément d'âme*, 1998) and a second monograph on the tradition of Quebec sociology (forthcoming).

Colin H. Williams is Research Professor at Cardiff University in the Department of Welsh, Adjunct Professor of Geography at the University of Western Ontario and a member of the Welsh Language Board and several European agencies concerned with issues of identity, language and social justice. Among his books are *Called unto Liberty* (1994), and the edited volumes *Linguistic Minorities, Society and Territory* (1991) and *Language Revitalization: Policy and Planning in Wales* (2000).

Introduction

Pierre Larrivée

The idea for this book began to form while I was living Birmingham, to which I had emigrated a couple of years before from Quebec City. British students, colleagues and the informed general population seemed to have a surprising amount of interest and sympathy towards Quebec, and much curiosity about the language situation and language laws there. Through various discussions, however, I came to realise that there were very few resources to which I could point my interlocutors on what is arguably the best-known case of language planning in the western world. Although there were some papers in scholarly journals and administrative publications, there was no recent, accessible, self-contained work that would present to a wider academic and general audience the Quebec language question. Although one hears of the linguistic situation in the press from time to time, the reports are often partial, one-sided snapshots; for which they cannot entirely be blamed, since it is not their purpose, any more than that of pamphlets for instance, to spell out objectively the views of the different linguistic groups in Quebec, and to answer the question of why the linguistic legislations came into being in the first place.

The objective of this book is to tell the story behind the existence of the linguistic legislations in Quebec. Language laws and language conflicts do not come out of the blue. They are shaped by history, they are influenced by demographic, economic and political factors, and they reflect cultural values and concerns.

The general issue of language planning is presented in Chapter 1. As a common action that characterises all human groups, language planning may concern any aspects of the social realm, including education, public services, work and commercial life. It can target aspects of languages themselves or the circumstances in which a language can be used, and takes a variety of implicit or explicit forms. These questions are articulated by Colin Williams. Chapter 2 discusses the turning points of the historical development of Quebec society. With the 1759 Conquest by the British Crown of what had been for a century and a half a French colony, each of the two French- and English-speaking communities had to ensure appropriate relations with the other group while promoting its own interests under various demographic, economic and political pressures. The tensions created by these conflicting necessities and their solutions at various times up to the present are defined by Jean-Philippe Warren.

Chapters 3 and 4 offer a thorough analysis of Canadian and Québécois linguistic laws. Michael MacMillan provides a comprehensive political discussion of the federal linguistic laws, how they have been informed by Quebec's concerns and how they impacted upon provincial legislation. He proposes that the Canadian measures of formal bilingualism have not significantly hindered the progression of French in Quebec, that it enjoys the support of the general population of that province while giving a legal basis for French-speaking communities outside Quebec to obtain, through litigation, a basic level of services in their language. As such, the federal and provincial laws are compatible, and should both be maintained, since the abrogation of federal legislation could be detrimental to Canadian political order.

Marc Chevrier gives a detailed account of the language legislation of Quebec. The disadvantaged economic and demographic position of Francophones in Canada encouraged successive Quebec governments over the last thirty years to assert the pre-eminence of French in the life of the province through Bill 63, Bill 22 and, most importantly, Bill 101, the French Language Charter. Because the objectives of the federal language policies are contrary to those of the Quebec instruments, the two series of legislation are seen to be incompatible. The provincial legislation should therefore become the unique linguistic reference within Quebec, in order to guarantee the position of French culture in its main homeland in the Americas.

Chapter 5 considers the public discourse on the French Language Charter developed by Quebec Anglophones. This minority group has, indeed, demonstrated a sustained negative reaction to the law. The public debate cannot, however, be explained by reference to factual elements of the linguistic laws or the community's subsequent material situation. It must instead be analysed as a strategy aimed at trying to maintain the dominant situation of the group, especially in the Montreal area where the demographic weight and economic importance of the community is most significant.

Finally, Chapter 6 brings together the questions of history, power and culture. Drawing a parallel with the example of the various Quebec Native Nations, this essay concludes by proposing that language laws are one medium that can ensure that the speakers of minority languages have a space within which they can participate fully in contemporary societies, not only to the cultural but also to the concrete economic benefits of all.

Putting this book together was an exciting adventure filled with all manner of twists and turns. The journey and the final destination would have been quite different but for the help of a number of people experienced at reading maps, repairing engines and knowing the right addresses. Among many other people, I would like to express my warmest thanks to Dennis Ager, André Bourcier, Richard Bourhis, Denise Deshaies, Louis-Jacques Dorais, John Gaffney, Guy Lachapelle, François Matte, Jacques Maurais, Georgios Varouxakis, Lynne Wilcox and José Woehrling for their enlightening comments all along the way; I am grateful to Claire Blanche-Benveniste, Ivan Evrard and Lene Schoesler for the input that they unsuspectingly had on the project by sharing with me their views on the topic in a Bucharest restaurant; my sincere thanks go to the anonymous reviewers involved towards the beginning and the end of the journey. I wish to acknowledge the indefatigable support of Emmanuel Kattan, the public affairs *attaché* at the Quebec House in London, who never tired of providing me with hints, leads and addresses; of Robert Laliberté and the *Association Internationale des Etudes Québécoises* for their exceptional encouragement both monetary and intellectual; of Jill Lake and her team at Palgrave for their expert professionalism that helped to smooth out the rocky bits of the ride. Above all, I would like to express my gratitude to the contributors. Not only were they probably the best designated drivers one could expect for the territories to be explored, they were also patient passengers, respecting various ground rules, showing gracious patience even when it seemed that we were going round in circles. To have the opportunity to publish their work here is, for me, both a lesson in humility and a subject of pride.

The story that we are about to tell is that of the patient and courageous discussion between conflicting values and cultures. If I were to dedicate this book, it would be to the spirit of all the actors of this story, past and present, famous and nameless, who showed an unflinching commitment to reconciling differences.

1
Language Policy and Planning Issues in Multicultural Societies
Colin H. Williams

State–civil society relations

Issues of language choice and behaviour are integral to the social, economic and political stability of multicultural societies. This chapter explores the role of language policy and planning as instruments of social development and examines selected dilemmas faced by multilingual states as they seek to formalise language choice through a variety of implicit and explicit language-related reforms. It is my conviction that although the Québécois material discussed in this volume is of great significance, it can only be properly understood when set alongside other examples of language planning as a form of socio-political intervention. Many take the view that language planning, as a discipline, has developed a certain objective detachment that allows it to be treated as if it were a form of scientific exercise. I accept that in certain aspects, such as corpus planning, translation and software development, such objectivity and precision is reached. However, language planning is in essence an extension of social policy aimed at behaviour modification. Given this, it is essential that the broader social and political context, within which language planning is exercised, be fully acknowledged. Consequently the first part of this chapter discusses the various implications of recognising some languages at the expense of others within liberal democratic practices. It then suggests comparisons between the European and African experiences of language planning, before focusing on power differentials between hegemonic language groups and dependent language groups.

As one of the chief components of group identity and the means by which the ideas and techniques of social development are diffused, language has become one of the most sensitive issues of the contemporary world. It is estimated that some 6,170 living languages (Mackey, 1991, p. 51), exclusive of dialects, are contained within the 187 or so sovereign states, and if we admit dependencies and semi-autonomous polities, the number rises to *c.* 200. Consequently there is a lack of congruence between the international political system and the cultural inheritance of its constituent citizens. This suggests that there will be a near-permanent crisis involving attempts to maintain linguistic diversity in the face of increasing linguistic standardisation in many parts of the world. Often language issues are an overarching mobilising factor within which other issues are pursued. Language-related tensions thus exacerbate normal socio-political strains. It follows that a sovereign state's language policy can be a key determinant of the degree to which political unity and the rate of economic 'development' are achieved. If a language policy is harmonious and effective, it releases collective energies into other more profitable avenues. If, on the other hand, it is authoritarian, divisive and dysfunctional, it can lead to alienation, pressures for regional separatism and ultimately to civil war or disintegration.

The multilingual character of most societies necessitates choices in communication at all levels from the individual to the state. Choice also implies conflict and tension, for one person's choice is another person's denial of opportunity; such is the competitive nature of languages in contact. The situation is complicated in many contexts because international migration and colonialism have introduced a new range of intrusive languages of wider communication (LWC), whose presence both challenge the indigenous languages and have a profound influence on the nature of the process of global development.

The state is central to any analysis of the impact of language policies on multicultural societies as the incorporation of ethnically differentiated territories has been a necessary precursor to the creation of the territorial-bureaucratic state. Normally incorporation strengthens central rather than local interests, and serves to threaten the material and spiritual sustenance that ethnic groups derive from the immediate locale. In consequence, patterns of state integration and development are often over-centralised, without corresponding attention to the needs of the 'periphery'; except, of course, the need to integrate it politically and strategically. This has led to charges of core discrimination, peripheral marginalisation and the denial of group rights and cultural reproduction. For some this is a necessary product of global development. But should the price of economic and bureaucratic incorporation into the mainstream involve the denial of distinctiveness? Must we, perforce, sacrifice cultural autonomy for political–economic advancement in multicultural societies? For far too many subject peoples, state-integration has resulted in the conquest of ethnic territory, the denial of popular rights, and the external development of their ethnic homeland. Whether through forced out-migration as a result of land enclosure (such as Scotland in the eighteenth-century clearances, or apartheid in South Africa after 1948), of famine (Ireland in the 1840s, Sudan in 1980–94, and Ethiopia in 1984–94), of resource exploitation (Maoris or Canada's First Nations and Inuit), rapid industrialisation (Euskadi in the late nineteenth century), most ethno-linguistic minority groups perceive their territory as having been under threat in modern history.

Because institutional means of dissent are denied them, subject peoples invariably focus on cultural diacritical markers, such as language or religion, as a means of asserting their own separateness and demonstrating their resistance to external state and commercial incursions into their territory. If we accept that most ethno-linguistic groups are relatively underdeveloped economically and politically, it is clear that questions of language, culture and identity are not merely supplementary to the more routinised socio-economic concerns of development. They can constitute the very essence of a subordinated group's relationship with the state in whose name the dominant group exercise power and control. As group identity and power differentials are rooted in their environment and expressed through material acts of construction or change, it is not surprising that any threat to the immediate territory of a subordinated group is interpreted as a challenge to culture and group survival. Place, boundaries and territory are critical in the process of control and development and their appropriation by external agencies has a long history related to the extension of state hegemony and strategic, capital projects of 'state-building' and 'nation-formation' which are essentially contestations over space.

The principle of equal recognition in liberal democracies

By the late twentieth century our conception of the rights of subjects and citizens had evolved to the extent that the principle of *freedom from* state direction or oppression in religious or linguistic matters had given way to a demand for *freedom to* be represented on the basis of equality within society as the determining essence of the participative state. Nowhere are these rights so fiercely conjoined and attacked than in the question of ethno-linguistic identities in the modern state. How to promote the mutual respect of individuals as they identify with particular social groups is a key challenge facing language policy.

The new politics of recognition is a belated attempt to compensate for the systematic exclusion of groups from the decision-making structures of society. Previous attempts to specify the rights and obligations of minority cultures often presumed that no permanent change would result from such reforms. A basic tenet of liberal democracy was that legislation to clarify the meaning of minority rights would not overly interfere with mainstream political business and economic development. But the current transition from representative democracy to participatory democracy, at least within parts of the European Union, requires the decoupling of the state majority from its hegemonic position (Habermas, 1996, p. 289). The framers of the European experiment must search for a binding substitute for the initial state nationalism which determined the process of nation-building.

Our conceptions of human rights have been formulated in an increasingly comprehensive manner to include elements which earlier theorists would have considered to have lain outside the proper remit of the citizen–state relationship. This relationship is central to the analysis since liberal democracy avers that citizens are entitled to certain minimum rights, chiefly those of participation in and protection by the state. However, the changing nature of the state, both as ideology and praxis, has encouraged a more pluralist view of its responsibilities.

The conventional, individual rights approach is that the state should not discriminate against or in favour of particular sub-groups, however they may be defined. This is justified by majoritarian principles of equality of all before the law, and is implemented through legislation enabling equal opportunity for socio-economic advancement to be based upon merit and application. The fact that many states persistently discriminated, by law, against Jews/Catholics/Protestants/Romanys in most multi-faith societies should never be marginalised in this discussion, for so often the state has exercised a malignant effect upon minorities, thereby blighting their historical development. Even when individual rights regimes have been extended to cover the interests of national minorities, they are rarely satisfied with such provision. Kymlicka (2001) cites three contentious issues: decisions about internal migration/settlement policies, decisions about the boundaries and powers of internal political units, and decisions about official languages. The partial improvement in the treatment of minorities and the resultant constructive dialogue between representatives of the various interest groups and governmental agencies at all levels in the political hierarchy of Canada and Western Europe offers a more realistic basis for the future enactment of minority rights.

Alternatively, the group rights approach, favoured of late, recognises that there are permanent entities within society whose potential and expectations cannot be met by reference to the recognition of individual rights alone. Such recognition is offered grudgingly, and reflects a minimalist stance which seeks to extend the individual rights tradition into a multicultural context. Such extensions tend to obscure the key issue of group tension, namely the ability of the minority to preserve, and if possible, develop its own group characteristics and desires, in the face of state inspired assimilation (Williams, 1989, 2000). Eisenberg (1998) illustrates from the Canadian North how the debate over Aboriginal rights have been distorted by the construction of a dualism between Western 'individualism' and Aboriginal 'collectivism'. By framing the debate thus, the real issue is masked, namely the ongoing effects of political subordination through colonisation, that is the majority's unilateral attempts to undermine the minority's institutions and powers of self-government (cited in Kymlicka, 2001, p. 77).

Three sorts of argument are posed to counter the 'special pleading' of constituent differentiated groups in the contemporary world (Williams, 1993a, p. 95). The first argues that the democratic state has a duty to treat its citizens equally, regardless of racial, national, ethnic or linguistic origin. Vaclav Hável (1991) maintains that minorities should not need 'extra rights' if the democratic guarantees are in place, an understandable interpretation in the Czech political context which stresses the role of the reforming state as the guarantor of individual freedoms. The second argument, heard most forcibly in the USA and France, is that minorities should meld over time into mainstream society.[1] But the greater recognition of the worth of constituent cultures, as *permanent* entities in society, is precisely what is at stake for those engaged in the politics of their group's survival within liberal democracies. When liberal democracy refuses to engage in the politics of recognition, it appears arrogant and denies the life-enhancing spirit upon which all forms of democracy are based. It accentuates societal fragmentation and anomie, ultimately leading to various forms of disengagement from public life and community responsibility. For 'democratic citizenship develops its force of social integration, that is to say it generates solidarity between strangers, if it can be recognised and appreciated as the very mechanism by which the legal and material infra-structure of actually preferred forms of life is secured' (Habermas, 1996, p. 290).

The third argument suggest that collective rights or community rights are difficult to articulate in constitutional–legal terms, which leads to obfuscation over both the target language and the defined holders of such rights. As we shall see in Chapter 4, if the protection of French in Quebec belongs to a collectivity, which is it? The francophone Quebecers, the population as a whole or the State of Quebec represented by the Attorney-General? Marc Chevrier teases out these relationships and navigates between conflicting impulses to protect, proscribe and encourage via legislation and marketing campaigns in Quebec.

The integrative challenge is in maintaining the active participation of all citizens in the resultant political process. It is tempting for many citizens to yield responsibility and to opt out of formal politics and to opt in to informal pressure groups or single-issue movements, leaving proponents of the community drained of their energies to mobilise and agitate on behalf of all. A concern for an active participatory democracy is surely relevant in most developed societies, where talk of 'the hollow state' and of 'the democratic deficit' reveal the shallowness of the general public's trust in professional politicians (Williams, 1994).

There is also an urgency to establish democratic credentials in the more 'liberal' post-communist societies after forty or so years of state totalitarianism. But the pristine democratic principles of co-equality, of majoritarian tolerance, of freedom under the law to reproduce individual or collective identity, have not necessarily guaranteed nor satisfied minority aspirations in Western European societies. In Central and Eastern Europe there is even less consensus about the nature of mass society, let alone the legitimacy of selected minorities in multi-ethnic societies. Social justice is not necessarily served by a compliant reliance upon a constitutional majority, whether it acts in a benign manner or otherwise. Indeed the contemporary situation in Eastern Europe is enigmatic, for many previously warring factions seem to be converging on a notion of a new conformity, which threatens to be every bit as stultifying as the old system, as new forms of radical dissent are squeezed out of the picture. We are set for a new round of language-related conflict as geo-strategic considerations clash with the emancipatory demands of mobilised minorities.

If the state adopts a diffusion perspective of ethnic change, viewing group identities as malleable and group membership as a purely private affair, it will conceive of group rights as a barrier to minority assimilation and as a basis for reproducing permanent divisions within society (Glazer, 1977). If the state conceives of its constituent cultural groups as forming part of an established ethnically plural society, then it must legislate and act on what the rights of each group shall be (Williams, 1986, p. 262). However, there is a profound difference between the stated policies of governments towards minorities enunciated at international conventions and the actual treatment of differentiated citizens at the local level. It is too facile to rest content with either individualist or collectivist paradigms of language legislation. Liberalism is not a neutral ideology. The liberal democratic state is much more than a referee for the warring factions contained within its bosom. Thus, rather than presume that there exists one universal solution to the question of managing ethno-linguistic pluralism, it is more instructive to draw attention to the sheer variety of assumptions about the nature of majority–minority relations inherent in models of social integration. Drawing on Canadian evidence, Evelyn Kallen (1995) has set forth an incisive account of inductive and deductive models of social reality, which conceives ethnic integration as a 'social doctrine that provides guidelines for the attainment of an ideal mode of accommodation of ethnic diversity in society' (Kallen, 1995, p. 163). These conceptual constructs are represented in Table 1 and inform the rest of the discussion.

Within Kallen's four models of melting pot, mosaic, dominant conformity and paternalism we have a differentiation between exclusive and inclusive definitions of civil rights. Europe and North America are witnessing a series of structural transformations which accord greater recognition to minorities. How do various forms of multiculturalism seek to promote the politics of mutual respect? Let us consider the difficulties of operating an ideology of multiculturalism within a model of liberal society which purports to recognise more than the mere survival of cultures by acknowledging their permanent worth.

The extreme delicacy of a rights-based approach to language policy is well recognised. 'Equality of rights is the precondition of recognition, but it is not sufficient to ensure it' (Ignatieff, 2000, p. 86). In similar vein, Tollefson (1991, p. 197) argues that 'Language rights are a fragile base for language policy, … constant struggle is necessary to protect rights, even in a country with a long historical commitment to – and a federal structure which supports it – a pluralist language policy.'

The recent recognition of religious and linguistic rights has encouraged the belief that increased cultural pluralism is a reflection of increased mutual tolerance. Yet tolerance *per se* does not necessarily follow, for it depends upon which groups have received recognition for what purpose and in which contexts. A major difficulty here is the threat posed to communitarian democracy by special interest groups. A further complication is that many indigenous minorities are being treated according to policies predicated on pluralism on the basis of equality, whilst non-indigenous minorities are treated according to policies predicated on pluralism on the basis of non-equality. How do these

Table 1 Assumptions behind models of integration in North American meritocracies

Variables	Melting pot (amalgamation)	Mosaic (cultural/ pluralism)	Dominant conformity (absorption)	Paternalism (colonialism)
1 Societal goal: (ethnicity and nationality)	one nation/ one people/ one culture	one nation/ many peoples/ many cultures	one nation/ one people/ one culture (dominant)	one dominant nation/ people/culture subordinated minorities
2 Symmetry/ asymmetry of political, economic and social power	symmetric (populations relatively equal)	symmetric	asymmetric (dominant population is superordinate)	asymmetric (dominant population monopolises power)
3 Ethnocentrism willingness/ability to maintain/shed	low ethnocentrism, willing and able to shed distinctiveness	high ethnocentrism, willing and able to maintain distinctiveness	dominant – high ethnocentrism, willing and able to maintain distinctiveness, minorities – low ethnocentrism, willing and able to shed distinctiveness	dominant – high ethnocentrism, willing and able to maintain distinctiveness, minorities – low ethnocentrism, unable to shed distinctiveness (racial/ascribed)
4 Levels of prejudice and discrimination	non-discriminatory low or absent prejudice	prejudice and discrimination not institutionalised	institutional and cultural discrimination; level of prejudice and discrimination	institutional, cultural, structural discrimination; level of prejudice and discrimination

			dominant – high, intolerant minority – low (willing to conform to majority norms)	dominant – high, intolerant, minority – stigmatised permanently
5 Criteria for social mobility	achieved	achieved	achieved and ascribed	dominant – achieved within stratum minorities – ascribed status is permanent: no mobility
6 Spheres of ethnocultural distinctiveness	none	variable public (political/economic/linguistic pluralism) private (multiculturalism) territorial (nationalism)	dominant – public and private minority – acculturation required	dominant – public and private minority – deculturation promoted/partial acculturation required
7 Collective identity	national identity (de-ethnicised)	hyphenated-identity (ethnic-national)	national identity = dominant ethnic identity	dominant – national entity + dominant ethnic identity; minority – negative valence of marginal identity
8 Human rights	individual human rights	individual and collective rights (collective, cultural and collective, national)	individual rights of minorities predicated on dominant conformity; collective rights of dominant group entrenched at societal-wide level	dominant – individual and collective rights, minority – no human rights, systematic violation of rights

Source: Adapted with permission from Kallen (1995), pp. 164–5.

two trends impact the one upon the other with regard to the recognition of rights in citizenship and language matters?

Taylor (1992) argues that the politics of equal respect embodied within the discourse of recognition does not serve us as well as we would like. This is because there is 'a form of the politics of equal respect, as enshrined in a liberalism of rights, that is inhospitable to difference, because (a) it insists on uniform application of the rules defining these rights, without exception, and (b) it is suspicious of collective goals'. Taylor calls it inhospitable because 'it can't accommodate what the members of distinct societies really aspire to, which is survival. This is (b) a collective goal, which (a) almost inevitably will call for some variations in the kinds of law we deem permissible from one cultural context to another' (Taylor, 1992, p. 61).

Clearly the dread hand of homogenisation can lie heavy on any attempt to maintain diversity through an appeal to universal considerations of human dignity and worth. Yet the filter process by which some decide the relative worth of others is far too imperfect. At its root there is an inherent paradox, between the demands for equality and the forces for efficiency as Taylor avers:

> The peremptory demand for favourable judgements of worth is paradoxically – perhaps one should say tragically – homogenising. For it implies that we already have the standards to make such judgements. By implicitly invoking our standards to judge all civilisation and cultures, the politics of difference can end up making everyone the same. (Taylor, 1992, p. 71)

Taylor argues that the demand for equal recognition is unacceptable. Rather what we need is a more humble approach which does not imply the pejorativisation of all other cultures. This, of course, presumes that cultural diversity is not only a growing feature of most societies, but also a positive and worthy feature. It has value, not only at the individual level of recognising human worth, but also at a societal level by legitimising access to political power and free participation in the democratic process. It follows that the ways of managing cultural diversity will vary according to why we think it has value.[2] Michael Ignatieff (2000, p. 87) argues that the real difficulty about recognition turns on the question of whether it means acquiescence, acceptance or approval. Demands for equal rights have become demands for approval and anything less than full approval by the majority denies the equal worth of the former discriminated party. In turn the rights revolution can 'engender a coercive culture of ritualised, insincere approval. So political correctness becomes a code word for a new form of moral tyranny: the tyranny of the minority over the majority' (p. 88).

However, a further stumbling block in the recognition of equal worth is the operation of the market and bureaucratic state, which in Taylor's view (1991, p. 11) 'tends to strengthen the enframings that favour an atomist and instrumentalist stance to the world and others'. Community solidarity and public participation in the decision-making process are weakened and religious or ethno-linguistic groupings intent upon their own survival, may be drawn closer into their own sub-cultures rather than forming a distinct part of the whole society, thus increasing the fragmented nature of mass society.

> This fragmentation comes about partly through a weakening of the bonds of sympathy, partly in a self-feeding way, through the failure of democratic initiative itself. Because the more fragmented a democratic electorate is in this sense, the more they transfer their political energies to promoting their partial groupings, and the less possible it is to mobilise democratic majorities around commonly understood programme.   (Taylor, 1991, p. 113)

Fragmentation and anomie seem to be winning the day for far too many previously committed citizens. And yet they all have, in principle, the right of free association, free speech and political representation, the hallmarks of a modern democracy. Religious and linguistic distinctiveness rests both on special interest recognition and on the maintenance of a common social order which not only affirms ordinary life but also recognises its *limits*.

This is an especially urgent consideration in South-eastern Europe, on the margins of Central Europe, in much of the developing world and, in a curious way, lies at the heart of the Québécois–Canadian impasse which is the crux of this volume. In order to sustain religious and sociolinguistic pluralism here, as elsewhere, a re-definition of the essence of political engagement is required.

When applied to current Canadian constitutional bargaining, Ignatieff argues that the politics of mutual recognition need not necessarily lead to fragmentation if the politics of reciprocity is engaged.

> This goes beyond balancing rights. It also means balancing acts of recognition. At the moment, the Canadian majority feels that it is faced with multiplying demands for recognition from various minority

groups, without these groups accepting any obligation to recognize the majority. This is the heart of the bitterness in English Canada over Quebec. It is the feeling that the Canadian majority is being asked to concede recognition of Quebec's distinct status without earning any commensurate recognition of Canada in return. This perceived inequality of recognition has led many English Canadians to refuse to be party to further concessions. What has proved insupportable is not the nature of Quebec's demands, but the threat of separation that accompanies the demands. Give us what we want or we will go is not a form of recognition but an expression of contempt.   (Ignatieff, 2000, p. 122)

Ignatieff (2000, p. 63) interprets the history of modern Canada as the story of the unwillingness of the majority to discard the connection between equality, individual rights and group assimilation. In response to francophone demands, Trudeau chose to emphasise the rights, not of one territorial community, Quebec, but rather the rights of individuals throughout the state. His programme of coast to coast bilingual federal services provided a commitment and a context to language policy and planning. But its basic premise, namely the recognition of individual rights within a programme of civic equality, was not enough. It failed 'to recognize and protect the rights of constituent nations and peoples to maintain their distinctive identities' (Ignatieff, 2000, p. 66). The Québécois response involved a territorial imperative, even though the rhetoric was couched in increasingly non-territorial, non-ethnic, terms, on the basis of an inclusive civil society. Kymlicka (2001, p. 79) points to the centrality of a language group exercising territorial hegemony when he writes that 'There is evidence that language communities can only survive inter-generationally if they are numerically dominant within a particular territory, and if their language is the language of opportunity in that territory. But it is difficult to sustain such a predominant status for a minority language, particularly if newcomers to the minority's territory are able to be educated and employed in the majority language (e.g. if newcomers to Quebec are able to learn and work in English).' We shall focus on the territorial ramifications of language policy below, but first we need to rehearse the varieties of language policy which influence inter-group contact in selected states.

Varieties of language policy and planning

As modern global control is increasingly related to language functions we may ask how these overarching socio-political forces are played out in linguistic terms and with what consequence for social policy and citizenship. As a mechanism for behaviour modification, language policy and planning depends largely on four attributes identified by Stewart (1968). These are the respective degrees of standardisation; autonomy; historicity; and vitality. These characteristics of language freedom are critical in helping planners to evaluate existing language functions and to harness the dynamic cultural interactions that characterise many multilingual societies.

As early as 1951 UNESCO developed a typology of the range of choice available to language planners that has been in use for two generations. It includes the following categories:

1 **indigenous language**: the language of the original inhabitants of an area;
2 **lingua franca**: a language used habitually by people who have different first languages so they can communicate for certain specific purposes;
3 **mother tongue**: the language one acquires as a child;
4 **national language**: the language of a political, social, and cultural entity;
5 **official language**: a language used to do government business;
6 **pidgin**: a language (formed by mixing languages) used regularly by people of different language backgrounds;
7 **regional language**: a common language used by people of different language backgrounds who live in a particular area;
8 **second language**: a language acquired in addition to one's first language;
9 **vernacular language**: the first language of a group socially or politically dominated by a group with a different language;
10 **world language**: a language used over wide areas of the world (a 'language of wider communication', or LWC).

(UNESCO, 1951, pp. 689–90)

Though useful in a heuristic sense such typologies have been criticised. Kay (1993) for example, argues that they are too imprecise to be used in any specific place or context. One may also query how 'original' a language must be to be classified as indigenous, and why a vernacular language is associated with subordination in the UNESCO classification, as if a dominant group could not also possess a vernacular language. Such imprecise definitions, however, were commonplace in the initial stages of language planning, which often transferred European or North

American models of social and linguistic behaviour to African, Asian or Latin American contexts.

Stewart (1968) proposes an alternative typology of language, which recognises the multiplicity of linguistic functions that can exist even within ostensibly one nation/one people/one culture states.

- official languages;
- provincial languages (such as regional languages);
- languages of wider communication (LWCs), which are used within a multilingual nation to cross ethnic boundaries;
- international languages, which are LWCs used between nations;
- capital languages (the means of communication near a national capital);
- group languages (often vernaculars);
- educational languages (used as the media of education);
- school-subject languages (those taken as second languages);
- literary languages (for example, Latin or Sanskrit);
- religious languages (such as Islamic Arabic).

Most developed societies retained the language policies which were critical to the project of constructing the territorial–bureaucratic nation-state. Consequently they face severe difficulties in matching their inherited institutional agencies and organisational structures to the reality of serving the legitimate demands of increasingly multilingual populations. Historically, we can identify four types of language policy implicated in the processes of state formation. The first and most common – as found in France, Spain and Britain – reinforced political and cultural autonomy by giving primacy to one indigenous language and thus enforcing it, and no other, as the language of government, administration, law, education and commerce. In so doing, a number of goals were achieved simultaneously. Among these was the search for national integrity, the legitimisation of the new regime and its state apparatus, the re-establishment of indigenous social organisation (often, but not necessarily incorporating an established religion), the reduction of dependence upon external organisations and influences, and the incorporation of all the citizenry in a wide range of para-public social domains. Foreign languages were reserved for the very specialised functions of higher education, international diplomacy and commerce.

A second type of language planning characterises those situations in which the 'national' goal has been to maintain cultural pluralism, so that the state might survive through containing its inherent tensions. Under this system, language was used to define regional associations rather than state or national citizenship. It is best exemplified in Europe by Switzerland's decentralised system, which incorporates cantonal unilingualism within a multilingual federal system, and the rigidly-enforced division of Belgium between its Walloon- and Flemish-speaking populations.

The third form of language planning has occurred when a recognised minority was granted some degree of geographical distinction, based upon the territoriality principle of language rights. In Finland, for example, high levels of language contact along the west coast, marked religious uniformity, a strong tradition of centralised government and the unifying effects of long-term external threats, led to a recognition that the minority Swedish-speaking population should be accorded official status. Following the 1922 Language Law, all communes were classified as unilingual Finnish, unilingual Swedish, or bilingual if they contained a linguistic minority of either group of 10 per cent or more; these classifications were revised after each decennial census to take account of changing linguistic geography (McRae, 1997). In comparative terms, the Finnish system of official bilingualism is characterised by a gross disparity in numbers, asymmetry in language contact and instability over time, leading McRae to conclude that such institutional arrangements for language accommodation have been functional in terms of conflict moderation and management, but less so for language stability.

A fourth option – the 'modernisation' or revitalisation of an indigenous tongue – characterises societies disengaging from colonial relationships and the cultural hegemony of a dominant state. This form of language planning was a key goal of the nationalist intelligentsia in Hungary, Ireland, Finland and Norway prior to independence, and remains critical to the political programme of nationalists and regionalists in Catalonia, Euskadi, Brittany and Wales today.

Clearly language planning in a multilingual society is not a precise instrument and is as capable of being manipulated as is any other aspect of state policy. Nevertheless, it is an essential feature of the economic and political restructuring of many states. The key issues are:

- who decides – and on what basis – such bi- or multi-lingualism is to be constructed?
- which languages are chosen?
- who benefits by acts of state-sponsored social and identity formation?
- how is language-related conflict managed and reduced?
- how is language planning to be related to all other forms of social intervention?

- how do citizens respond to reformed language regimes?
- how do such reforms relate to international trends in education, human rights, freedom of mobility of labour and skills acquisition?

Space does not permit a detailed evaluation of the various models and methods which underpin language planning systems.[3] Nevertheless, by employing a series of illustrative tables some insight into language planning aims and models may be gained. The first and fundamental insight is that language planning processes may be viewed conventionally either from a predominantly societal (status planning) or language (corpus planning) focus.[4] Table 2 charts Einar Haugen's formulation which can be used to focus either on language policy and its implementation or on language teaching and development (for details see Kaplan and Baldauf, 1997, pp. 28–58).

Haarmann (1990) has added a behavioural dimension to such considerations, arguing that as status and corpus planning are both productive activities, what is missing is the perceptual filter by which people relate to the *prestige* factor of language planning. Haarman also emphasises the multilevel contexts within which language policy has to be received and implemented by the target audience. Thus Table 3 is an attempt to inject promotional and contextual elements to status and corpus planning.

In their excellent overview of the discipline, Kaplan and Baldauf (1997), provide a summary of the various aims which underpin language planning. How plausible such schemes are depend in large part on

Table 2 Haugen's revised language planning model with additions

	Form (policy planning)	Function (language cultivation)
Society (status planning)	1. Selection (decision procedures) a. problem identification b. allocation of norms	3. Implementation (educational spread) a. correction procedures b. evaluation
Language (corpus planning)	2. Codification (standardisation procedures) a. graphisation b. grammatication c. lexication	4. Elaboration (functional development) a. terminological modernisation b. stylistic development c. internationalisation

Source: Haugen (1983), p. 275.

Table 3 An ideal typology of language cultivation and language planning (Haarmann, 1990, pp. 120–1)

	Ranges of language planning		Ranges of language cultivation	
	Activities of government	*Activities of agencies*	*Activities of groups*	*Activities of individuals*
Status planning	4.1	3.1	2.1	1.1
Prestige planning	official promotion	institutional promotion	pressure group promotion	individual promotion
Corpus planning	4.2	3.2	2.2	1.2
	Level 4	Level 3	Level 2	Level 1
Maximum ←	Efficiency in terms of the organisational impact		→	Minimum

Source: Kaplan and Baldauf (1997), p. 50.

the political context within which such goals are to be realised, and thus the next section focuses on alternative methods of implementing the principles of language rights (see Table 4).

Personality and territoriality principles of language policy and planning

Conventionally, language policies are predicated on either a personality or territoriality principle of planning.[5] Two conditions are necessary for competition to arise between language groups. First, the languages must share a common contact space. Secondly, the relationship between these two languages must become the symbolic stakes of the competition, which takes place on the level of the shared space. Laponce (1987, p. 266) has advanced the following four propositions about languages in contact:

- 'languages tend to form homogenous spatial groupings';
- 'when languages come into contact they tend either to specialize their functions or to stratify';
- 'the specialization and the stratification of languages is determined by the socially dominant group';
- 'the social dominance of a language is a function of the number of its speakers and the political and social stratification of the linguistic groups in contact'.

Table 4   A summary of language planning goals

	Alternative formulations	*Examples*
Macro level[a]		
Language purification		
External purification		
Internal purification		French[e]
Language revival	Language revival[c]	Hebrew[e]
	Restoration	
	Transformation	
	Language regenesis[d]	
	Language revival	
	Revitalisation	
	Reversal	
Language reform		Turkish[e]
Language standardisation	Spelling and script standardisation[b]	Swahili[e]
Language spread		
Lexical modernisation	Term planning[b]	Swedish[e]
Terminological unification	Discourse planning[b]	
Stylistic simplification		
Interlingual communication		
Worldwide IC		
Auxiliary languages		
English LWC		
Regional IC	Regional identity[b]	
Regional LWC	National identity[b]	
Cognate languages IC		
Language maintenance		
Dominant LM		
Ethnic LM		

Auxiliary code standardisation

Meso level planning for[b]
Administration: training and certification of officials and professionals
Administration: legal provisions for use
The legal domain
Education equity: pedagogical issues
Education equity: language rights/identity
Education elite formation/control
Mass communication
Educational equity: language handicap[f]
Social equity: minority language access[f]

---

[a] Nahir (1984); [b] Annamalai and Rubin (1980); [c] Bentahila & Davies (1993); [d] Paulson *et al.*
(1993); [e] Eastman (1983); [f] Kaplan and Baldauf (1997).

Source: Kaplan and Baldauf (1997), p. 61.

Research in contact linguistics demonstrates that it is a chimera to search for a universal model for conflict reduction. On the contrary, procedures must be considered that are adaptable to each situation.

The recognition of the need to honour rights and plan language services normally involves the use of a previously disallowed language within public administration and the legal system, a religious-based education provision, or differentiated access to the media. Such reforms may be predicated on the basis of a personality or a territoriality principle or some expedient admixture of both, but they are not in themselves sufficient to avoid conflicts. Research in Canada, Belgium, Finland and Switzerland (Domenichelli, 1999; McRae, 1997; Nelde *et al.*, 1992) suggest that some conflicts can be partially neutralised if the following conditions are observed:

- The territoriality principle should be limited to a few key areas like administration and education.
- The institutional multilingualism that emerges should lead to the creation of independent unilingual networks, which grant equal opportunity of communication to minority and majority speakers. These networks should also exclude linguistic discrimination connected with speakers of the prestige language.
- Measures of linguistic planning should not be based exclusively on linguistic censuses carried out by the respective governments. Rather, they must genuinely take account of the situational and contextual characteristics of the linguistic groups.
- Minority linguistic groups in a multilingual country should not be judged primarily on quantitative grounds. On the contrary, they should be awarded more rights and possibilities of development than would be due to them based on their numbers and their proportion to the majority.

(Nelde *et al.*, 1992)

Nelde *et al.* believe that according such equality to minorities by assuring them of more rights could result in fewer people adopting an intransigent ideological position. Unless far more attention is paid to the rights of lesser-used language speakers, then more conflict will ensue.[6] It is a matter of some considerable debate as to whether territorial principles of language protection, in general, offer adequate means to bolster language loss and whether language legislation in Quebec, in particular, has enabled successive governments sufficient control to regulate language choice and behaviour within their purview.[7] Chevrier, below, discusses the options for Quebec highlighting Stéphane Dion's (1992) conclusion that the personality solution should be adopted throughout Canada except in Quebec where territorialism should be acknowledged as a political fact. Such asymmetrical paradigms mask the more substantive issue namely the federal system's attempt to contain, rather than energise a coast to coast francophone population and Chevrier like Castonguay (1999a) and Cardinal (2000) is particularly acerbic in his accurate portrayal of the impact of federal policies on French language maintenance, even if supporters of the federal programmes would debate that the intent was not to subvert, but to maintain, the French fact throughout the state.

What is not subject to debate is the fact that Quebec's move toward territorial specification of language choice and regulation has been challenged as being discriminatory from a Canadian majoritarian point of view, as discussed later in this volume. Such demands for language rights and territorial control, as Kymlicka (2001, p. 79) makes clear, are taken as evidence of the minority's 'collectivism'. But the minority are merely seeking the same opportunities to engage in public life and in the economy that the majority take for granted. In their own way, majorities are just as collective, perhaps more so, for they have internalised such values as 'common sense' notions of democratic civility, while simultaneously denying such values to minorities.[8]

Language erosion also involves the potential loss of creativity and spontaneity mediated through one's own language(s), thus contributing to a quenching of the human spirit, and a reduction in what some have termed the ecology of 'linguodiversity' (Williams, 1991a; Skutnabb-Kangas, 1997). This reason alone may prove convincing to many. But need linguistic decline sound the death-knell for particular ethnic or immigrant identities in Europe or North America? No necessary correspondence exists between linguistic reproduction and ethnic/immigrant identity (Edwards, 1994; Williams, 1991a). Indeed cultural activities and symbolic manifestations of identity often continue long after a group's language declines. None the less, increased interdependence at the superstructural level implies more harmonisation for the already advantaged groups. The EU has harmonised state and community policies so as to strengthen its majority language regimes, which when combined with other globalising processes, open up new forms of inter-regional interaction such as cable television and global multi-service networks, but also poses a threat to conventional territorial relationships of both regional and immigrant minorities.

A further difficulty is the lack of adequate data by which to analyse demo-linguistic trends, and the attempt by government agencies to put a positive gloss on official language trends. Extra and Gorter (2001, pp. 7–16) have raised the issue of the criteria used for identification of population groups in multicultural Europe. They argue that data on Regional Minorities are recorded on the basis of (home) language and/or ethnicity, while those on Immigrant Minorities are collected on the basis of nationality and/or country of birth. Due to the decreasing significance of nationality and country of birth criteria in the EU it is probable that the combined criterion of self-categorisation and home language will characterise future language planning policy. However, one should be alert to the political implications of choosing certain criteria by which to include and exclude residents in specific programmes. Consequently the advantages and disadvantages of various criteria are outlined in Table 5 and their implications for the Canadian/Québécois dialogue which follows should not be lost, especially if the discussion is informed by the insightful analysis of census-interpreters such as Charles Castonguay (1997, 1999b). Precisely because Statistics Canada has chosen to define and interpret official language data in a certain manner, successive Federal governments have placed a more positive gloss on official language policy than is warranted by reality. Castonguay points to trends such as the demographic advantage of English, the collapse of Canada's French-speaking population, the impact of allophone language shift and the increasing anglicisation of francophones outside of Quebec as evidence that the 'personality principle' approach to official bilingualism is inherently assimilationist, thus subversive. Cardinal (1999) offers a cautionary rider to such trends, arguing that the federal language regime has placed francophone minorities outside Quebec in an unhealthy state of dependency on government and the courts. The acute political point she makes is that they thereby become part of the Trojan Horse federal strategy *vis-à-vis* Quebec, as discussed by Castonguay (1999a) and Williams (1981, 1996b).

> The quid pro quo for this federal generosity toward official-language minorities has been that they accept being used – especially when the Liberals are in office – as accomplices in campaigns designed to undermine Quebec's demands on language and other matters. Such a situation prevents the building of links with Quebecers. It accentuates the fragility of the small francophone communities outside Quebec since they are in constant political conflict with the overwhelming majority of the Canadian francophone population – who are Quebecers.   (Cardinal, 1999, p. 84)

The emancipation of long-discriminated minorities has also to be set within the context of an enabling infrastructure which allows them to

Table 5   Criteria for the definition and identification of population groups in a multicultural society

Criterion	Advantages	Disadvantages
Nationality (NAT) (P/F/M)	• objective • relatively easy to establish	• (intergenerational) erosion through naturalisation or double NAT • NAT not always indicative of ethnicity/identity • some (e.g. ex-colonial) groups have NAT or immigration country
Birth-country (BC) (P/F/M)	• objective • relatively easy to establish	• intergenerational erosion through births in immigration country • BC not always indicative of ethnicity/identity • invariable/deterministic: does not take account of dynamics in society (in contrast to all other criteria)
Self-categorization (SC)	• touches the heart of the matter • emancipatory: SC takes account of person's own conception of ethnicity/identity	• subjective by definition: also determined by language/ethnicity of interviewer and by the spirit of times • multiple SC possible • historically charged, especially by World War II experiences
Home language (HL)	• HL is most significant criterion of ethnicity in communication processes • HL data are cornerstones of government policy in areas such as public information or education	• complex criterion: who speaks what language to whom and when? • language not always core value of ethnicity/identity • useless in one-person households

P/F/M = person/father/mother.

Source: Extra and Gorter (2001), p. 9.

use their new found rights. However, deciding between the promotion of one or many languages in public services or in the educational domain is becoming less of a 'free choice'. The increasing burdens of economic, social and cultural development crowd in on the limited resources available for language planning and its implementation. This will be exacerbated when the next stages of EU enlargement are completed as it is estimated that there will be an additional 50 or 60 languages within the remit of European governments and NGOs. These will comprise border minority languages, autochthonous languages (Kashubian in Poland, Carpatho-Rusyns in Slovakia), partially migrant languages (Russian in the Baltic states), official languages (Maltese in Malta) and linguistic islands (the Tartars).

But there is also the counter-trend of regional diversity, which emphasises the value of cultural diversity and the worth of each specific language, not least as a primary marker of identity. In the EU, ethno-linguistic minorities have reacted to these twin impulses by searching for European-wide economies of scale in broadcasting, information networking, education and public administration, meanwhile establishing their own EU networks and entering into new alliances to influence decision-making bodies. They believe that by appealing to the superstructural organisations of the EU for legitimacy and equality of group rights, they will force individual states and the Community to recognise their claims for political/social autonomy within clearly identifiable territorial/social domains.[9]

But the wider question of the relative standing of official languages makes political representatives wary of further complicating administrative politics by addressing the needs of approximately 55 million citizens who have a mother tongue that is not the main official language of the state which they inhabit. Historically, the recognition of linguistic minority demands is a very recent phenomenon. Since 1983, the European Commission has supported action to protect and promote regional and minority languages and cultures within the EU. In 1996 some four million ecus were allocated to European socio-cultural schemes. Equally significant is a raft of recent legislation and declarations upholding the rights of minorities to use their languages in several domains (Williams, 1993b; *Declaració de Barcelona*, 1996).

The previous expansion of the EU in 1995, and its imminent further enlargement in 2004–5, has increased the difficulties in translating multicultural communication and guaranteeing access to information and hence power for all groups. At the heart of the debate on European identity lies a consideration of the role of hegemonic languages as both symbol and instrument of integration. English – the premier language for international commerce and discourse – is used by over 1,700 million people world-wide as an official language, of whom some 320 million have it as a home language (Gunnermark and Kenrick, 1985; Crystal, 1987). Should English be encouraged as the official language enabling most Europeans to communicate with each other? Or is it desirable to attempt to slow down its inevitable global spread? Critics claim that the spread of English perpetuates an unequal relationship between 'developed' and 'developing' societies. While access to information and power demands fluency, it also requires institutional structures, economic resources and power relationships.

Modernised indigenous languages, such as Irish or Catalan are capable of expansion but are unlikely to displace hegemonic languages, especially within the civil service, or in technological and commercial sectors. Renewed languages such as Welsh, Frisian or Basque have penetrated into new domains, such as local administration, education and the media, but even here the impression given is that much of this activity is tokenistic or reaches only the superficial structures of society. In contrast, threatened minority languages such as Romany or Skolt Lapp will be further marginalised. Because of high fertility rates, some groups are experiencing linguistic reproduction rates greater than one, and their prospects for survival look promising, especially in constructing an infrastructure for domain extension in education, government and broadcasting. Conversely, however, some autochthonous language speakers are rapidly losing their control in traditional core areas as a result of out-migration, capital-intensive economic development and increased mobility. The fact that lesser-used languages have become highly politicised in the last twenty years, should not divert attention away from their fears of cultural attrition.

An additional consideration is than many migrants who settled in another European country, often as a consequence of two World Wars, have lost the native language capacities of their forebears. For them diacritical markers, such as diet, music or the visual arts, have replaced language as the link with the wider cultural community. Fundamental questions surround the symbolic bases of their culture and the degree to which one may characterise residual elements as either authentic or as expressing an integral identity. This is a major feature of Europe's cultural heritage and will prove a testing ground for more sensitive and flexible applications of any policy of multiculturalism. This is most acute in the recent re-discovery among many residents of Central Europe of their German heritage and of their potential relationship with a unified and re-invigorated German *MittelEuropa* policy.

Perhaps the greatest challenge facing framers of European identity comes from non-European migrants and their descendants, especially as globalising perspectives will reinforce the need for link languages other than English in this realm. Initially this will result from private and commercial-oriented demands, but as the total size and significance of link languages – especially Islamic-related variants – grows, then there will be pressure to reform public agencies and the educational system, particularly in France, the UK, Germany, Belgium and the Netherlands. The increased presence of non-nationals within European states will add to the alienated feelings of many recent migrants who feel that they do not belong by right to any particular state.

Clearly the state is deeply implicated in the direction of change with regard to multicultural policy. As society becomes more pluralised, and social mobility increases, greater tensions occur between the functional provision of bilingual public services and the formal organisation of territorial-based authorities charged with such provision. These conflicts are exacerbated by immigration into fragile language areas, which leads to the public contestations of language-related issues as each new domain is penetrated by the intrusive language group. Such sentiments are hard to gainsay. The difficulty lies in determining what proportion of the public purse is to be expended on satisfying the legitimate demands of this policy. Issues of principle, ideology and policy are frequently no more than thinly disguised disputes over levels of resource expenditure. One arm of government is involved in extending the remit of pluralism whilst another is reigning in the fiscal obligations to so act. Either way, dependent cultures are tied inexorably to the largesse of the state. Governments are obliged to maintain their support for many multicultural projects, albeit simultaneously signalling their intent to withdraw public finances and welcome private sector funding. Either way, the languages and cultures of visible minorities are in danger of being expropriated by external forces, while cultural dependency is being increased. As they become better organised, however, astute minority groups will press for greater recognition of their cultural rights, seeking the individual choice and empowerment required to decide their lifestyle and future prospects as participative citizens. From this perspective, multiculturalism is a set of institutional opportunities for individual and group advancement in a competitive environment. In other words it becomes a platform for social progress.

The politics of mutual respect presuppose a historically well-entrenched democratic order. The watchwords of an open society are redistributive social justice, participatory democracy and mutual tolerance. These concepts, in turn, presuppose a political–juridical framework adequate to ensuring that increased cultural contact will not lead to escalating conflict. Cultural communities are best represented when the state guarantees individual freedom of association.

Language planning as an instrument of development: African and Asian perspectives

Many of the modernisation processes observed in Europe since the *Aufklarung* have been repeated in the so-called 'developing world'. Development theory often assumes that language-choice behaviour is utilitarian and rational and can be measured through techniques such as a cost–benefit analysis of language switching. It also assumes that the broad tenets of modernisation theory influence patterns of language maintenance and shift. Eastman (1983, p. 148) has summarised the development assumptions of language planning which may be modified as follows:

- people with language skills are favoured over those without; people with linguistic disabilities are held back in economic advancement;
- population increases via birth rate *or* migration affect the relative strength of languages or speech varieties;
- a quality increase as well as a quantity increase in *per capita* growth requires an expansion of linguistic knowledge; that is, people need to know and use more of a language as they acquire more and better goods;
- people need to be aware of, and know how to use, different language features (such as social dialects, special vocabularies, argots, jargons or special-purpose languages) to adjust to changes in professional and industrial growth;
- international trade requires people to be able to use and have access to LWCs;
- linguistic homogeneity adds to the ability of people to cross occupational, industrial and status lines;
- where the spread of modern economic growth is sequential, modern linguistic growth is also sequential – the need for vocabulary development makes it likely that the world languages will be chosen for adoption in preference to attempts to enhance local languages.

(Eastman, 1983, p. 148)

Value recognition is not an essential part of language planning, although one might argue that it should be, for how can planning of any kind be effective without explicit recognition and practice of this principle? Hegemony prevails and will continue to do so until minority people band together and form a common front to push for their perspectives to be incorporated into the development planning process. This will involve a clash of discourses and a conflict over the very definition of what counts as the problem that development is seeking to overcome. From a local, community perspective the problem may be a lack of real power to transform their immediate situation. From the point of view of the central state apparatus, it may be that ethno-cultural differences are perceived as an impediment to the creation of a state-wide programme of economic development where institutional agencies can redefine the populus as workers and consumers regardless of ethnic criteria. The commodification of identity is thus an essential feature of economic and political restructuring in the advanced stage of the development of organic capitalism when production and consumption in the semi-periphery remain so unbalanced.

Conscious of this ideological struggle, some language planning and development studies theorists have recognised the contextual effects on language maintenance and language loss and have sought to incorporate environmental and politico-economic factors more directly into their analyses (Williams, 1991a). This bodes well for a realistic, holistic assessment of language change in developing societies. However, any attempt at language planning will depend on the resources available and the capacity of the public sector and educational system to realise the explicit goals of policy. Structural adjustment in most of Africa has exasperated the lack of a settled civil society and too often language promotion is linked to exhausted nationalism or to a variant of elite manipulation of the masses advocating an anti-neoliberal philosophy. Rising debt and the inability of many states to renegotiate their role within the global pattern of uneven development has damaged many of the earlier grand designs, partly because of an over-accumulation problem, partly because hard currency financing renders economies vulnerable and partly because many political leaders have 'talked left and acted right' when it comes to their dealings with the World Bank or the IMF.[10]

The work of Conklin and Lourie (1983), summarised by Baker (1996) offers a very useful framework and balance sheet for the factors influencing language maintenance and loss. Table 6 illustrates the complexity of the issues involved, but I would argue that all three sets of factors need to be addressed simultaneously if a practical set of proposals is to be constructed in any particular context. In addition, as with nearly all examples of language planning schema it also needs to identify the role of language in economic development and modernisation.

Table 6   Factors encouraging language maintenance and loss

Factors encouraging language maintenance	Factors encouraging language loss
A Political, social and demographic factors	
1 Large number of speakers living closely together	Small number of speakers well dispersed
2 Recent and/or continuing in-migration	Long and stable residence
3 Close proximity to the homeland and case of travel to homeland	Homeland remote
4 Preference to return to homeland with many actually returning	Low rate of return to homeland and/or little intention to return
5 Homeland language community intact	Homeland language community decaying in vitality
6 Stability in occupation	Occupational shift, especially from rural to urban areas
7 Employment available where home language is spoken daily	Employment requires use of the majority language
8 Low social and economic mobility in main occupations	High social and economic mobility in main occupations
9 Low level of education to restrict social and economic mobility, but educated and articulate community leaders loyal to their language community	High levels of education giving social and economic mobility. Potential community leaders are alienated from their language community by education
10 Ethnic group identity rather than identity with majority language community via nativism, racism and ethnic discrimination	Ethnic identity is denied to achieve social and vocational mobility; this is forced by nativism, racism and ethnic discrimination
B Cultural factors	
1 Mother-tongue institutions (e.g. schools, community organisations, mass media, leisure activities)	Lack of mother-tongue institutions
2 Cultural and religious ceremonies in the home language	Cultural and religious activity in the majority language
3 Ethnic identity strongly tied to home language	Ethnic identity defined by factors other than language
4 Nationalistic aspirations as a language group	Few nationalistic aspirations
5 Mother tongue the homeland national language	Mother tongue not the only homeland national language, or mother tongue spans several nations
6 Emotional attachment to mother tongue giving self-identity and ethnicity	Self-identity derived from factors other than shared home language
7 Emphasis on family ties and community cohesion	Low emphasis on family and community ties. High emphasis on individual achievement

Table 6 Contd.

Factors encouraging language maintenance	Factors encouraging language loss
8 Emphasis on education to enhance ethnic awareness or controlled by language	Emphasis on education if education in mother-tongue community
9 Low emphasis on education if in majority language	Acceptance of majority language education
10 Culture unlike majority language culture	Culture and religion similar to that of the majority language
C Linguistic factors	
1 Mother tongue is standardised and exists in a written form	Mother tongue is non-standard and/or not in written form
2 Use of an alphabet which makes printing and literacy relatively easy	Use of writing system which is expensive to reproduce and relatively difficult to learn
3 Home language has international status	Home language of little or no international importance
4 Home language literacy used in community and with homeland	Illiteracy (or aliteracy) in the home language
5 Flexibility in the development of the home language (e.g. limited use of new terms from the majority language)	No tolerance of new terms from majority language; or too much tolerance of loan words leading to mixing and eventual language loss

Source: Reproduced by permission from Colin Baker (1996), *Foundations of Bilingual Education and Bilingualism* (Multilingual Matters: Clevedon, Avon). Adapted from Conklin and Lourie (1983).

A staggering range of variables faces the language planner concerned with mobilising the state's educational system in order to produce functional bilingual or multi-lingual citizens. There is enough case study experience in the literature for us to be able to predict weak and strong forms of education for bilingualism and biliteracy. Table 7 illustrates the available range which will be illustrated below by reference to specific examples in East Africa and Western Europe. It is my contention that the construction of an articulate bilingual or multi-lingual citizenry is an essential prerequisite of a developing state. Only when we can anticipate the utilitarian power of a language in particular economic contexts can we begin to talk of the pragmatic links between language processes and development processes.

Types of language choice

'Africa invented language; Asia sacralised language; and Europe universalised it' (Mazrui and Mazrui, 1992, p. 96). Africa's triple linguistic heritage makes it an acute case of linguistic dependency event though

Table 7 Weak and strong forms of education for bilingualism and biliteracy

Type of programme	Typical type of child	Language of the classroom	Societal and educational aim	Aim in language outcome
Weak forms of education for bilingualism				
Submersion (Structured immersion)	Language minority	Majority language	Assimilation	Monolingualism
Submersion with (Withdrawal classes/ sheltered English)	Language minority	Majority language with 'pull-out' L2 lessons	Assimilation	Monolingualism
Segregationist	Language minority	Minority language (forced, no choice)	Apartheid	Monolingualism
Transitional	Language minority	Moves from minority to majority language	Assimilation	Relative monolingualism
Mainstream with foreign language teaching	Language majority	Majority language with L2/FL lessons	Limited enrichment	Limited bilingualism
Separatist	Language minority	Minority language (out of choice)	Detachment/ autonomy	Limited bilingualism
Strong forms of education for bilingualism and biliteracy				
Immersion	Language majority	Bilingual with initial emphasis on L2	Pluralism and enrichment	Bilingualism and biliteracy
Maintenance/ heritage language	Language minority	Bilingual with emphasis on L1	Maintenance, pluralism and enrichment	Bilingualism and biliteracy
Two-way/dual language	Mixed language minority and majority	Minority and majority	Maintenance, pluralism and enrichment	Bilingualism and biliteracy
Mainstream bilingual	Language majority	Two majority languages	Maintenance, pluralism and enrichment	Bilingualism and biliteracy

Notes: (1) L2 = Second language; L1 = First language; FL = Foreign language. (2) Formulation of this table owes much to discussions with Professor Ofelia Garcia.

Source: Reproduced by permission from Colin Baker (1996), *Foundations of Bilingual Education and Bilingualism* (Multilingual Matters: Clevedon, Avon). Adapted from Conklin and Lourie (1983).

Mazrui and Mazrui (1992) argue that the cultural interplay between *indigenous*, *Islamic* and *Western* legacies promoted a functional complementarity within the continental array of languages.

A central issue for developing countries, especially in Africa, is what should be the relationship between colonial languages and indigenous African languages? The question is just as urgent in Tanzania, where Kiswahili, rather than a European language is promoted nationally. Conventionally multilingual approaches to communication are adopted in such societies. How is this promotion of language spread best formalised in policy? What steps would be necessary to ensure that multilingual strategies in, for example, education, are not hijacked once more by an élite (Robinson, 1994)?

New political, economic and cultural forces have infused a spirit of linguistic competition in social domains and have created different sociolinguistic dynamics and formations. These changes are important, because recent strands of development theory are increasingly 'concerned with the impact of development on groups which are distinguished through *cultural* criteria rather than by their function in the production process' (Hettne, 1984). If true, how does cultural complementarity and competition affect the process? The determining factor is, of course, colonial history and peri-colonial contemporary reality. Africa, no less than any other part of the world, is differentially integrated into a global division of labour which is mediated through ideology and culture. But the language of this integration is primarily Western, essentially English or French, or Afro-Islamic, particularly Arabic. Thus whilst Afro-Islamic or Western languages are transnational or national in their communicative range, most Afro-ethnic languages are subnational, and limited to specific regions within state boundaries.

This suggests that as development relates to the global division of labour and international/universal technologies, then transnational languages are essential to development and indigenous languages are a barrier hindering access to the wider world. However, such implications are politically unacceptable, and therefore states must search for a modern version of a 'hybrid' communication system which relate both to the heritage of traditional cultures and to global structures and opportunities. A language which is capable of embracing both requirements is thus essential and should be the one with the greater versatility, vocabulary and functional utility (Kay, 1993).

When the question is whether to use an LWC as a 'national' and 'official' language, planners should consider the six socio-political variables that characterise three modal types of 'nation' (Eastman, 1983, pp. 58–9). Joshua Fishman (1969) argues that whether a 'nation' is modal type A, B or C depends largely on whether nationism (instrumental attachment and operational efficiency) or nationalism (ethnic authenticity and sentimental–primordial attachment) is the goal.

A-modal nations initiate language choices so that they may integrate a linguistically heterogeneous area with a primarily oral rather than written tradition. Eastman (1983, p. 13) comments that many developing states are of this type and frequently choose an LWC as an official and as a national language. Often indigenous language standardisation is also initiated so that people can learn to read and write their first regional language as well as the LWC, as is illustrated through the promotion of six regional languages together with the employment of English and French in Cameroon.

Type B nations are called uni-modal and are characterised by an indigenous language with a literary tradition, plus an LWC usually dominant because of former colonial policy. The intelligentsia and employees of the bureaucratic-territorial state tend to favour the LWC, while the indigenous language with the literary tradition is promoted as both the symbol and the substance of nationalist mobilisation. Swahili's challenge to English in Tanzania would exemplify the uni-modal nation's choice of national language.

Type C nations are multi-modal and have a range of competing languages with their own literary traditions. The selection of one all-purpose indigenous national language undoubtedly creates tension, especially in the ranks of supporters and speakers of the discriminated languages, but this may be a necessary price to pay for communicative efficiency in the new state. In multi-modal nations, bi- or tri-lingualism is a political goal, and in the case of India, for example, the indigenous national, all-state language, Hindi, has been championed at the expense both of other regional Indian languages and to a lesser extent, at the expense of English, the LWC.

Developing this distinction between 'nationism' and 'nationalism', Ralph Fasold (1988) has distinguished three main functions of national languages: (1) nationalist/national, or identificational; (2) nationist/ official or administrative; and (3) communicative. Brann (1991) has added a fourth element, the territorial or 'son-of-the-soil' function, and suggests that in most former colonial situations new states must take account of all four criteria – territoriality, communality, representation and status – when choosing one or several 'national' languages.

The difficulty facing politicians and language planners in Africa is that very few indigenous languages are capable of satisfying both preservation and modernisation. Thus Mazrui and Mazrui (1992, p. 89) aver that the proportion of Afro-ethnic languages which have the potential to be truly national or transnational is rather small. They include Amharic (Ethiopia and Eritrea), Bemba (Zambia and Zimbabwe), Kituba (Zaire and Congo), Lingala (Zaire, Congo, Angola, Central African Republic, Sudan and Uganda), Lwena (Angola, Zaire and Zambia), Nyanja or Chewa (Malawi and Zambia) and Sango (Central African Republic, Cameroon, Chad, Congo and Zaire). Such claims are open to question, but what is not in doubt is that many attempts are currently being made to redefine indige-nous languages as 'national' languages, which could become the com-mon inheritance of most or all of the citizens of post-independent states.

It is often argued that speakers of Afro-ethnic languages tend to be mostly rural in terms of their core area of demographic concentration and linguistic value (though this is not true of Amharic, for example). This gives them an authenticity in both time and space, and a certain lit-erary and psychological legitimacy in that most Afro-ethnic language speakers 'tend to regard the rural homeland as their real home' (Mazrui and Mazrui, 1992, p. 90). However, functionally it limits their geo-graphical spread and domain usage in an increasingly technological world. Examples of urban African concentrations which are growing quickly tend to weaken this claim, but the principle of low relative util-ity for Afro-ethnic languages in an increasingly inter-connected world holds true. In contrast, most Afro-Islamic languages depend upon the dynamics of urbanisation, they prosper as regional *lingua francas* serving commerce, politics and leisure pursuits. Thus the top five *lin-guae francae* in terms of speakers are all Afro-Islamic languages, namely Arabic, Kiswahili, Hausa, Fulfulde and Mandinka, with the first three named growing at the expense of the latter (Mazrui and Mazrui, 1992, p. 90).

In the majority of cases, African societies have retained the repertoire of language policies which they inherited from their colonial past. In consequence, many societies are faced with severe difficulties in match-ing their institutional agencies and organisational structures to the real-ity of serving the legitimate demands of a multilingual population. As a central feature of post-colonial development, language planning has become a crucial tool of 'state-formation' and 'nation building'. The key question was whether the national linguistic communication was to be based upon the use of indigenous or foreign languages. The new state may either seek to promote one exclusive 'national' language, at the expense of all others – the 'one-nation-one-language plan' – or it may seek to recognise important languages within its boundaries and employ one or more for official functions, that is the 'one-nation-more-than-one-language plan' (Stewart, 1968; Eastman, 1983).

As we have seen, the first type of plan was common in European state formation, as in the French, Spanish and British versions of 'national' development. It is best represented in Africa by post-war Rhodesia and to a lesser extent by Tanzania's political determination to create a 'national' culture by replacing English with Swahili as its 'official' language. Other examples of endoglossic nations would be Somalia (Somali), Sudan (Arabic), Ethiopia (Amharic) and Guinea (which has employed eight languages, Fula, Manding Susu, Kisi, Kpelle, Loma, Basari and Koniagi) (Heine, 1992, p. 24).

Such endoglossic policy seeks to institute political and cultural autonomy by giving an indigenous language full opportunity to be developed as the language of government, administration, law, education and commerce. This policy strengthens national integrity, the legitimisation of the new regime and of its state apparatus, the re-establishment of indigenous social organisation, the reduction of dependence upon Western organisations and influence, and the incorporation of the citizenry in a wide range of para-public social domains. Again foreign languages are reserved for higher education, international diplomacy and commerce.

Of those nations which do not practise an active endoglossic policy, Heine (1992, p. 24) cites Botswana (Tswana), Burundi (Rundi), Lesotho (Sotho), Malawi (Chewa), Ruanda (Kinyarwanda) and Swaziland (Swati). They may aim to encourage an indigenous language, but as most are derived from colonial units with centralised political organisation and one dominant language, they tend to favour the use of the colonial language for official purposes. In this respect there is a wide gap between the rhetoric of the declared national language policy and the actual experience of daily communication in the colonial *lingua franca*.

The second type of language planning exists when the 'national' goal is to maintain cultural pluralism. It is best represented in Africa by the commitment of the Bureau of Ghanaian Languages to introduce eleven languages in the education system, including three variants of Akan. A quite different interpretation of such planning was the extension of the apartheid system in the Republic of South Africa from the initial Bantustans to the creation of the putative independent Homelands. Under this system, language was used to define national citizenship, even if language affiliation was an ascribed label rather than a measurable attribute, as in the case of all the people of mixed descent who, by being allocated to a Homeland, were automatically denied South African citizenship. South Africa's over-concern with the fit between language and political boundaries expressed in its homeland policy (language = culture = homeland) derives from the cornerstone of the *Genootskap van Regte Afrikaaners* (Fellowship of True Afrikaners), founded in 1875, 'our language, our nation and our land'. Herbert (1992, p. 5) comments that this trinitarian conception which formed the homelands tribalisation policy stems from 'the projection of the Afrikaner's sense of ethnic particularism and linguistic chauvinism onto other people' (Van den Berghe, 1968, p. 221). A radically different version of the pluralist goal of achieving unity through diversity has now been implemented in South Africa with the recognition of eleven languages to serve its enfranchised citizens. Current patterns in residential segregation between English- and Afrikaans-speaking citizens show more positive trends as the Coloured, Indian and White population revert to pre-apartheid urban distributions based upon socio-economic differentiation and educational criteria. Indigenous African language groupings vary, but in most cities tri-lingualism is the norm, with speakers from the immediate rural hinterland strengthening the particular ethnolingusitic mix. Only the industrial heartland of Galtung demonstrates a mix of all eleven official languages to any significant degree. Thus language planning in the RSA will have to come to terms with both a 'national' level and a 'regional' or 'metropolitan' level set of policies which simultaneously promote the political and economic advantages of a language of wider communication without necessarily damaging the ethno-lingusitic vitality of several smaller, more vulnerable, language groups. Socialisation through formal education is perceived as a key to such stability, however, it is doubtful if education alone can perform such a task and consequently additional resources will be required if a real language choice is to be offered to citizens in domains as varied as the health system, public administration and the legal system.

The 'national language question' in Africa has always reflected the triumph of political zeal over the realisation of bilingual or multi-lingual communicative competence. The will has always out-paced the reach. In consequence one might argue that language planning in such cases is an acute expression of political social engineering. Yet Mackey avers that 'In the development of standard languages, edict has been less effective than example, the ideologies of the practitioners more powerful than the ideas of the planners' (Mackey, 1991, p. 56). The Tanzanian example would suggest that edict and example, ideology and plan must be synonymous if such planning is to be truly effective. That there are so few examples of effective planning in Africa suggests that there is very little consensus over both means and ends in this domain of language policy.

On the macro-scale, languages tend to specialise according to their utility and function. The trend is 'that Afro-ethnic languages fulfil intra-ethnic communicative and social-psychological needs in non-formal, and many formal, domains of discourse. Afro-Islamic and Afro-Western language facilitate inter-ethnic communication and horizontal mobility' (Mazrui and Mazrui, 1992, p. 91). However, this old divide between vernacular and vehicular languages is no longer so tenable. One cannot simply juxtapose indigenous with exogenous, rural with urban, traditional with modern. Kay's (1993) powerful argument in favour of language and cultural displacement as a means of escaping structural poverty and the open prison of ethnic identity certainly seems like a rational justification for the encouragement of the 'new African'. His 'pragmatic' solution of the adoption of English in multi-lingual Zambia, as elsewhere, as an LWC appears rational. But is it reasonable? Is the North's globalising role in reforming African identity through technology, bureaucracy and ideology inevitable and therefore to be incorporated within development strategies and political policies? What are the consequences of adopting a Western language in multi-ethnic contexts on both the constituent ethno-linguistic groups and upon the universal language 'community'? Let us illustrate by asking whether English should be encouraged as the official co-equal or second language of many African states? Is it better to anticipate the inevitable or to resist the spread of English as the globalising language? What are the immediate implications of encouraging such global language spread in Africa?

One obvious consequence is the relative functional decline of many African languages, whose communicative power and symbolic purchase is reduced by changing socio-economic circumstances. Systematic exposure to external influences has revealed the limited functional utility of most African languages in a changing context. Roland Breton (1991, pp. 172–4) avers that without energetic language defence policies, most African languages will be submerged within three generations. He recognises that the old pattern based upon language complementarity is being challenged by the pervasive spread of more functional 'official' and inter-ethnic languages. 'Today Africa is involved in a vertiginous breath-taking process of urbanization which has already lead to cities where all ethnic groups are mixed together, half of the population of many countries; there is the central "melting pot" whose pestle is the state language; there, there is nothing to compare with the old rural complementarity between vernacular and vehicular' (Breton, 1991, p. 174).

Language dependency

The process of language dependency obtains at all levels of the socio-political and spatial hierarchy from the individual to the state and international level. Individuals have to perform daily cost–benefit analyses on the economics of language choice. This is not a new situation, as, from ancient times, traders and travellers throughout Africa exercised the same diglossic fluency as do modern taxi drivers in Cairo, or government officials in Lagos. But what changes the situation today is that the freedom to exercise such choice is increasingly determined by state-influenced infra-structural decisions. The individual and the state are conjoined by

> the drastic law of economy which commands language development [for] here through language planning, psychology meets economics, and individual identity joins national design. The options faced by the man in the street are those of the man in power. Masses and governments, in this case at least, are alike – time and money are limited; emergency drives you in one way, the highway of modernity, which is a no return route. (Breton, 1991, p. 174)

This lack of freedom and creativity is exacerbated when alternative power bases promote different languages for different reasons. Thus Tanzania and the apartheid Republic of South Africa were both cases where economic, commercial power required English, but political power promoted a rival tongue, namely Swahili or Afrikaans respectively. This lack of congruence added a further element to the already difficult process of modernisation.

The 'new Africans', the 'men of power', were until recently in a privileged position, in part, because of their command of a Western or other international language. Military, political and commercial leaders have exercised their multi-lingual skills to great effect such that the 'credentials for ruling an African country are disproportionately based on a command of the Euro-imperial language. In Africa south of the Sahara it has become impossible to become a member of parliament or President without being fluent in at least one of the relevant European languages' (Mazrui and Mazrui, 1992, p. 84). The same observation can be made about senior executives in business, senior civil servants and academia.

Should the élite's diglossic capacity be extended to the masses? This is one of the biggest questions of social development policy. Kay argues that certain international languages should become available to all forthwith in order to liberate and develop people in Africa (Kay, 1993). In a similar vein, Carol Eastman has advocated an institutional diglossia with 'English as a medium of instruction, at all levels, while at the same time encouraging first language in home, neighbourhood and regional activities' (Eastman, 1991, p. 148). Others may not be so persuaded by the functional necessity of massive language switching from African to European languages, therefore let us demonstrate a series of alternative answers to the key question of whether most Africans should possess, at the least, both an indigenous and an international language.

Alternative strategies

Pragmatists have a well-established pedigree in language planning. They urge the adoption of a universal language, such as English, in order to provide a 'passport to the modern world'. This perspective views ethnicity as a dualistic concept, reflecting both its potential for dynamic change and for reactionary conservatism. Because it is essentially a behavioural phenomenon reflecting acquired values, it can be manipulated for good or evil. Given the conviction that a Western language would better serve the developmental needs of sub-Saharan Africa than would an indigenous tongue, Kay (1993) has argued that 'plural societies (in Europe no less than Africa), are better served by pragmatic, "neutral", *non*-racial and *non*-ethnic policies which are fairly cognizant of the nature and needs of all individuals, groups and peoples whom they serve'. His Zambian illustration demonstrates that the people are divided by seventy-two ethnic and seven regional languages and are united by one official language, English. 'Like all human constructs, this language policy evidently is not without either history or ethnic origins; but it is pragmatic and seeks to serve the best interests of 8,000,000 people. English is their passport to the modern world' (Kay, 1993).

Such pragmatism, whether by design or default, is also encouraged by technological developments and by the globalisation of culture and economy (Williams, 1993b). There is an acute inevitability surrounding the universalisation of English and, to a lesser extent, of French. The question arises as to whether such inevitability is welcomed and adapted to specific 'national', group and individual needs, or resisted and restricted only to the functional domains of an élite communication network, thereby perpetuating privilege and access to material and intellectual power bases?

Clearly the reasons why this form of pragmatism does not automatically endear itself to all is that both English and French symbolise and realise a colonial inheritance, and perpetuate a neo-colonial intellectual and political dependency. Virulent anti-colonial nationalism fed on this obvious manifestation of inequality and forced incorporation into a European imperial system. Post-colonial nationalism was faced with an acute dilemma of either rejecting the colonial instruments of subjugation, or somehow incorporating them into the new nation-state project, as described above by Hettne (1984). Kay (1993) counters this observation by arguing that Western languages *per se* were not instruments of subjugation *except* by their policies of exclusion. The stark choice facing educators was either to 'revert to "tribal obsolescence" or to "modernise" – including the adoption of a *MODERN* (Western) language. Here we encounter a major misconception, it is the Tanzanian (Swahili) and RSA (Afrikaans) language policies which are the policies of subjugation.' This attitude is intricately bound up with the perceived status differentials between constituent groups in the respective states.

The linguistic hegemony of English

Critics of English, as an instrument of imperialism and modernisation, claim that the spread of English perpetuates an unequal relationship between 'developed' and 'developing' societies because access to information and power does not depend solely upon language fluency. It also depends upon institutional structures, economic resources and relationships. Tollefson reminds us that:

> in order to gain access to English-language resources, nations must develop the necessary institutions, such as research and development offices, 'think tanks' research universities, and corporations, as well as ties to institutions that control scientific and technological information. From the perspective of 'modernising' countries, the process of modernisation entails opening their institutions to direct influence and control by countries that dominate scientific and technical information, the result is an unequal relationship. (Tollefson, 1990, p. 84)

The spread of English is also deeply implicated in the creation of new forms of inequality within societies. Most post-colonial societies are characterised by a dual institutional system, which though linked, nevertheless present different ranges of opportunities to their respective members in the conventional and modernised sectors. In a powerful critique of the role of ELT (English Language Teaching), Phillipson (1992, p. 270) has demonstrated how arguments used to promote English can be classified into three types based upon the language's

1   capacities: English-intrinsic arguments, what English *is*;
2   resources: English-extrinsic arguments, what English *has*;
3   uses: English-functional arguments, what English *does*.

Each element is mediated by the structure of the world order in which English is dominant and each develops its own discourse which locates English *vis-à-vis* competing languages. Thus

> English-intrinsic arguments describe English as rich, varied, noble, well adapted for change, interesting, etc. English-extrinsic arguments refer to textbooks, dictionaries, grammar books, a rich literature, trained teachers, experts, etc. English-functional arguments credit English with real or potential access to modernization, science, technology, etc.; with the capacity to unite people within a country and across nations, or with the furthering of international understanding. (Phillipson, 1992, pp. 271–2)

The functions of English are nearly always described in positive terms. Whether the argument for its extension is couched in terms of persuasion, promise or threat, they represent various ways of exerting and legitimating power. This was well understood during colonial times and is reproduced today in more subtle, sophisticated ways as is demonstrated in the rhetoric of the British Council. When the British 'do not have the power we once had to impose our will ("sticks"), cultural diplomacy must see to it that people see the benefits of English ("carrots") and the drawbacks with their own languages, and then, consequently, want English themselves for their own benefit ("ideas"): "the demand is insatiable." And that means that British influence, British power has not diminished, because Britain has this "invisible, God-given asset". Thus "Britain's influence endures, out of all proportion to her economic or military resources" ' (*British Council Annual Report*, 1983/4, p. 9; quoted in Phillipson, 1992, pp. 286–7).

Language, and the ideology it conveys, is thus part of the legitimisation of positions within the global division of labour. Attempts to separate English from its British and North American value system are misguided, for English should not be interpreted as if it were primarily a *tabula rasa*. Any claim that English is now a neutral, pragmatic tool for global development is disingenuous, because it involves a 'disconnection between what English *is* ("culture") from its structural basis (from what it *has* and *does*)'. It disconnects the *means* from *ends* or *purpose*, from what English is being used for. This type of reasoning 'is part of the rationalisation process whereby the unequal power relations between English and other languages are explained and legitimated. It fits into the familiar linguistic pattern of the dominant language creating an external image of itself, other languages being devalued and the relationship between the two rationalised in favour of the dominant language. This applies to each type of argument, whether persuasion, bargaining, or threats are used, all of which serve to reproduce English linguistic hegemony' (Phillipson, 1992, p. 288). A summary of the manner in which English hegemony is 'glorified' in a competitive situation is presented in Table 8.

Such points emphasise that conflict is inherent in language issues and helps to explain why bilingual and multicultural education – far from encouraging the positive aspects of cultural pluralism – has hitherto been characterised by mutual antagonism, begrudging reforms and ghettoisation. Attempts to overturn pejorative judgements about the normalcy of bilingual education or the promotion of minority languages as normal and as essential elements in society come up against powerful hegemonic discourses which negate the salience of such languages for general developmental issues and social intercourse. There are signs that such discourses are being challenged all over Europe and beyond (Phillipson, 1992; Skutnabb-Kangas, 1999) especially in relation to the urgent need to bring together basic human rights and economic rights within a more participative democratic process. The dilemma is encapsulated in this prescient quotation from the outstanding analyst

Table 8 The labelling of English and other languages

Glorifying English	*Devaluing other languages*
World language	Localised language
International language	(Intra-)national language
Language of wider communication	Language of narrower communication
Auxiliary language	Unhelpful language
Additional language	Incomplete language
Link language	Confining language
Window onto the world	Closed language
Neutral language	Biased language

Source: Philippson (1992), p. 282.

in this field, Tove Skutnabb-Kangas, who writes:

> Globalising access to information has enabled counterhegemonic forces to ensure that there is growing sensitivity to human rights. But at the same time there is also a growing inability to secure them by progressive forces in civil society. The gap between rhetoric and implementation is growing, with all the growing inequalities. Behind this lies the collapse of institutions of democratic political control of trade and capital. In this light, it is completely predictable that states commit linguistic genocide; it is part of the support to the homogenising global market forces.... At present, though we can hope that some of the positive developments might have some effect, overall there is not much cause for optimism ... we still have to work for education through the medium of the mother tongue to be recognised by states as a human right. And if this right is not granted, and implemented, it seems likely that the present pessimistic prognoses of over 90 per cent of the world's oral languages not being around anymore in the year 2100, are too optimistic.   (Skutnabb-Kangas, 1999, pp. 56 and 63)

Globalisation and European minorities

Ethno-linguistic minorities have reacted to globalisation and European integration by searching for European-wide economies of scale in broadcasting, information networking, education and public administration. They have also established their own EU institutions and bureaux and entered new alliances to influence EU decision-making bodies. They believe that by appealing to the superstructural organisations for legitimacy and equality of group rights, they will force member states to recognise their claims for varying degrees of political/social autonomy within clearly identifiable territorial/social domains.

Logically, if globalisation and interdependence can enhance the productive capacity of majority, 'nation-state' interests, they can also be harnessed to develop the interests of lesser-used language groups. Historically the recognition of linguistic minority demands is a very recent phenomenon. In accordance with the resolutions of the European Parliament (Arfé, 1981; Kuijpers, 1987; Killilea, 1994), the European Commission since 1983 has supported action to protect and promote regional and minority languages and cultures within the European Union. In 1996 some 4 million ecus was expended on European socio-cultural schemes (budget line B3-1006 of DGXXII). Equally significant has been a raft of legislation and declarations upholding the rights of minorities to use their languages in several domains (Williams, 1993a). However, linguistic minorities face many structural barriers to their full participation within the EU system.

Recent expansion of the EU has increased the difficulties in translating multi-cultural communication and guaranteeing access to information and hence power for all groups. The real geolinguistic challenge is to safeguard the interests of all the non-state language groups, especially those most threatened with imminent extinction. A critical aspect of constructing these safeguards is access to knowledge, thus we need to ask and act upon the answers to questions such as who controls access to information *within the mother tongue and the working languages* of European minorities? Are such languages destined to occupy a more dependent role because of superstructural changes favouring dominant groups or will they achieve relative socio-cultural autonomy by adopting aspects of mass technology to suit their particular needs?

Additional issues concern the adaptation by speakers of lesser-used language to the opportunities afforded by changes in global–local networks, the growth of specialised economic segments or services and of information networks which are accessed by language-related skills. Accessibility to or denial of these opportunities is the virtual expression of real power in society which must be taken on board in any discussion of the politics of regional cultural representation. The general pattern is expressed thus by Castells (1997) in his monumental three-volume study *The Rise of the Network Society*:

> Cultural expressions are abstracted from history and geography, and become predominantly mediated by electronic communication networks that interact with an audience and by the audience in a diversity of codes and values, ultimately subsumed in a digitised, audio–visual hypertext. Because information and communication circulate primarily through the diversified, yet comprehensive media system, politics becomes increasingly played out in the space of the media. The fact that politics has to be framed in the language of electronically based media has profound consequences on the characteristics, organisation and goals of political processes, political actors, and political institutions. Ultimately, the powers that are in the media networks take second place to the power of flows embodied in the structure and language of these networks.   (Castells, 1997, p. 476)

Why is a common language so often seen as essential to 'nation-building' or state development? If conflict is such a predictable outcome why not opt for linguistic and cultural pluralism as a dominant ideology? Is it merely a post-imperial reaction to a European model of state formation and citizen socialisation? Is the faculty of imitation, and the search for legitimacy through national congruence, so strong as to impel political élites on such a conflict-ridden trajectory?

The answer is surely that language is power to confer privilege, deny opportunity, construct a new social order and radically modify an inherited past which is not conducive to the pursuit of hegemonic aims. Language choice is thus a battleground for contending discourses, ideologies and interpretations of the multi-ethnic experience.

> At a deeper level, the material foundations of society, space and time are being transformed, organised around the spaces of flows and timeless time. Beyond the metaphorical value of these expressions a major hypothesis is put forward: dominant functions are organised in networks pertaining to a space of flows that links them up around the world, while fragmenting subordinate functions, and people, in the multiple space of places, made of locales increasingly segregated and disconnected from each other. ... The social construction of new dominant forms of space and time develops a meta-network that switches off nonessential functions, subordinate social groups, and devalued territories. By so doing, infinite social distance is created between this meta-network and most individuals' activities and localities around the world. The new social order, the network society, increasingly appears to most people as meta-social disorder. Namely, as an automated, random sequence of events derived form the uncontrollable logic of markets, technology, geopolitical order or biological determinations.   (Castells, 1997, p. 477)

As a result of imperialism, neo-colonialism, the modernisation of technology and the globalisation of information flows, there is an acute inevitability surrounding the universalisation of hegemonic languages, such as English, French or Spanish. Transnational languages have been significant elements of imperial rule since Persian, Greek and Roman times and greatly influenced the spread of capitalism and the modern world system. The roles of English and French are crucial to the development of former overseas possessions, by relating former colonies to the motherland and to each other through the Commonwealth and *la francophonie* (Gordon, 1978; Bostock, 1988; Williams, 1996a). Should this inevitability be welcomed, or resisted by being restricted to élite communication networks, thereby perpetuating privilege and access to material and intellectual power bases?

Key domains: education, public administration and the economy

Within the European system, official languages, other than Russian, French, German, Spanish and Italian, are coming to terms with the reality of specifying their specific domain competence in spheres as varied as education, international jurisprudence, military technology and logistical planning, international environmental co-ordination and human rights. Of the major languages German is likely to spread as a result of its revitalised East European commercial and foreign policy. However, it is Spanish which is set to be a major international, transcontinental bridge language. In global terms, if Spanish can be seen as a resource for socio-cultural growth as well as commercial gain, there could be a win–win situation rather than a zero-sum stand off between supporters of English and those of Hispanic-based bilingualism, especially in the Americas (Baker, 1996, p. 358).

As a result of all these tendencies there is growing pressure for a pan-European educational policy in which

> isolated instruction in separate foreign languages should be replaced by instruction for multilingual communication. This requires training in the ability to quickly shift actively or passively from one language to another. In order to make accessible as many European languages as possible, each European school should teach the following languages:
>
> (a) the student's mother tongue
> (b) the world's language (English)
> (c) a language from a language family that does not include the student's mother tongue (i.e. a Romance or Slavic language for Germans, a Germanic or Slavic language for French, a Germanic or Romance language for Poles etc.).   (Posner, 1991, p. 134)

This general maxim is laudable, and would need to accommodate the situation of speakers of lesser-used language such as Breton, Catalan or Friulian, for whom the state language would be co-equal with the mother-tongue instruction.

Specialists stress education's potential in promoting cultural awareness which is predicated on the following assumptions (from Bakes,
1996, p. 379):

1 There is a fundamental equality of all individuals and all minority
   groups irrespective of language and culture.
2 In a democracy, there should be equality of opportunity irrespective
   of ethnic, cultural or linguistic origins.
3 Any manifest or latent form of discrimination by the dominant
   group against minorities requires elimination.
4 A culturally diverse society should avoid racism and ethnocentrism.
5 While generalisations about cultural behaviour may be a natural part
   of humans making sense of their world, cultural stereotypes are to be
   avoided.
6 Minority cultural groups in particular need awareness of their culture as
   a precondition and foundation for building on intercultural awareness.
7 In mainstream monocultural education, language minority parents
   tend to be excluded from participation in their children's education.
   In multicultural education parents should become partners.
8 A pluralist integration is established by interaction and not a mosaic,
   by intermingling and a discovery of others to improve mutual understanding, break down stereotypes, while increasing self-knowledge
   and self-esteem.

Does promoting a common educational approach imply that ultimately
the European Union will become the first post-modern, post-sovereign
multicultural system of the twenty-first century? For the optimist, this
emphasis on accommodation, openness and diversity is an expression
of a highly developed pluralist society which demands mutual respect
and tolerance of its constituent cultures. For the pessimist, such openness is a recipe for continued strife, inter-regional dislocation, inefficient
government and the artificial reproduction of often misleading cultural
identities which deflect attention away from more pertinent social categories. Rather than being a springboard for action such a conception is
seen as an open prison which will hamper the unfettered development
of the individual in a free and burgeoning society.

The basic issue relates to the relative autonomy of constituent groups
within any European policy of multiculturalism. What started as an
attempt to preserve a common Western heritage now has to adjust to
the reality of managing divergence in a multiracial society. How vibrant
are Europe's constituent cultures? How dependent are they on official

patronage? Are they self-sustaining or are many perpetuating a generation-specific conception of a sub-culture, subsidised by public coffers? Clearly such questions draw attention to the dualistic relationship of culture and the modern state. Most minority cultures are increasingly dependent upon the state for legitimising their access to the media, for granting them permission to establish bilingual or religious-based schools, for upholding in law several of their key fundamental values and principles. However, when language and the culture it represents becomes institutionalised in new domains via new agencies, such reforms change the relationship between the individual and the state. Power for enfranchisement is the key to how successful such a relationship will be in serving the needs and expectations of a multicultural society.

It is imperative that European integration should take account of minority rights, without halting the emergence of new forms of ethnic and cultural identification. Only if people are incorporated within the process on equitable terms will the development of society operate at a reasonable political level, otherwise it is the tyranny of the powerful masquerading as progress and social change. In tackling the underlying fears and aspirations of the language reformers we need to ask a further set of questions.

1 What are the key needs for language development in Europe?
2 Whose interests are served in language development?
3 To what extent is democracy undermined by the unsatisfied aspirations of threatened language groups?
4 Are OLS (other language speakers) considered as competitors to autochthonous groups in the crowded arena of minority rights?
5 Are the non-territorial claims of OLS groups sufficiently well developed to have a socio-spatial impact on local services and public provision?
6 What is the role of language in education for the adequate rendering of social services and how does one avoid creating a demand for particular languages at the expense of others?
7 What are the different critical masses required for particular services/classes/liaison?
8 In considering various levels of governmental recognition of language needs, in which domains are there well-recognised multicultural rights, in which is differentiated service provision still a privilege, and in which domains is there unlikely to be any progress whatsoever?

9   How do the central agencies of social reproduction, such as the law, education and health, relate to the increased demands of pluralism and strive to satisfy such demands within a multicultural system?

In tackling such questions pessimists argue there is little chance for the reconciliation of starkly contrasting ethno-linguistic pressures. Conflict is inherent in the situation and far from encouraging the positive aspects of cultural pluralism multicultural education hitherto has been a history of mutual antagonism, begrudging reforms and ghettoisation, where spatial segregation and social isolation have become mutually reinforcing patterns in far too many communities. The drift toward single-issue politics and fragmentation cannot be adequately captured through conventional theorising based around the grand ideas of the nineteenth century. This is why much of the earlier discussion centred upon Charles Taylor's critique of democratic involvement within divided societies is so timely and urgent.

Conclusion: Canada and Quebec in comparative perspective

How do these considerations inform the analysis of language policy and planning in Quebec in the remainder of this volume? Cognisance has been taken of the following factors which determine the range of possibilities for language policies within multicultural societies:

- the state-system and political infra-structure;
- models of social integration and state–civil society relations;
- evolution of language legislation;
- personality and territoriality principles of language service provision;
- education's key role in socialising citizens and immigrants alike;
- the linguistic hegemony of English;
- the rise of the network society;
- types and strategies of language choice;
- the economic and political resources needed to implement different types of language policy;
- conflict resolution through language policy and economic development.

Taken together these are some of the suggested parameters by which language policy may be translated into social practice. But language policy, as successive authors in this volume will testify, is reflective of fundamental political and philosophical differences which revolve around the tension between the state, the collective good and the individual citizen. Calls for tolerance and mutual understanding abound. But they do not necessarily translate into vital, active support for the promotion of French wherever it is spoken in this northern set of spaces. Consequently, the struggle continues, and the geo-linguistic facts do not give comfort to those who would argue that shared sovereignty is the best guarantor of French language survival. Many will pin their hopes on reconciliation and heed Ignatieff's (2000, p. 134) call for the construction of a shared common truth. Others will argue that interdependence and partnership merely serve to perpetuate dependency, however much it is dressed up in the language of equal rights and an overarching legitimate legal order. For my part, as an outsider, coping rather than controlling seems to be the watchword for the twenty-first century in Quebec and Canada as elsewhere. It is my conviction that volumes such as these help us realise the magnitude of the forces we are seeking to change and the inherent fragility of socio-linguistic realities in plural societies.

Acknowledgements

The African material in this essay draws on Williams (1996a) with permission. I am grateful to the Canadian High Commission, London, and the Canadian Studies in Wales Group for their research support, and to Jesus and Mansfield Colleges, Oxford University, for electing me as a Visiting Fellow during 2002 which enabled me to develop this essay.

Notes

1 A recent example of the intransigence of the French system in this respect is the decision of the French Court (November 2001) to strike down as unconstitutional an agreement between the Ministry of Education and the Breton schools movement, Diwan. The court declared that French was the sole official language of the state, and this has obvious implications for language use in Alsace, North Catalonia, North Euskadi and Occitania, to say nothing of the condition of Arabic and other 'immigrant' languages.
2 In discussing these value conflicts in the Canadian context, Ignatieff (2000, p. 134) reveals the crux of the problem 'The real issue is that we do not share the same vision of our country's history. The problem is not one of rights or powers, but one of truth. We do not inhabit the same historical reality. And it is time we did. For two generations, English Canada has asked, with earnest respect, "What does Canada want?". It's time for English Canada to say *who* we are and what *our* country is. The answer is: we are a partnership of nations, a community of peoples united in common citizenship and rights. We do possess a common history, and like it or not, we had better begin to share a common truth.'

3   I favour Robert Cooper's broad definition of language planning, which states that 'language planning refers to deliberate efforts to influence the behaviour of others with respect to the acquisition, structure, or functional allocation of their language codes. This definition neither restricts the planners to author-itative agencies, nor restricts the type of target group, nor specifies an ideal form of planning. ... Finally, it employs the term influence rather than change inasmuch as the former includes the maintenance or preservation of current behaviour, a plausible goal of language planning, as well as the change of current behaviour' (Cooper, 1989, p. 5).

4   Many critics argue that such a division is artificial and untenable and that the sequence in Haugen's model is too idealistic to be of any practical worth.

5   However, many critics argue that this is a naïve division, which can lead to confusion and conflict as language behaviour, and demographic trends nul-lify the principles upon which original language policy was predicated.

6   As will be suggested later in Chapter 3 below, the status of language rights in Canada is now a fundamental constitutional principle of political life. It is thus less amenable to the asymmetrical, territorial solutions that are advo-cated by critics of the current policy.

7   On this see the discussion in Chapter 3 'The Quebec language legislation offers ample testimony that the Quebec government already possesses the main factor in language survival, namely political control over language within its territorial space. In conjunction with its other strengths, the French language exercises control of the education system, and experiences widespread use through the family, community and economic life.'

8   Kymlicka (2001, p. 79) expresses it thus: 'In reality, the anglophone majori-ties in both the United States and Canada zealously guard the right to live in a state where they form a majority, and their right to have English recognised as a language of public life. This defence of boundaries and linguistic policies of existing nation-states is as "collectivist" as the demands of minorities for protection of their self-government and language rights'.

9   Robert Mugabe of Zimbabwe illustrated this tendency throughout the 1990s. In an attempt to appease several dissenting groups he provided a monthly pension to the war veterans, engaged in widespread land reallocation which implicated over 800 white farms. In the global capitalist crisis, he reduced exchange controls which led in 1997 to a 74 per cent crash of Zimbabwe's currency. Four consequences followed: (1) imported inflation; (2) a rise in VAT; (3) the IMF riots; (4) rises in petrol prices and transport fares triggered an 'autonomist' response which in December 1997 led to the worst melt-down in its history. Black Friday was followed by Red Tuesday. Mugabe responded by utilising 38 per cent of export earnings as foreign debt repay-ment. *Source*: Patrick Bond, seminar on Zimbabwe, Oxford University, 15/2/2002.

10   The most recent example was the establishment of a European network of language planning agencies in October 2001 at the instigation of the Basque Government and the Welsh Language Board. This brings together civil ser-vants and professional language planners from Foras na Gailge, Ireland Folktinget, Finland, the Fryske Akademy, Friesland, Netherlands, the Language Planning Departments of the Basque Country, Galicia and Catalonia, Spain, the Welsh Language Board, UK and EBLUL. Three results

may be reported: (1) the Basque Government has provided the secretariat for this network; (2) the EU has recognised the legitimacy of involving this network in their language policy deliberations; and (3) a division of labour whereby the EBLUL will concentrate more on the relatively poorly represented linguistic minorities within the EU and more significantly within the enlarged EU in Central and Eastern Europe.

References

Ammon, U. and Kleineidam, H. (1992) (issue eds), 'Language Spread Policy: Languages of Former Colonial Powers'. *International Journal of the Sociology of Language*, **95**.

Amyot, M. (1980) *La situation démolinguistique au Québec et la charte de la langue française* (Quebec: Conseil de la langue française).

Arfé, G. (1981) 'On a Community Charter of Regional Languages and Cultures and on a Charter of Rights of Ethnic Minorities', resolution adopted by the European Parliament, Strasbourg.

Baker, C. (1996) *Foundations of Bilingual Education and Bilingualism*, 2nd edn (Clevedon, Avon: Multilingual Matters).

Bohman, J. and Rehg, W. (eds) (1999) *Deliberative Democracy* (Cambridge, Mass.: MIT Press).

Bostock, W. W. (1988) 'Assessing the Authenticity of a Supra-National Language Based Movement: La Francophonie', in C. H. Williams (ed.), *Language in Geographic Context* (Clevedon: Multilingual Matters), pp. 73–92.

Bourhis, R. H. (ed.) (1984) *Conflict and Language Planning in Québec* (Clevedon, Avon: Multilingual Matters).

Brann, C. M. B. (1991) 'Review of F. Coulmas, "With Forked Tongues: What are National Languages for"?' *History of European Ideas*, **13**: 131–5.

Breton, R. (1991) 'The Handicaps of Language Planning in Africa', in D. R. Marshall (ed.), *Language Planning: Focusschrift in Honour of Joshua A. Fishman* (Amsterdam: John Benjamins).

British Council (1993/4) *Annual Report* (London: British Council).

Caldwell, G. and Waddell, E. (eds) (1982) *The English of Québec from Majority to Minority Status* (Quebec City: Institut Québecois de Recherche sur la Culture).

Canadian Heritage (1998) *Multiculturalism: Respect, Equality, Diversity* (Ottawa: Department of Canadian Heritage).

Cardinal, L. (1999) 'Linguistic Rights, Minority Rights and National Rights: Some Clarifications'. *Inroads*, **8**: 77–86.

Cardinal, L. (2000) 'Le pouvoir exécutif et la judiciarisation de la politique au Canada: Une tude du programme de contestation juriciaire', *Politique & Sociétés*, **9**: 43–64.

Cardinal, L. and Hudon, M.-E. (2001) *The Governance of Canada's Official Language Minorities: A Preliminary Study* (Ottawa: Office of the Commissioner of Official Langauges).

Cartwright, D. G. and Williams, C. H. (1982) 'Bilingual Districts as an Instrument in Canadian Language Policy'. *Transactions of the Institute of British Geographers*, **7**: 474–93.

Cartwright, D. G. and Williams, C. H. (1997a) 'Les enclaves linguistiques ne régleraient rien'. *Le Devoir*, 18 November, p. A9.

Cartwright, D. G. and Williams, C. H. (1997b) 'If Quebec is Divisible, so is Ontario'. *The Gazette*, 22 November, p. B6.

Castells, M. (1997) *The Rise of the Network Society* (Oxford: Blackwell).

Castonguay, C. (1996a) 'Assimilation Trends among Official Language Minorities, 1971–91'. *Towards the XX1st Century: Emerging Socio-Demographic Trends and Policy Issues in Canada* (Ottawa), Proceedings of the Federation of Canadian Demographers Symposium, St Paul's University, Ottawa, 23–25 October 1995, pp. 201–5.

Castonguay, C. (1996b) 'L'intérêt particulier de la démographie pour le fait français au Canada', in J. Erfurt (ed.), *De la Polyphonie à la Symphonie* (Leipzig: Leipziger Universitätsverlag), pp. 3–18.

Castonguay, C. (1997) 'The Fading Canadian Duality', in J. Edwards (ed.), *Language in Canada* (Cambridge: Cambridge University Press).

Castonguay, C. (1999a) 'Getting the Facts Straight on French: Reflections Following the 1996 Census'. *Inroads*, **8**, pp. 57–76.

Castonguay, C. (1999b) 'French is on the ropes: Why won't Ottawa admit it?' *Policy Options*.

Chevrier, M. (1997) *Laws and Languages in Québec: The Principles and Means of Québec's Language Policy* (Quebec: Ministère des Relations internationales).

Chevrier, M. (2003) 'A Language Policy for a Language in Exile', Chapter 3 in the current volume.

CLF (1988) *Le Projet de loi fédéral C-72 relatif au statut et à l'usage des langues officielles au Canada* (Quebec: Conseil de la langue française).

COL (1980) 'Mother Tongues in Canada and Québec'. *Languages of the World* (Ottawa: Commissioner of Official Languages 2).

Conklin, N. and Lourie, M. (1983) *A Host of Tongues* (New York: Free Press).

Cooper, R. (1989) *Language Planning and Social Change* (Cambridge: Cambridge University Press).

Coulmas, F. (ed.) (1988) *With Forked Tongues: What are National Languages Good For?* (Ann Arbor: Karoma).

Crystal, D. (1987) *The Cambridge Encyclopaedia of Language* (Cambridge: Cambridge University Press).

Declaració de Barcelona (1996) *Declaració universal de drets lingüístics* (Barcelona: International PEN and CIEMEN).

Dion, S. (1992) 'Explaining Quebec Nationalism', in R. Kent Weaver (ed.), *The Collapse of Canada* (Washington, DC: Brookings Institute).

Domenichelli, L. (1999) 'Comparaison entre les stratégies linguistiques de Belgique et du Canada'. *Globe: Revue internationale d'études québécoises*, **2**(2): 125–46.

Eastman, C. M. (1983) *Language Planning: An Introduction* (San Fransisco: Chandler and Sharp).

Eastman, C. (1991) 'The Political and Sociolinguistic Status of Planning in Africa', in D. F. Marshall (ed.), *Language Planning: Focusschrift in Honor of Joshua A. Fishman* (Amsterdam: John Benjamins), pp. 135–51.

Edwards, J. (1994) *Multilingualism* (London: Longman).

Eisenberg, A. (1998) 'Individualism and Collectivism in the Politic's of Canada's North', in Joan Anderson, Avigail Eisenber, Sherrill Grace and Veronica Strong-Boag (eds), *Painting the Maple: Essays on Race, Gender and the Construction of Canada* (Vancouver: University of British Columbia Press).

Elliott, J. L. (ed.) (1979) *Two Nations: Many Cultures – Ethnic Groups in Canada* (Scarborough, Ont.: Prentice Hall).

Extra, G. and Gorter, D. (eds) (2001) *The Other Languages of Europe* (Clevedon, Avon: Multilingual Matters).

Fasold, R. (1988) 'What National Languages are Good For', in F. Coulmas (ed.), *With Forked Tongues* (Ann Arbor: Koroma), pp. 180–5.

Fishman, J. A. (1969) 'National Language and Languages of Wider Communication'. *Anthropological Linguistics*, **11**: 111–75.

Fishman, J. A. (1989) *Language and Ethnicity in Minority Sociolinguistic Perspective* (Clevedon, Avon: Multilingual Matters).

Fishman, J. A. (1991) *Reversing Language Shift* (Clevedon, Avon: Multilingual Matters).

Fishman, J. A. (2001) *Can Threatened Languages Be Saved?* (Clevedon, Avon: Multilingual Matters).

Glazer, N. (1977) 'Individual Rights against Group Rights', in E. Kamenka (ed.), *Human Rights* (London: E. Arnold).

Gordon, D. G. (1978) *The French Language and National Identity* (The Hague: Mouton).

Gunnermark, E. and Kenrick, D. (1985) *A Geolinguistic Handbook* (Gothenburg: Gunnermark).

Haarman, H. (1990) 'Language Planning in the Light of a General Theory of Language: a Methodological Framework'. *International Journal of the Sociology of Language*, **86**: 103–26.

Habermas, J. (1996) 'The European Nation-state – its Achievements and its Limits', in G. Balakrishnan and B. Anderson (eds), *Mapping the Nation* (London: Verso), pp. 281–94.

Harley, B. (1994) 'After Immersion: Maintaining the Momentum'. *Journal of Multilingual and Multicultural Development*, **15**(2 and 3): 229–44.

Harries, L. (1983) 'The Nationalisation of Swahili in Kenya', in C. Kennedy (ed.), *Language Planning and Language Education* (London: George Allen and Unwin), pp. 118–28.

Haugen, E. (1983) 'The Implementation of Corpus Planning: Theory and Practice', in J. Cobarrubias and J. A. Fishman (eds), *Progress in Language Planning* (Berlin: Mouton), pp. 269–89.

Havel, V. (1991) 'A Freedom of a Prisoner', Opening address to the Bratislava Symposium II, and reproduced in J. Plichtová (ed.) (1992), *Minorities in Politics: Cultural and Language Rights* (Bratislava: European Cultural Foundation).

Hechter, M. (2000) *Containing Nationalism* (Oxford: Oxford University Press).

Heine, B. (1992) 'Language Policies in Africa', in R. K. Herbert (ed.), *Language and Society in Africa* (Johannesburg: Witwatersrand University Press), pp. 23–35.

Herbert, R. K. (ed.) (1992) *Language and Society in Africa* (Johannesburg: Witwatersrand University Press).

Hettne, B. (1984) *Approaches to the Study of Peace and Development: A State of the Art Report* (Tilburg: EADI Working Papers).

Horowitz, D. L. (1985) *Ethnic Groups in Conflict* (Berkeley: University of California Press).

Horowitz, D. L. (1991) *A Democratic South Africa?* (Berkeley: University of California Press).

Ignatieff, M. (2000) *The Rights Revolution* (Toronto: Anansi).

Joy, R. J. (1972) *Languages in Conflict* (Toronto: McClelland and Stewart).

Joy, R. J. (1992) *Canada's Official Languages: The Progress of Bilingualism* (Toronto: University of Toronto Press).

Kallen, E. (1995) *Ethnicity and Human Rights in Canada* (Toronto: Oxford University Press).

Kaplan, R. B. and Baldauf, R. B. (1997) *Language Planning from Practice to Theory* (Clevedon, Avon: Multilingual Matters).

Kay, G. (1970) *Rhodesia: A Human Geography* (New York: Africana Publishing).

Kay, G. (1993) Personal communication.

Kay, G. (1993) 'Ethnicity, the Cosmos and Plonomic Development, with Special Reference to Central Africa', Stoke on Trent, Staffordshire Polytechnic, mimeo.

Kennedy, C. (ed.) (1983) *Language Planning and Language Education* (London: G. Allen and Unwin).

Killilea, M. (1994) 'On Linguistic and Cultural Minorities in the European Community', resolution adopted by the European Parliament, Strasbourg.

Kingwell, M. (2000) *The World We Want* (Toronto: Penguin).

Kuijpers, W. (1987) 'On the Languages and Cultures of Regional and Ethnic Minorities in the European Community', resolution adopted by the European Parliament, Strasbourg.

Kukathas, C. (1995) 'Are There any Cultural Rights?' in W. Kymlicka (ed.), *The Rights of Minority Cultures* (Oxford: Oxford University Press), pp. 228–55.

Kymlicka, W. (1998) 'Multinational Federalism in Canada: Rethinking the Partnership', in R. Gibbins and G. Laforest (eds), *Beyond the Impasse: Towards Reconciliation* (Montreal: Institute for Research on Public Policy), pp. 15–50.

Kymlicka, W. (2001) *Politics in the Vernacular* (Oxford: Oxford University Press).

Laitin, D. D. (1992) *Language Repertoires and State Construction in Africa* (Cambridge: Cambridge University Press).

Laponce, J. (1984) 'The French Language in Canada: Tensions between Geography and Politics', *Political Geography Quarterly*, 3: 91–104.

Laponce, J. A. (1987) *Languages and their Territories* (Toronto: University of Toronto Press).

Mackey, W. (1991) 'Language Diversity, Language Policy and the Sovereign State'. *History of European Ideas*, 13: 51–61.

Mackey, W. (1992a) *Assessing Canadian Language Policy* (mimeo).

Mackey, W. (1992b) Personal communication, May.

McRae, K. (1997) 'Language Policy and Language Contact: Reflections on Finland', in W. Wölck and A. de Houwer (eds), *Recent Studies in Contact Linguistics*, Plurilingua XVII (Bonn: Dümmler), pp. 218–26.

Marshall, D. (ed.) (1991) *Language Planning: Focusschrift in Honour of Joshua A. Fishman*, 3 vols (Amsterdam: John Benjamins).

Mazrui, A. and Zirimu, P. (1990) 'The Secularization of an Afro-Islamic Language: Church, State and Market-Place in the Spread of Kiswahili'. *Journal of Islamic Studies*, 1: 24–53.

Mazrui, A. M. and Mazrui, A. A. (1992) 'Language in a Multicultural Context: the African Experience'. *Language and Education*, 6: 83–9.

Msanjila, Y. P. (1990) 'Problems of Teaching through the Medium of Kiswahili in Teacher Training Colleges in Tanzania'. *Journal of Multilingual and Multicultural Development*, 11: 307–18.

Moore, M. (2001) *The Ethics of Nationalism* (Oxford: Oxford University Press).

Nelde, P. (1997) 'On the Evaluation of Language Policy', in Generalitat de Catalunya (ed.), *Proceedings of the European Conference on Language Planning* (Barcelona: Department de Cultura), pp. 285–92.

Nelde, P. H., Labrie, N. and Williams, C. H. (1992) 'The Principles of Territoriality and Personality in the Solution of Linguistic Conflicts'. *Journal of Multilingual and Multicultural Development*, **13**(5): 387–406.

Phillipson, R. (1992) *Linguistic Imperialism* (Oxford: Oxford University Press).

Posner, R. (1991) 'Society, Civilisation, and Mentality: Prolegomena to a Language Policy for Europe', in F. Coulmas (ed.), *A Language Policy for the European Community* (Berlin: Mouton), pp. 121–37.

Robinson, C. L. D. (1992a) *Language Choice in Rural Development* (Dallas: International Museum of Cultures).

Robinson, C. L. D. (1992b) 'Where Minorities are in the Majority', paper presented at the International Conference on the Maintenance and Loss of Minority Languages, Noordwijkerhout, the Netherlands, 1–4 September.

Robinson, C. L. D. (1994) 'Is Sauce for the Goose, Sauce for the Gander? Some Comparative Reflections on Minority Language Planning in North and South'. *Journal of Multilingual and Multicultural Development*, **15** (2 & 3): 129–45.

RCBB (1967) *Report of the Royal Commission on Bilingualism and Biculturalism*, Chairmen: Laurendean and Dunton (Ottawa: Queen's Printer).

Rubagumya, C. M. (ed.) (1990) *Language in Education in Africa: A Tanzanian Perspective* (Clevedon, Avon: Multilingual Matters).

Skutnabb-Kangas, T. (1997) 'Language Rights as Conflict Prevention', in W. Wölck and A. de Houwer (eds), *Recent Studies in Contact Linguistics*, Plurilingua XVII (Bonn: Dümmler), pp. 312–24.

Skutnabb-Kangas, T. (1999) 'Language, Power and Linguistic Human Rights – the Role of the State', in *Proceedings of the International Conference on Language Legislation* (Dublin: Comhdháil Náisiúnta na Gaeilge) February, pp. 50–68.

Stewart, W. A. (1968) 'A Socioloingistic Typology for Describing National Multilingualism', in J. Fishman *et al.* (ed.), *Language Problems of Developing Nations* (London: Wiley), pp. 503–53.

Taylor, C. (1991) *The Malaise of Modernity* (Toronto: Anasi).

Taylor, C. (1992) 'Multiculturalism and "The politics of recognition" ', in C. Taylor and A. Guttman (eds), *Multiculturalism and 'the Politics of Recognition'*. (Princeton, NJ: Princeton University Press), pp. 25–74.

Taylor, C. (1994) 'Reply and Re-articulation', in J. Tully (ed.) *Philosophy in an Age of Pluralism* (Cambridge: Cambridge University Press), pp. 213–57.

Tollefson, J. W. (1991) *Planning Language: Planning Inequality* (London: Longman).

Tully, J. (1999) 'Liberté et dévoilement dans les sociétés multinationales'. *Globe: Revue internationale d'études québécoises*, 2(2): pp. 13–36.

UNESCO (1951) *The Use of Vernacular Languages in Education* (Paris: UNES).

Van den Berghe, P. L. (1968) 'Language and Nationalism in South Africa', in J. A. Fishman, C. A. Ferguson and J. Das Gupta (eds), *Language Problems of Developing Nations* (New York: Wiley), pp. 215–24.

Williams, C. H. (1981) 'Official-language Districts, a Gesture of Faith in the Future of Canada'. *Ethnic and Racial Studies*, **4**: 334–47.

Williams, C. H. (ed.) (1982) *National Separatism* (Cardiff and Vancouver: University of Wales Press, and the University of British Columbia Press).

Williams, C. H. (1986) 'The Question of National Congruence', in R. J. Johnston and P. J. Taylor (eds), *A World in Crisis?* (Oxford: Blackwell), pp. 196–230.

Williams, C. H. (1989) 'The Question of National Congruence', in R. J. Johnston and P. J. Taylor (eds), *A World in Crisis?*, 2nd edn (Oxford: Blackwell), pp. 229–66.

Williams, C. H. (1991a) 'Language Planning and Social Change: Ecological Speculations', in D. Marshall (ed.), *Language Planning: Focusschrift in Honour of Joshua A. Fishman*, 3 vols (Amsterdam: John Benjamins), pp. 53–74.

Williams, C. H. (ed.) (1991b) *Linguistic Minorities, Society and Territory* (Clevedon, Avon: Multilingual Matters).

Williams, C. H. (ed.) (1993a) *The Political Geography of the New World Order* (London: Belhaven/John Wiley).

Williams, C. H. (1993b) 'The European Community's Lesser Used Languages'. *Rivista Geografica Italiana* **100**: 531–64.

Williams, C. H. (1994) *Called unto Liberty* (Clevedon, Avon: Multilingual Matters).

Williams, C. H. (1996a) 'Ethnic Identity and Language Issues in Development', in D. Dwyer and D. Drakakis-Smith (eds), *Ethnicity and Development* (Chichester: John Wiley), pp. 45–85.

Williams, C. H. (1996b) 'A Requiem for Canada?' in G. Smith (ed.), *Federalism: The Multiethnic Challenge* (London: Longman), pp. 31–72.

Williams, C. H. (1998b) 'Introduction: Respecting the Citizens – Reflections on Language Policy in Canada and the United States', in T. Ricento and B. Burnaby (eds), *Language and Politics in the United States and Canada* (Mahwah, New Jersey: Lawrence Erlbaum Associates Publishers), pp. 1–33.

Williams, C. H. (ed.) (2000) *Language Revitalization: Policy and Planning in Wales* (Cardiff: University of Wales Press).

2
The History of Quebec in the Perspective of the French Language[1]

Jean-Philippe Warren

Introduction

It would be impossible here to recapitulate the whole of the history of Canada or to enumerate every event that has had an impact on the shaping of the Canadian nation. We only wish to discuss in this chapter some of the major challenges that the French-speaking community in the Province of Quebec has faced during its 400 years of existence.

The issue is seen here from a historical bias. On the one hand, the question of language did not become an autonomous issue in Quebec until recently. As the traditional elements of identity gradually disappeared, the main vector of identification and definition has become linguistic. On the other hand, the population of Quebec underwent several identity changes, as evidenced by their definition first as 'Frenchmen', then as 'Canadians', then as 'French Canadians', before calling themselves '(French) Quebecers'. In this chapter, we will try to explain how and why this rapid transformation of the identity of the French speakers in Canada took place. That is, why and how the French speakers went from colonial settlers to citizens of a Province. Therefore, the following pages do not so much trace the history of some part of a country: they try to trace the history of a nation in the making. From the colony of New France, to Lower Canada, to United Canada, to the Province of Quebec of the Dominion of Canada and the Province of Quebec as we know it today, the historian can retrace the affirmation of the French-speaking community, while he is witness to the complexification and radicalisation of the challenges of its survival.

1534–1760: the 'discovery' of Canada and the colonisation of New France

Although the drakkars of the Vikings did venture as far as Newfoundland, and although the boats of the Basque fishermen followed the cod right up the St Lawrence Gulf, Jacques Cartier, having erected a white cross in the name of his king on the ground of a land unknown to the European cartographers, is considered the official European discoverer of Canada (1534). From St Malo, Cartier navigated, during his second trip, far up the St Lawrence river, but could not push further to the west, being stopped by the rapids of Hochelaga (Montreal).

Despite past hagiographies, the intentions of Cartier were neither glorious nor heroic. François I, envious of the military exploits of the Spanish Conquistadors in Mexico, had mandated Cartier to find a passage to India and to discover natural resources that could be plundered. Despite the beauty and the vastness of the landscape, the terrible living conditions in this part of the world could not be ignored. During the winter of 1535, more than half of Cartier's companions died of scurvy and cold, and it would have been much worse without the help of the native populations. The Amerindian people were open to exchange with the Europeans, but they were hostile to the colonisation of their territory. In contrast to the more hierarchically structured societies of South America, the Amerindian societies of that time were, for the most part, lightly structured, with the consequence that it was impossible to subdue them by simply overthrowing a prince. Moreover, they were very skilled in the art of war and diplomacy. Most of the north-east of the American continent was organised through alliances, treaties and commercial exchanges.

Thus began the adventure of the French Empire in America: with a terrible deception. Cartier did not discover gold and he did not find a maritime route to India. Canada was really, to use an expression popularised later by Voltaire, 'quelques arpents de neige', without any interest and profit for the king of France. At that time, nobody seemed to want to launch any colonisation project, not the king, who was preoccupied by his continental politics, nor the merchants, hoping for rapid gains, nor the peasants, strongly attached to their land. During the period following the 'discovery' of Canada, the fishermen continued to anchor along the American coasts, but every attempt to establish permanent settlement proved disastrous.

We have to wait until the arrival of Samuel de Champlain at Quebec (1608) to witness the foundation of the first permanent base in

Canada – eventually to become the capital of New France. The beginnings were hard: twenty out of twenty-eight of Champlain's companions died the first winter. The 'habitation' (as it was called) was nothing more than a small fur trade post. It was established on a strategic bluff on the St Lawrence river so as to block the access of other European merchants (mainly English and Dutch). It also served as a commercial counter toward exchange with the Amerindians. In 1632, Quebec City was peopled by about 100 inhabitants; in 1660 it had only 2500, with a dramatic ratio of 7 men to each woman.

The (almost) unique economic activity was the fur trade, in particular beaver fur, which still accounted for 75 per cent of exports from the colony in 1760. Beaver fur was used in the fabrication of hats in Europe. The fashion was so popular that the pelts were sold in tens of thousands each year. This flourishing market helped the colony to establish itself. The King decreed that the colonisation of this part of his Empire would be the price to pay to acquire the monopoly on fur trade. In other words, the money made from the fur trade would serve to finance the colonisation of New France.

The suppliers of pelts being the Native population, the colony had no other choice but to ensure their collaboration. More than anything, this meant signing military treaties. The King of France promised to help his allies in war with enemy tribes. For their part, the Amerindians promised to defend the colony against the possible attacks of enemy nations, whether Amerindians or Europeans, and never to trade with Dutch or English colonies. The entire history of the young colony is thus filled with skirmishes, battles and negotiations, followed by further battles, skirmishes and negotiations. Too weak to maintain itself alone, relying almost entirely on the fur trade for its economic survival, having to deal with the competition and the military pressure of the Dutch and English colonies, New France was forced to become involved in a diplomatic and military entanglement that it did not control but tried to manipulate as much as possible to its profit. It was in large part because the Huron tribes sided with them that the men and women of New France were able to resist through the seventeenth century. Of course, the wars were to be bloody, but less deadly than the viruses and bacteria brought by the Europeans. At least 90 per cent of the north-east Amerindians died as a result of epidemics less than a century after the arrival of the Europeans. The colonisation of North America took place on a land that was not deserted, but widowed.

In 1642, Montreal was founded by a group of mystics dreaming of establishing a missionary city. The goal was to achieve the conversion of the indigenous people. That meant making them Frenchmen. The missionaries tried to teach them the French language and how to behave according to French manners; most importantly, they tried to convince them to give up their traditions and adopt the Christian faith. The religious communities left us numerous and fascinating accounts of both their religious adventure and the life of the Natives. The *Jesuits' Relations*, for example, are a literary monument. But the idealism and the courage of the Montreal founders were not enough to make their assimilation project a success. Not impressed by the European way of life, Amerindians were hostile to conversion and 'frenchifying'. The superiority of the Europeans appeared to them to be without foundation; they were not convinced of the enlightened character of the European culture. Most often, it was in fact the Europeans who realised, in the mirror of the Other, that their values were often arbitrary and artificial. The traditions and customs are all relative, wrote LeJeune at the end of his life. He was a Jesuit missionary who came to adopt a relativistic perspective (except of course for the Christian faith!), realising the diversity, the complexity and the richness of the Native cultures.

In the meantime, as the clergy and members of the religious communities tried to 'civilise' the Amerindians, numerous Canadians, who had become *coureur de bois* (trappers), adopted the 'savage' way of life. They learnt the Iroquoian and Algonquian languages, become interpreters, lived like Indians, were hired as intermediaries by the fur companies, penetrated deep into the forest to explore the territory. Cavelier de La Salle was typical of this race of men who came from the old continent to seek fortune. He fought other trappers, contracted alliances with Native people, bartered with them, and covered by foot or canoe the new continent, from North to South, in search of wealth and a way to Asia that was not to be found. Radisson was another of those men, who was captured by the Iroquoians and adopted as a member of the tribe, before escaping them. As a trapper and an explorer, he continued to travel the American continent for twenty years, always staying in close contact with the Indians, the fur companies and the governments of the European Empires.

The organisation of the colony on the fur trade was very different from the systems of the Dutch and British. Their colonies' contacts with the Natives were less common. Their economies were based first on agriculture (that of, among others, tobacco, for exportation). Their settlements slowly progressed to the West without being dispersed over a vast territory. The difference between the 'coureur de bois' of New France and the puritan farmer of New England gives a clear image of the gulf between the two forms of settlement. The consequences of this difference on the future development of New France were to be decisive.

On the one hand, the frontiers of New France were constantly expanding with the intensification of trapping. At the beginning of the seventeenth century, New France stretched from Newfoundland to the Great Lakes, and from the South of Hudson's Bay to Louisiana. By comparison, the thirteen colonies of New England occupied a narrow strip of land on the Atlantic coast. Today's toponymy shows traces of the French American Empire: in Deschutes River (Oregon) or South Loup River (Nebraska), and Louisiana (named after Louis XIV), New Orleans (Nouvelle Orléans), Castine (a deformation of Saint-Castin), Detroit, Vincennes, Saint-Louis, etc. We do not need to point out that the possession of territory was often nominal: the other European powers remained unimpressed with the construction of forts scattered over vast regions, and the Native nations gave no indication of wanting to give up their land and rebelled occasionally against the European intrusion.

On the other hand, being in constant contact with the Native nations, the inhabitants of the colony 'canadianised' themselves. Marie de l'Incarnation, an Ursuline nun freshly arrived in Ville Marie (later Montreal), wrote, in a letter of 1640, of her amazement at 'this part of the world where people are savages all year long, except when the boats arrive and we take up our French language again'. The influence of Native languages on French were, on the whole, limited, except for a few words related to wildlife and flora – such as *achignan* (a fish), *atoca* (cranberry), *babiche* (strap of raw leather), *carcajou* (a mammal), *ouaouaron* (a giant frog) – and names of places, such as Quebec, Tadoussac, Chicoutimi, Témiscaming. The impact of Native cultures on French attitudes was, in contrast, far-reaching; the Canadian spirit, more independent and more open to cultural differences than the French spirit at that time, was strongly influenced by this initial contact. Uprooted from France and resettled on the American continent, the Canadian settlers thus developed some original traits of character.

The destiny of the colony, nothing more than a small trade post until then, changed after 1660, thanks to the policy of Colbert, the Minister of Louis XIV. For the first time, the royal power was committed to ensuring its presence and influence in North America. A relatively audacious policy of settlement helped the consolidation of New France. A true colony was formed with the arrival, between 1663 and 1675, of settlers, 'filles du roi' and soldiers from the Carignan's regiment. The clearing of land for cultivation was slow. Less than 70,000 acres were cultivated in 1721. But this still represented three times more than sixty years earlier.

The fur trade gave way to farming, the field replaced the forest. A seigniorial system organised the concession of lands. The Crown gave land on condition that the seigniors recruited 'censitaires' and developed agriculture. This system was not very efficient, but it nevertheless marked the landscape of the colony: it cut long strips of land perpendicular to a river (without which there could be no trade nor rapid transportation), between Quebec and Montreal.

At the beginning of the eighteenth century, the three main traditional characteristics of New France were henceforth well established. The *coureur de bois* disappeared deep into the territories of North America to bring back the main exporting good of the colony, furs. The clergy began to assert itself by creating parishes, and thus entering into competition with the royal power (over the social organisation of the colony) and the fur companies (over preserving the Natives from the bad European influence). Loosely attached to a seigniory, the peasants had a liberty and a status that were far greater than in France. Each of the inhabitants had a different image of what New France should be: the trapper would have liked it to be as wide as North America itself, the priest would have liked it to be limited to the parish, and the peasant hoped it would be small enough for the military protection of its farm to be ensured but big enough to ensure his prosperity.

New France had about 18,000 inhabitants in 1700, and, supported by a high fertility rate, 70,000 by 1760. The thirteen British colonies had a population twenty times bigger, with 1,500,000 people in 1760. These populations put pressure on New France, as they expanded to the West and to the North. Fishing for cod and whales, added to the competition for furs, fuelling the continuous rivalry between the two colonial powers (the Dutch colony had been taken over by that time by the British colonies). The disproportionate size of the military resources of the two colonies, the scattered nature of New France settlements, stretching from the St Lawrence to the Mississippi, the parsimonious help available from the metropolis, all these factors contrived to force the capitulation of New France in 1760, after the siege of Quebec by British troops. The far too vast French North American Empire was in fact very fragile: it ended in 1763 with the Paris Treaty by which France officially abandoned its colony to England.

1760–1867: Lower Canada under British governance

On the verge of its return to France, an officer of the French army, Lévis, was not the only one to be astonished by the way the people of Canada welcomed the new regime. The end of military struggle, the commercial peace, a bilingual and francophile administration and the assurance, given by the conqueror, to respect the possessions, the religion and the rights of the inhabitants all contributed to a spirit of concord. Although the majority of the population suffered little trauma from the Conquest, the state bureaucracy, aristocracy and upper bourgeoisie making up the ruling class deserted the colony, with the consequence that social and economic development, from a French Canadian point of view, was stalled for several years. For better or worse, the Union Jack was flying over Quebec City, Trois-Rivières and Montreal.

The British government created the Province of Quebec, a territory on the two banks of the St Lawrence river. It was later split, in 1791, into Upper Canada (now Ontario) and Lower Canada (now Quebec). The government of Newfoundland and the government of Nova Scotia were associated with them. The English Empire chose to treat the newly conquered territories like all its other colonies. The colony was to be one of geographically limited settlements, based on agriculture or the production of goods for the metropolis market. The fur economy passed into the control of the English, as did the growing wood industry. Lands were distributed to friends of the governor. Nevertheless, the English did little for their compatriots. As described by the Anglican Bishop Inglis, the last conquest of the British Empire was 'a French colony with an English garrison'. In 1764, the Province of Quebec comprised 300 English speakers and 65,000 French speakers.

This was one reason why the colonial government was not overly oppressive toward its new subjects. There was a fear that the latter might be tempted to call for their annexation to the American republic that had declared its independence in 1776. There was also the danger of riots if the government imposed its presence too heavily on subjects who were accustomed to independence and who were skilled in the art of war. With the Quebec Act in 1774, England gave Canada a constitution that abolished the Test Act and restored the French civil laws, the seigniorial regime and the rights of the Catholic Church. The Quebec Act was completed by the 1791 Constitutional Act, which created a House of Commons, empowered, jointly with the Legislative Council, to adopt laws for the administration of the country. This apparent democracy was, however, smothered by the non-elected Executive Power and the Legislative Council which were responsible only to the governor. The parliamentary government was invalidated because those upper powers were sold to British interests, even though in the province of Lower Canada, at the turn of the century, there were only 20,000 English speakers in a total population of 160,000 inhabitants.

The French Canadians, who called themselves simply Canadians, in opposition to the British, missed no opportunity to protect their rights. In 1792, at the new assembly of the House of Commons, Jean-Antoine Panet was elected President, despite the opposition of the English deputies. His speech before the governor strongly advocated the use of the French language. He was granted permission, as were all the French deputies with him, to express himself in his mother tongue. From then on, politics became the French Canadians' favourite way to fight their battles and ensure the development of their nation.

This preference for public affairs is demonstrated by the fact that the main borrowings from English at the time came from the vocabulary of the court and of parliamentary debates. *Coroner, foreman, writ, warrant, bill, speaker*, all these words entered the juridical and political language, and from there the common language. French thus became filled with English terms. Those loanwords from the occupying power were decried by some as a sign of the degeneration of the French Canadian language. 'Their style [of the lawyers],' wrote Tocqueville after a short inquiry in Lower Canada, 'is vulgar and filled with barbarisms and English locutions... The whole picture shows something bizarre, incoherent and even burlesque.'

The French Canadians borrowed much more than the mere words of the occupiers, they also adopted their way of life: social clubs, food and drink (beer, tea and potatoes), hair styles, furniture design, the mode of greeting (by shaking hands instead of kissing cheeks). The evolution of the language not only illustrates the anglicisation of the vocabulary, it tells of the assimilation of ways and manners brought from London. Economic growth, stimulated by the boom of the wood industry, enabled the settlers to buy many imported goods that the advertisements in the newspaper did not bother to translate: *brown bread, ketchup, groceries, teaboard, boiler, drab*. However, the French inhabitants continued to wish each other *la pinouillère* (happy new year) and store their belongings in the *cocron* (cook room).

Furthermore, the movement of English liberalism influenced colonial debates. Etienne Parent, one of the most famous French Canadian intellectuals of the nineteenth century, was influenced by the masters of English political economy. In a time, however, where national feelings were growing and the right of nations to determine their own future was being recognised, it was the American republic that fascinated the Canadians. The 1830s were filled with declarations about the democratic success and the material prosperity of the United States. There, the rich and the poor seemed to be equals, because the poor were rich, and the rich not so far from the poor. And, most importantly, their Southern neighbour was ruled not by the whim of an hereditary king, but by an elected democracy.

These adaptations of and concessions to the English and American spirit did not lead the French Canadians to an abdication of their mother tongue. If they were influenced by the Anglo-Saxon manners and philosophy, they did not adopt English as their common language. On the contrary, they were keen to protect their rights, their faith and their traditions. The director of the newspaper *Le Canadien*, Etienne Parent, advocated the importance of maintaining a rightful place for the French speakers in the colony, to broaden liberty under the Union Jack and to liberalise the colonial regime. He argued that a nation speaking the language of Molière would be in no way less truly Canadian. 'As far as we know, there is not a French Nation in this province, but a Canadian nation, a moral and religious nation, a loyal Nation attached to liberty and at the same time able to benefit from it; this Nation is neither French, nor English, nor Scottish, nor Irish, nor Yankee, it is Canadian', wrote Parent in 1831. The Canadians were longing for a destiny of their own in North America, one that would differ from that of England and from that of the United States.

The governors and their counsellors were irritated to see the Frenchmen resist assimilation. They were annoyed to see them progress in number and in force. They worried about their influence on the administration of the colony. This conquered nation was acting as though it were equal to the conqueror! One can read, in the *Quebec Mercury* of October 27, 1806: 'This province is already too much a French province for an English colony. To "unfrenchify" it, as much as possible … should be a primary object. … After forty years' possession of Quebec, it is time the province should be English.' This kind of speech was not uncommon in the English press. A majority of the English-speaking population hoped to establish a British society in Canada, ruled by a landed or leisure aristocracy, open to commercial activities and dominated by a Protestant ethic. Convinced of their own racial superiority and participating in the anti-papist movement, the English saw the French-speaking group as an obstacle for economic progress and for the social harmony of the colony.

The policy toward the Canadians seemed to be hardened by the Napoleonic Wars, the rise of the imperialist ideology (Rule Britannia!), the clashes over the economic organisation of the young colony (the English favoured commerce and the French Canadians favoured land revenues) and, above all, by the demographic expansion of the English population (they were 600 in 1765, 30,000 in 1812, 200,000 in 1851, the year they exceeded the French population in Canada). Irish and English immigration reached its peak during that period, when tens of thousands of immigrants, escaping political turmoil or economic crisis, arrived each year at Quebec City's harbour. It was openly hoped by some that, soon, the French would drown in the English sea, leading to an untroubled Anglo-Saxon North America.

Resisting the assimilationist projects of some English colonial administrators, a French Canadian petite bourgeoisie had emerged through the first three decades of the nineteenth century. Newspapers spread over the colony the words of liberal and republican ideals. Social and political networks were developing. Meetings followed assemblies, and were followed by more meetings. Calls for a totally responsible government became persistent. The social and political climate became tense, political skirmishes multiplied. Conflicts became radical, and previously unclear issues took shape. The central question became the control of power. A group of notaries, doctors, lawyers, gentlemen farmers and businessmen united against the will of the 'opulent and haughty gouverning powers'.

The Patriot Party, guided by a 'Canadian O'Connell', Louis-Joseph Papineau, and animated by a republican ideal, increasingly opposed the royal power, on the grounds of favouritism and administrative incompetence. Given the refusal by the metropolis to accept some reforms that were thought to be absolutely necessary, and because of a radicalisation of the colonial regime, the leaders of the Patriot Party put out a call to arms to declare the independence of the colony, hoping to replicate the American republican model in Canada. The Troubles of 1837–8 broke out with little preparation. The leaders denounced the partiality of the judges and the bad administration of the governors, pressing for an elected Legislative Council. Public political speeches galvanised the population, but the bishops fiercely condemned the armed uprising. The clergy distrusted a movement that criticised its control of provincial affairs, that refused to submit to the lawful royal authority, and put in peril the pact with the British, where colonial dependence was the price to be paid for liberty. In addition, the clergy were frightened by a rebellion that cherished the flag of an impious American republic, referring to the immoral principles of the French revolution.

In part because the clergy refused to give them its support, in part because their military preparation was poor, and also because they were unable to stir up a larger mass of the population, the small numbers of patriotic troops were easily crushed by the British armies and militias. Papineau and other leaders of the rebellion were forced into exile, while others were executed for their crimes. Those events were to have a tremendous impact on Canadian history.

A high-ranking civil servant of the Empire, Lord Durham, was mandated to examine the reasons for the conflict and to propose some solution to it. After a short period spent in the colony, Durham drew a surprising conclusion in his Report in 1838: 'I expected to find a contest between a government and a people: I found two nations warring in the bosom of a single state: I found a struggle, not of principles, but of races, ... two races, so long habituated to regard each other with hereditary enmity, and so differing in habits, in language, and in laws.'

On that precise point, it must be said that Lord Durham was only partly right. Beneath the race issue, even more important economic and democratic conflicts can be found. In their opposition to the English, the Canadians did not want to protect their mother tongue so much as to resist the pressure of the English merchant bourgeoisie and ask for true democratic institutions, in place of what they saw as a political comedy played by an aristocratic bureaucracy. As a matter of fact, a proportion of the English population of Upper Canada did support the Patriots of Lower Canada and applauded their will for reforms. The rebellious groups' motives do not exactly fit the linguistic frontiers, even if the conservatism of the Royalists who emigrated after the American revolution was unfamiliar to the liberalism of the Patriots. That is what Durham did not understand, or what he did not want to understand, and that is why the first recommendation of his Report appears so unjust and so raw: 'The language, the laws, the character of the North American continent are English; and every race but English ... appears there in a condition of inferiority. It is to elevate them from that inferiority that I desire to give the Canadians our English character. ... that any plan which may be adopted for the future management of Lower Canada, the first object ought to be that of making it an English province; and that, with this end in view, the ascendancy should never again be placed in any hands but those of an English population.' The solution proposed by Durham was a simple rendition of a two-term equation: remove one of the two terms, and since the equation does not exist anymore, it is therefore solved.

It is during this period that what will be called the 'two solitudes' were created, each community distancing itself from the other. As much as the English extremists were afraid of the Papist threat, the French Catholics were frightened by the Anglo-Protestant. The intensification of communications did not overcome a growing incomprehension. Let us not forget that this epoch was one of great nationalistic fervour all over the western world; some centres of protest spread in Europe (Belgium, Poland, Italy and Ireland) and in South America. This nationalist mood was not without consequence for the development of the Canadian nationalities.

The years 1840–90 saw the formation of the messianic myth of French Canada, a myth that continued to develop until the 1960s. Parallel to the myth of the civilising destiny of the United States, it stated that French Canada was promised a great destiny in North America. It was an idealised compensation and a rationalisation of the precarious situation in which the French Canadian Nation found itself after the defeat of the Patriots. This Nation is poor? Who cares, when it is rich with a Catholic faith that is the promise of the kingdom of heaven. This Nation is without glory? Do not worry, since it lives from the eternal values that keep it away from the cupidity, the sensual pleasures and the moral decadence of Protestant America. This Nation is French? It is therefore a part of a more refined, less cupid civilisation than the Anglo-Saxon. Greed, unrestrained individualism, the narrow calculation of shopkeepers and the harsh desires of cupidity that were all said to be the essence of the English world, were considered foreign to the pleasant rusticity and fraternity of the French Catholic families. 'One goes to heaven, ultramontane catholics would say, by way of the cross, not by railway!' Even though America was no more the land of 'savages', the enterprise of conversion and of proselytising was still necessary. The dream of a French America was thus perpetuated, and has been summed up by a theologian at the beginnings of the twentieth century in the following way: while the English were building industries and manufacturing, the French Canadians had a mission to find peace and accomplishment under the shadow of their parochial church.

Following the recommendation of Durham, the Union of the two Canadas was voted in 1840. Some articles of the law denote undeniable unfairness to the French Canadians. The deputation of Eastern Canada was the same as the one of Western Canada, but their population was not; Eastern Canada was made to share a part of the major debts of Western Canada; English was recognised as the only official language and French was thus banned by the Legislative Assembly.

The difficulties of this period were not accepted passively by French Canadians. They fought to restore the rights of their scorned language. In 1848, the interdiction to use French was raised. LaFontaine participated in a government of reconciliation, because, according to him, there was no other choice, for the French Canadians, but to work with the British. His alliance with the reformists of Western Canada gave him the opportunity to unite the two nations in an effort to modernise a United Canada. This did not, of course, stop the conflict between the supporters of Georges Brown and the liberal–conservative coalition. For example, the leaders of Eastern Canada were unhappy that Toronto was becoming the economic and political rival of Montreal.

The American Civil War and the new conditions created by the end of the mercantilist system posed important challenges for all during the 1860s. The need to build a transcontinental railway, the alliance of the high finance and the business bourgeoisie, the will to unite the American British colonies against their giant Southern rival, the hope that had never been completely abandoned of a country in which the French and English could unite their destiny, are some of the motives which led, in 1867, to the signing, by the deputies of both linguistic communities, of the British North America Act. Even though still a Dominion of the Empire, Canada as we know it was born. The Act brought together the provinces of Nova Scotia, New Brunswick, Ontario and a Quebec that had been recreated from the former Lower Canada of 1791–1841. Seven other provinces have joined the Dominion over the years (the last one being Newfoundland in 1949) or have been created as Canada expanded to the West.

A major achievement of those battles conducted in the political arena over a quarter of a century has been the recognition of a political and juridical status for the French language. A great number of commentators consider that this secured the future of the French-speaking community in Canada, that the long struggle for its recognition was over, and that a prosperous period awaited the French Canadians. The election of Wilfrid Laurier, a French speaker, as Premier of Canada in 1896, raised great hopes. But these were soon to be tarnished.

1867–1918: between colonisation and exile

One of the articles of Durham's programme was to marginalise the French group with massive English immigration. This part of his programme was a definite success. The Canadians had opened the continent and founded cities, dreaming of a French America. But the continent was closing in on them; they were now surrounded, besieged, on the defensive. They tended to think in terms of survival of their language, their religion and their traditions. The liberals who were challenging their compatriots to venture into commerce and business, and to catch up with a North American continent that was progressing fast received a somewhat conservative answer. Without capital, the French inhabitants were more and more attached to the work of the land, by their own natures and by necessity.

The Patriots' ideology of liberation gave way to the Catholic Church's conservatism. It was a period of ultramontanism, an ideology that gives priority to the spiritual in temporal affairs and thinks the Church should rule the institutions of civil society, particularly the schools, although ultramontanism was balanced by a liberal ideology well established in the financial circles of Quebec and Montreal. The parish was more than ever the natural structure of the French Canadian social organisation. The Church was progressing rapidly. It became involved in the temporal order and attacked liberalism as a pernicious and harmful ideology. Above all, it became increasingly nationalist. Aspiring to replace the petite bourgeoisie in the protection of the national interest, it was guided by the utopian vision of creating a new Christendom, preserved from the errors of modernity (free thinking, compulsory education of youth by the state, divorce) and inspired by an idealised past modelled on a feudal society. Industrialisation, materialism and cosmopolitanism represented its favourite *bêtes noires*, and there was not one pastoral written without a condemnation of whatever could get in the way of the realisation of its dream of harmony based on the Catholic family. The epithets and adjectives associated with the American way of life were very pessimistic: egoism, individualism, materialism, paganism, cult of material comfort, anarchy, moral decadence were all alleged. It was not a question of catching up with the United States on the road to progress, but of avoiding, protected by a great ideological wall all around the Quebec reserve, the insidious influences of liberalism.

Although the influence of the Church over French Canada was not as absolute as it might wish, it remained strong. The strength of the Church seemed to vary with that of the feeling among Francophones that they were soon to disappear. The first national historian, François-Xavier Garneau, wrote some poetry in which he described the destiny of his nation as identical with that of the Hurons: decimated, exterminated, assimilated, in other words conquered.

In this social context, the great question, the question that seemed vital more than ever before, was demographic. The numbers were alarming. In 1851, the population of Upper Canada exceeded the population of Lower Canada. The French Canadians were becoming a minority in the country they discovered and founded. After 1867, their marginalisation continued. They represented 31 per cent of the Canadian population in 1871, 29 per cent in 1911 and 28 per cent in 1921; they comprise about 22 per cent today. Those numbers can be explained by English emigration. The climate and the low economic opportunities were among the reasons why Canada did not attract many immigrants before the Napoleonic Wars. From then on, however, everything changed. A million British nationals emigrated to Canada between 1816 and 1851. In twenty years (1880–99), another million had been added, and another three million between 1899 and 1919. It is feared that the destiny of Louisiana, once a French colony and now an American state where French is virtually no longer spoken, will soon mirror that of French Canada.

These questions explain what has been called the *revenge of the cradles*. The strong fecundity of the French Canadians helped them deal with the consequences of the British immigration. The French Canadians had a birth rate 20 per cent higher than their English compatriots. Families with fifteen children, whilst not common, were not exceptional. Large families ensure the survival of the national group. But having children is one thing, establishing them so that they can prosper in strength and numbers is another.

At the end of the nineteenth century, a colonialist ideology had put forward the possibility of French Canadians conquering the *Pays d'En Haut*, identified in the past with the regions of the Great Lakes to the West, and now located in the North of the Saint-Lawrence Valley, in Abitibi, Laurentides, Saguenay and Lac Saint-Jean. Advised by colonialist-priests, the settlers travelled many miles through the forest. The colonialist ideology was not a project that aimed to reproduce a traditional society, but a utopia of economic and national conquest. It organised railways and the wood industry, it searched for allies in the press and the government, and it initiated a movement to learn new techniques. But it was also nostalgic for the old country, and the impossible dream of complete independence for the descendents of the settlers of New France.

Despite these efforts, the economic situation of the Quebec province, and of Canada in general, forced the French Canadians to emigrate to the South to find fortune. The manufacturers of New England hired labour chased from their homes by the economic crisis that had struck agriculture in Quebec. The fact that Quebec had neither coal nor iron ore prevented it from exploiting the resources of steam machinery. That allowed New England's businessmen to increase and diversify their production, and to raise their profits. The boom of American industry was phenomenal. It not only attracted the inhabitants who were vegetating on their lands and the urban populations who were out of work, but also all those seeking better remuneration. From 1840 to 1940, 900,000 people permanently crossed the Quebec border to find a better life in the United States.

While trying to stop the flow of emigration, the élites continued to dream of a French America that was shattered by the Conquest of 1760. Having considered emigration to be a national disaster, they began to think of it as a providential phenomenon. Compiling statistics on the birth rates of each linguistic group, an anonymous contributor to *La Presse* wrote in 1899 an enthusiastic review of the future situation: 'In the exclusively English-speaking ridings, the birth-rate is as low as in any New England State, whatever the number of families and weddings. The head of the bureau of statistics does not hesitate to state publicly that this state of affairs is due to public morality, which is perverted and degraded to the highest degree. With similar results, it will inevitably be the case that the previously essentially English-speaking province, will become French and will be integrated by the fecundity of French Canadians.' Speaking about the heroism of French Canadian mothers, without whom the nation would have disappeared, the correspondent praised with the greatest enthusiasm, the joys of a marital life filled with numerous children. 'In less than a century, if things go the way they are, the French Canadian population of the American continent will be over 70,000,000. The French Canadian newspapers are already predicting a time when French Canadians will control the destinies of the Province of Ontario and maybe also that of the Northern States.' This analysis was confirmed by well-known intellectuals. In 1900, Edmond de Nevers foretold the dissolution of the Canadian confederation, its absorption by the United States and the constitution in the middle of the twentieth century of three main linguistic zones: English in the centre, German in the West, French in Quebec and in a great part of New England.

Of course, emigration to New England did not have the consequences foreseen by the élites. The French speakers would soon melt, after two or three generations, into the dominant English-speaking society. They have left a trace in some of the most frequent family names of the United States (Bernier, Fortier, Grenier, Plamondon), although some have been anglicised over time (O'quin for Aucoin, Besset for Bessette, Clutter for Cloutier, White for Leblanc, Miller for Meunier). With the suppression by the English Canadians of the Metis' rebellion of Louis Riel in 1885 in the West, and the proportional demographic decrease of the French Canadians in the Prairies (in Alberta, they accounted for 7 per cent of the population in 1881, against 16 per cent twenty years before), the political élite could see dark clouds gathering over the skies of the Province of Quebec and wherever else the French Canadians established themselves during their peregrination and immigration. The spectre of assimilation haunted their conversations like never before.

In this respect, the Irish bishops did everything, except help the cause of the French-speaking Catholics. At the same time, they wished that Catholics would assimilate as soon as possible to the English population, so that Protestant America would convert to the 'true faith'. The Pope himself gave his support to this policy of assimilation in the hope that the Anglican Church would return to the Catholic fold. It was not only the English Protestants who stood in the way of the French Catholic future, but the English Catholics, too, took their side against those who shared their faith without sharing their idiom.

Mgr Francis Bourne, Archbishop of Westminster, had exposed this policy in a statement at the twenty-first Eucharist congress, held in Montreal in 1900. For him, Catholicism would prosper in America on the condition that it would be practised in English. A sharp answer came from Henri Bourassa, who protested by stating that, 'for three million Catholics, descending from the first apostles of Christianity in America, the best safeguard of faith is the conservation of the idiom in which for three hundred years, they have adored Jesus Christ'. The question was not that of protecting the language in and for itself, but rather that of making the language the best defence of the Catholic faith in a continent where, some said, apostasy often followed linguistic assimilation.

The ideology of the first half of the twentieth century has been described as a Church-based nationalism, for the essential reason that it binds together language and faith in the defence of French Canada. The Church being the most important institution of the French Canadian social fabric, this union of the faith and the language was a decisive element in the history of the Province of Quebec. As a matter of fact, during the all-important years before the Second World War, the Catholic Church was somewhat the state of a nation without a state. The religious communities took care of the hospitals and of the education, the clergy organised parochial life. Virtually everything was officially Catholic: unions (*Confédération des Travailleurs Catholiques du Canada*), colleges, press (*L'Action catholique, Le Droit*), universities (they have a papist charter), cooperatives (*Caisses populaires Desjardins*), social clubs, and so on. The clergy's conversion to nationalism, after a century of collaboration with the British power, was thus a decisive event.

For example, the *Association catholique de la jeunesse canadienne-française* (ACJC) was a youth movement which called for the preservation of the idiosyncratic character of the French Canadians. The *Société du parler français*, supported by members of the clergy and some intellectuals, was created in 1902. The *Ligue des droits du français* was founded by Father J.-P. Archambault with the aim of disseminating the use of

French. The first edition of the newspaper *Le Devoir*, the voice of the ultramontane Henri Bourassa, was sold in 1910; the journalists spoke of the cutting of the imperial cord with England and of the protestation of the French compatriots for the protection of their traditions and their language. *L'Action française* (1917), headed among others by Abbot Lionel Groulx, launched campaigns to improve the quality of the language spoken in the cities and in the Canadian parish, to encourage national pride and to make Canadian socio-economic life as French as possible. The nationalism of this period was less political and more cultural, and this is why it applied itself mainly to the revitalisation of the French idiom.

France became a normal reference, the centre toward which the leaders turned, and the guiding light that indicated the shining future of the nation. But so was Rome, because Catholicism is considered of course a factor of national homogenisation and an irreducible characteristic of the French Canadians. The past of New France took on the appearance of grandiose, fabulous heroism. Its miraculous birth was the promise of a brilliant future. In his books, Lionel Groulx, the first history teacher at the University of Montreal, continuously provided the victorious image of the fatherland while preserving the initial inspiration of the Latin and Christian cultures. 'French of America, sons of pioneers and conquerors of the land, call with an overcome voice the soul of your country.... And the soul of your race and your country will come to say, in the rumor of an epic poem, that no history holds a better place than yours in the prime glory of this continent, and that in its testimony lies maybe your oldest and most certain claims to respect from other Nations.' Thus Groulx wrote in the conclusion of his most famous book, *Notre maître, le passé*, published in 1924.

In their efforts to ensure the persistence and the progress of the French in Canada, the French Canadian nationalists encountered strong resistance from their English compatriots. The schools represented the new battleground, after the political arena, where the future of the languages in Canada was fought. With compulsory schooling and the growing importance of technical instruction came the crucial issue of education in one's own mother tongue. 'School, people would say, can be the fortress of a race, or its grave.' This, the English Canadian nationalists understood well. They tried to block or to impede the teaching of French in primary schools. In 1905, the law that created the Provinces of Alberta and Saskatchewan had insignificant dispositions to make sure French would be respected in schools; in fact, those dispositions were abolished in 1918. In Manitoba, a weak compromise between the Province and the federal government ensured a minimum of opportunities for French speakers who wished to have a couple of hours a day of teaching in French. In 1912, the *Règlement 17* greatly restricted the teaching of the mother tongue for French Ontarians. On the one hand, Howard Ferguson, an Orangeman who was to become the Premier of the Province of Ontario, applauded a bill that would make for a more homogenous Canada. On the other hand, Henri Bourassa fulminated and compared the iniquity of Ontarians to that of Germans, with whom Canada was at war at the time. It had become incredibly difficult to give credence to the idea of a pact between the two founding nations of 1867.

1918–45: the backwardness of the French-Canadian economy

The last three decades of the nineteenth century witnessed the definitive establishment of the industrial era: iron had replaced wood as the basic raw material and coal was the new source of energy. In this new context, a majority of French Canadians first saw salvation in agriculture and colonisation. 'Let us get hold of the land!' was the rallying cry of the élite. At the beginning of the twentieth century, economic reality brought changes in a way that seemed to be to the advantage of the Province of Quebec. The demand for pulp and paper soared, aluminium conquered a vast market, hydro-electric energy replaced coal at a lower cost. The Province experienced an industrial revival. But the revival did not initially seem to benefit French-Canadian businessmen, as they lacked sufficient capital to launch major commercial and industrial enterprises. In Marxist terms, it could be said that the national economy did not benefit from a primitive accumulation of capital. In 1905, for example, the total capital of the three banks controlled by French Canadians (Banque provinciale, Banque d'Hochelaga and Banque Nationale) amounted to 32 million dollars, compared to more than 150 million for the Bank of Montreal alone.

In the nineteenth century, surprised by the situation of the French Canadians, Tocqueville had written that the worst destiny for a nation is to be conquered. The French face of Montreal or Quebec was mutilated by English advertising. 'Albeit French is almost universally spoken, most of the newspapers, bills, and even the shops signs are in English. The commercial concerns are almost entirely in their hands.' Although there is a slight exaggeration in the remark of the famous sociologist, it sums up nicely the dramatic situation of the French Canadians. If commentators should beware of casting the situation of Quebec during the

1920s as a simple conflict between French-speaking proletarians and English capitalists, this rendering none the less contains an element of truth.

In 1917, Edouard Montpetit, professor at the *Ecole des Hautes Etudes Commerciales* (HEC), claimed in *L'Action française* that the national question had, in fact, become an economic question. After Errol Bouchette (1905), he proposes the rallying cry: 'Let us get hold of the industry.' Some analysts were forecasting a second defeat for the French Canadian group, this time on the battlefield of the economic war in which every other Western nation was involved. French-speaking Quebec was not getting its fair share of the benefits and opportunities of the industrial revolution. The turn of the twentieth century was characterised by the penetration of powerful English Canadian and American capital, and the eviction of the French Canadians from commanding positions in the business world. And the situation showed no signs of getting any better. On the eve of the Second World War, Victor Barbeau denounced, in a book that caused quite a stir, the level of inferiority of his compatriots. 'Despite the gild of our lounges, the tin of our churches, we are poor, terrifyingly poor. We are proletarians, workers, manufacture fodder.' Consulting a directory of Canadian industry, Barbeau listed some of the main names: Canadian Goodrich, Goodyear, Bendix, Imperial Oil, Crane, Champion Spark Plug, General Electric, Westinghouse. Were any of the listed names French? Very few, in fact almost none, except for the small companies Papeterie Rolland and the Fonderie de Plessisville. French-speaking Quebec was at the bottom of the ladder in most economic sectors, including the field of natural resources, exploited again by foreign interests.

To resolve the situation of economic inferiority, two alternative political programmes were proposed.

On the one hand, Quebec liberals tried to attract Anglo-Saxon investors at any price, even if that meant sacrificing the national traditions and abandoning the promotion of French. The liberal attitude of *laissez faire* allowed Anglo-Saxon companies to exploit Quebec's natural resources, and to subsequently stall the efforts of French-Canadian businessmen. In a world where the only rule was the survival of the fittest, and where the State refused to play a substantial part, foreign, mainly American enterprises, were free to manage the French Canadian market.

On the other hand, nationalists like Groulx, Montpetit and Minville proposed that the economic situation could not be solved without returning to traditions, even if that meant exacerbating latent xenophobia. They proposed a programme based on a return to the land and the support of agriculture. This traditional agenda would, however, delay industrial progress by making business careers less prestigious than sacerdotal vocation and the liberal professions.

The crisis of 1929 fuelled the nationalist fervor. Trusts were criticised both as anti-Christian enterprises, because they benefit only a minority, and as anti-French, because they were in the hands of Anglo-Saxon interests. Even though their foundation had taken place earlier, Catholic unions during the 1920s took on the shape of a national movement. Against the international unions, perceived as a factor of Americanisation, they proposed not only the restoration of the economic order on the grounds of Christian values, but the defence of national traditions. They took the side both of the worker and the French Canadian against the foreign trusts and savage capitalism. The *Ecole des Hautes Etudes Commerciales* (HEC) developed a line of thought based on economic nationalism. The State should invest in the economy and sustain the efforts of economic recovery by French Canadians. A programme of social restoration was elaborated in 1932, aiming to block the influence of the CCF, a socialist party founded in the Canadian west. The authors of this programme denounced the individualism of liberal economy and its uneven economic development. The crisis was so deep and the liberal system so corrupt that an improvement could not be expected without substantial adjustments. A global reform should be tried. But, all the same, stated the authors, the reforms must avoid the temptation of resorting to any socialist nonsense that might hold only contempt for Catholicism. What nationalists wanted to find was a third path between 'vitiated capitalism' and 'vicious communism'. They did not hesitate to cite the example of the corporatist state of Portugal, and even of the fascist state of Italy.

Paradoxically, if the nationalists enjoyed great popular success, it was the liberals who reigned throughout almost all the period between the two great wars. In a way, Quebec was divided in two. The dominant discourse was for the time, radical, bent on revenge and interventionism, but the concrete actions of the state were in the continuation of the classical liberal tradition. In the tracts published by the *Ecole Sociale Populaire*, an institution of propaganda controlled by the Jesuits, one can read virulent diatribes against capitalism, but the consolation is that the great enterprises had never been so well protected, and never had fewer social actions been conducted, charity still being in the hands of the private institutions.

This explains, in great part, the ambiguous position of the nationalist groups. They did seek the recovery of the provincial economy, yet they did not want to sacrifice the ancestral customs of the French Canadians for fear that they might lose their traditional values. That is why they proposed reforms that were significantly different from mainstream North American economic practices. They dreamt of creating an industrial, financial and commercial system independent from the one in place in the rest of America: a rural economy instead of a manufacturing economy, mutual funds in the place of banks, cooperatives rather than large capitalist businesses. The Church and the nationalists united to limit the access of French Canadians to a modern world that was thought to be threatening their Catholic identity (due to its materialistic aspect) and their French identity (due to its essentially English character). This fear of modernity was thus also a fear of assimilation. A young oblate who was to become Cardinal Villeneuve, proclaimed in the 1920s: 'Whole provinces are already entirely americanized, not only in the common language, but also in their ideas, feelings and tastes, in their interests, its businesses, its entertainment; by sects, schools, theatres, magazines and dailies; by a licentiousness in moral life, in the indifference for religion, in divorces, birth-control, feminism, by an equal materialism in ideals, by a shameful paganism in pleasure.' In the cities, the windows of the boutiques and stores advertised in English: Dry Goods Store, Groceries Store, Merchant Taylor, Watch and Clock, Boot and Shoe Maker. The anglicisation of public signage was a foreboding sign, the nationalists believed, of the anglicisation of the heart.

This anglicisation did not spare the rural zones, but it seemed to be less important than in the urban centres. In the course of the twentieth century, as a consequence of its progressive industrialisation, Quebec had become, on the whole, an urban province by 1931. The statistics of urbanisation made even the most optimistic commentators anxious. The nationalists were increasingly nervous, as they associated cities not only with linguistic assimilation, but also with cosmopolitanism, condemned because it leads to the repudiation of one's origins and the loss of identity. The virtues of a race could be better maintained by rural life. Thus, because the loss of the personality of the French Canadian workers and the devaluation of the French culture was supposed to be the inevitable consequence of urbanisation, agriculture seemed to be the best answer to an economy besieged by foreign capital. 'The return to the land,' wrote Esdras Minville in the 1930s, future director of the HEC, 'appears as the easiest and happiest solution to the problems that the crisis is provoking and multiplying. This appears, in particular to us French Canadians, as the only solution to the extremely worrying problem, that existed before the crisis and that will exist after it, of the economic restoration of our people.' With the Catholic faith and the ancestral traditions, land represented the foundation of the nation. Only there, people believed they had a grip on their destiny that they could not have elsewhere. 'In a world ruined by the orgies of speculation,' declared Minville, 'the land remains the great resource that, in the absence of uncertain millions, gives the modest and soothing certainty of everyday bread – will we not take this providential opportunity to give back to our people its historical vocation, to people the countryside, to establish for good our economic organization? Such an attitude would amount both to folly and crime.' In a time when the economy was going to the dogs and when the poor were getting packed into shelters and refugee centres, the nationalists were repeating the old refrain going back to the nineteenth century about the agricultural mission of the French Canadian people. For them, an unemployed was a settler away from his field.

To sum up, the period between the two world wars was a difficult one for the French Canadian community. But the historian must not exaggerate those difficulties. The twentieth century was not only a time of despair, of unemployment and economic alienation. Two universities were founded (Montreal, Sherbrooke), in addition to great schools (HEC), newspapers (*La Patrie, La Presse, L'Action catholique, Le Devoir*), periodicals (*L'Action nationale, Relations, La Relève*) and publishing houses (Beauchemin, Fides). Some important literary works were published by very talented authors (Desrosiers, Saint-Denys Garneau, Grandbois, Ringuet, Savard, etc.). Two main literary streams were in opposition in the first half of the twentieth century: the literature of the land tells the virtues of rural life and ancestral traditions, while a more exotic, but also more marginal literature, is involved in symbolism, believes in art for art's sake, and soon discovers surrealism. Slowly, patiently, a community was giving itself the means to make its voice heard. Science (notably botany, medicine and chemistry), the social sciences (political economy and sociology) and history progressed. Many intellectuals were trying to conciliate the values of America and those of French Canada. We have no choice, they said: geography has placed Quebec where it is, and this gives it as a neighbour a populous and dynamic nation. How can this be ignored any longer, they asked?

1945–2000: the temptation of independence

Post-war prosperity pre-empted the economic debate. Liberalism and capitalism emerged through crises unaffected by left-wing or right-wing political thinking. The implosion of liberal Protestant North America did not occur. On the contrary, between 1946 and 1961, the average *per capita* income had doubled. More than ever before Quebecers were willing to join the consumer society: cars, telephones, television sets, electric appliances all made their way into average households. In 1953 for instance, 37 per cent of homes owned a vacuum cleaner, 82 per cent a washing-machine, 68 per cent a refrigerator, 78 per cent a phone; in 1959, 90 per cent of them owned a television. The American way of life was not something to be resisted anymore, it was already becoming an integral part of French Canadians' everyday life.

This new state of affairs did not put an end to the language debate, however, it merely shifted its boundaries. Whereas the French Canadian diaspora had been, even for French-speaking Quebecers, the basic reference of their wider society, it was to be slowly but surely replaced by the Province of Quebec. Authored by Toronto, Montreal and Quebec social scientists, the 1953 *Les Essais sur le Québec contemporain* were a sign of things to come: they broke from the 'French Canada' model to focus on Quebec, while the 1964 *Etats généraux du Canada français* defined Quebec as the homeland of French-speaking North America. French Canadians would henceforth be known as Quebecers (it is indicative that the lyrics of a widely played song by folk-singer Claude Gauthier were modified from 'Je suis de nationalité canadienne-française' to 'je suis de nationalité québécoise-française'.) The Acadians, the Francophone in Ontario, Manitoba and Alberta, not to mention the New England 'Canucks', hence would be seen as isolated islands of minority French-speaking groups, lacking the resources to ensure their status and self-development. Indeed, outside of Quebec, only 3 per cent of the Canadian population were French-speaking.

This collective identity from Canadien-français to Québécois can be explained by several factors: from 1850, when, on the whole, language was the cause of few concerns, except maybe among the élite, in the discussions of anglicisms found in Quebec French, to 1900, when French was becoming an element of the Catholic identity, to 1950, when the issue took a central political role, and a clear progression towards language as a cultural and national marker can be identified.

In a paper published around 1950, Father Richard Arès quoted sobering data proving that the assimilation of Francophones was directly proportional to their distance from Quebec. The only Province in Canada where the French fact, as precarious and as threatened as it may have been, resisted assimilation was Quebec. This was where Francophones constituted a majority and possessed the institutions by which they could define their destiny. In Arès' eyes, therefore, the only solution for the future of French in Canada appeared to rest on the gathering of Francophones inside the boundaries of Quebec, maybe even on the independence of that Province. To control the state of Quebec, to focus on its territorial base, would be, during the 1960s, the watchwords of the nationalist élite who, by then, had given up all hope of maintaining a French-speaking community spread across North America.

Let us illustrate this trend by an example. In 1959, André Laurendeau signed, as the editor of the high-brow Montreal newspaper *Le Devoir*, an article deploring the sorry state of schoolchildren's language. A concurring reply was immediately written and published in the paper by an obscure teacher under a pen-name. The 'Frère Untel' went further in denouncing the appalling mediocrity of his pupils' spelling, speech and vocabulary. Whereas fifty years earlier the confection of a dictionary of anglicisms and frequent linguistic mistakes would have been called for, the Brother proposed a bold plan: no less than the direct intervention of the state. 'LANGUAGE IS A COMMON GOOD', he wrote, 'it is up to the state to protect it. The state protects mooses, partridge and trout, it should protect language with the same rigor. An idiom is well worth a moose and trout.' Edited in book form, the *Insolences du Frère Untel* was to become one of the strongest runaway bestsellers in Quebec's publishing history.

Long considered as the guardian of the nation, the Roman Catholic Church lost its appeal quite rapidly after the Second World War, and especially from the 1960s onwards, because of its reactionary streak bound in the past. Enlightened journals decried conservative Catholicism as being incompatible with modernity, and denounced its unchallenged monopoly over the hearts and souls of the faithful as being contrary to the true Christian tradition. During the 1960s, in a matter of years, the Church lost its central role in education, public charity and health, all of which were to become the biggest Quebec government departments. The important fact is that this role was previously assumed way beyond the borders of Quebec, extending from New Brunswick to Alberta down to New England. Thus, the decline of Church control over community institutions led directly to the end of French Canada.

These massive political, social and cultural changes through the 1960s were known as the Quiet Revolution. This period was not so much a break from the French Canadian past than the outcome of dreams and expectations expressed since the 1930s, even if their proponents did not necessarily recognise their ideals in the new reforms. Indeed, the Quiet Revolution can be said to present in a new light the social question and the national issue debated by the contributors to *L'Action française*.

On the one hand, the creation of the Ministère de l'Education (1964), the Office de la langue française (1961) and the Ministère de la Culture (1961) endowed the government with a new mission, a fully national one. Far from stopping at culture, the expansion of the role of the state continued in all directions, in all spheres of activity: leisure, health, communications, land management, hydroelectricity, mines and forests, etc. In 1966, during the electoral campaign, Daniel Jonhson, soon to become Premier, castigated this extravagance: 'Words, words, words! Taxes, taxes, taxes!' To no avail: even Jonhson wouldn't turn the clock back. In his view, words would keep on flowing to clarify common goals, as sure as taxes would have to be raised to achieve them! Between 1945 and 1963, provincial government revenues soared from seven million dollars in 1914 to ninety-six million in 1945, to 851 million in 1963, and to twelve billions in 1981.

In place of the discredited corporatist ideology, socialism gained an appeal it had never had before. The social movements in Quebec hardened their positions in the 1960s and 1970s. Committed Catholics, such as the philosopher and sociologist Fernand Dumont, came out in favour of socialist policies. Labour leaders announced their intention to break the back of the capitalist system. A string of proximate Marxist, communist and self-management utopian small magazines gained credence in those years (*Parti Pris, Socialisme 64, Maintenant, Possibles*). Marcel Rioux, a highly respected professor at the University of Montreal, believed that Quebec's history made it a favourable foothold for the establishment of a true socialist regime: for him, French Quebecers as a whole formed an 'ethnic class' of proletarians, united over and above their inner economic disparities and social hierarchies; moreover, they had, thought Rioux, the unique opportunity to build a flexible and adapted welfare state promising equality and social justice for all. Such wide-eyed pronouncements, tied in with the spectacular growth of the government in the 1960s and 1970s, enticed some American observers to believe that Quebec might be developing into some kind of 'Cuba of the North'.

On the other hand, in a context of rapid social change, the independence movement, connected with decolonisation movements around the world, became increasingly militant in its demand for a sovereign Quebec. 'We do not want to be a province different from the other Canadian provinces anymore', it claimed, 'we want to be a country like every other.' The *Rassemblement pour l'Indépendance Nationale* (RIN, 1960) dissolved in favour of a larger sovereignist *Parti Québécois* (PQ, founded by René Lévesque in 1968), which benefited from the opportune political and social climate. The support for independence lost some of its momentum with the 1970 October Crisis, when the War Measures Act was promulgated and the Canadian army was sent into the streets of Quebec in response to the abduction of a British diplomat and a provincial minister by the small terrorist group *Front de Libération du Québec* (FLQ). Although terrorism frightened the general population, the latter none the less elected the *Parti Québécois* in 1976, which, with 40 per cent of the votes in a divided political landscape, formed a majority government.

Two conflicting positions faced each other in 1976. In Ottawa, Pierre-Elliot Trudeau, the federal Prime Minister, proposed a vision of a Canada that would be bilingual from the Atlantic to the Pacific coast, reviving the old dream of a country created by a pact between two founding nations. In Quebec City, René Lévesque, the Prime Minister of Quebec, opposed across-the-board bilingualism, which had always been historically a vector of assimilation for Francophones; he advocated the construction of a strong Quebec where French would have pre-eminence over English. This view was put forward in Bill 101, preceded by the similarly inspired Bill 22 and Bill 63, which were causes of pride for some, of profound annoyance for the conservative few, while the most alarmist decried the totalitarian nature of these language laws. The English Canadians, a majority in Canada, were becoming a minority in Quebec: not only because of the revolution taking place amongst the French Quebecers, but because immigrants from all over the world were establishing themselves in Montreal.

Bill 101, enacted by the various Quebec governments, none the less achieved some of its objectives. Mixed with public investment, a strong social legislation and spectacular growth in higher education, the imposition of French at work was to have spectacular results. In 1970, Francophones represented 38 per cent of managers in Quebec businesses, compared to 58 per cent in 1988. The gap between work revenues of Anglophones and Francophones jumped from 31 per cent in 1970 to 10 per cent in 1985. The proportion of Francophones working in French only is now 63 per cent. The economic rise of the Francophones in Quebec did not benefit only the most qualified as the whole nation went on to benefit from this.

Even if the 1970s were a period of strong nationalistic fervour, the social trends were towards individualism. A decade earlier, Gilles Vigneault, a chansonnier, was singing the 'land', its landscape, winter, language, inhabitants and customs. In 1972, Beau Dommage, a young musical group, was singing of everyday life in Montreal, trivial love stories and personal sadness. Individualism was making inroads into national unity. The community of the rural parish was no more, the dream of a nation-state was considered impossible with the end of unanimity, and the cohesion of a common culture was progressively torn to pieces with a new ideology of personal freedom bound to the consumer society.

A social and national question waiting for an answer

During the 1980s, the old national question, far from calming down, intensified; and for good reason. In 1980, the Government of Quebec called the electors to vote on the question of Quebec sovereignty, which 60 per cent rejected. The results were greeted with relief by the Federalists. The federal Prime Minister, Pierre Trudeau, used his last mandate to 'patriate' the Canadian constitution from London, with the agreement of the nine Anglophone provinces but without that of Quebec, which was excluded from the process through what is known as the 'night of the long knives'. Quebec found itself in effect outside the Canadian constitutional order.

In order to satisfy the request made by Quebec to integrate the new constitutional arrangements, the conservative government of Bryan Mulroney, a French-speaking Quebecer, agreed to negotiate a new constitutional agreement. The Meech Lake Accord appeared to satisfy all parties, until last-minute objections from English Canada, in particular against the clause asserting the distinct status of Quebec, prevented its ratification by all provincial governments. The Accord fell through, bringing unprecedented levels of nationalist feelings in Quebec.

In 1995, a new referendum was held, and was lost once again by the advocates of Quebec sovereignty, if only by a few thousand votes: 60 per cent of Francophones voted for independence, 95 per cent of Anglophones and Allophones opposed it. Those statistics are important. Immigration was rapidly changing the face of the ethnic composition of the province. For example, Montreal numbered about 52 per cent French, 45 per cent Britannic and 3 per cent Others in 1871; in 1961, the proportion was, respectively, 67 per cent, 12 per cent, and 21 per cent; and, in 1991, 59 per cent, 6 per cent, and 34 per cent.

In 2001, the PQ was still leading the province, with the mandate to create the right conditions for the sovereignty of Quebec. In Ottawa, the Bloc Québécois had roughly the same number of deputies as the Liberal Party. But the debate over sovereignty was getting bogged down and the prospect of independence looked more uncertain than ever; moreover, the prospect of a renegotiation of the Canadian constitution that would take into account the distinct character of Quebec had never seemed so unlikely.

But, from another point of view, that of the federalist, the political situation was nothing less than perfect. If Canada was not broken, they said, why fix it? Indeed, for several years, Canada had been elected by the United Nations as the best country in which to live. The Free Trade Treaty with the United States (1989) brought a wave of prosperity. While the provincial state of Quebec was poor, Ottawa was tremendously rich. Furthermore, French Canadians benefited from several federal institutions (Radio-Canada, Conseil des Arts, etc.) and from the Bill on Official Languages (1969) of the federal government. Since 1990, the Prime Minister of Canada has been Jean Chrétien, who keeps repeating that there is no national question in Canada, but only a stubborn and backward extremist group of separatists.

On the other hand, the social question has not yet been solved. The economic recession of 1982–3 put the Providence State in a difficult position, and the apparently impressive financial success of Quebec businesses was equally affected. Many institutions did stand the test of time and are still the object of collective pride, notably Hydro-Québec and the Caisse de Dépôt et de Placement; none the less, the inability to face world competition, the debt-ridden ventures and bankruptcies gradually led the government to pull out of several sectors.

The first source of employment for Quebecers during the 1960s and 1970s became inaccessible to the younger generations. The demographic structure of the population is a cause for concern, with people over fifty being more numerous than the generations to come. The 'baby boom' group, highly influential on the political agenda, was in favour of education in its youth, in favour of the working class in its forties and, now, more and more in favour of health care and retirement programmes.

In general, the economic prospect is gloomy: the Province of Quebec is an increasingly insignificant region in North America. In a context of globalisation and world market, it is losing its economic influence. Montreal, for instance, is the shadow of the great port and financial centre of the past. The institutions put in place during the Quiet Revolution to help boost the national economy have been abolished or are being marginalised. Compared to twenty years ago, the standard of living for a young couple at the turn of the century is 20 per cent lower.

In other words, the 1990s, much like the 1980s, have been difficult years for French-speaking Quebecers. They could bring about neither the full reunion of the two linguistic solitudes, nor the abolition of

es. From the movement initiated in the 1930s, the Quiet
the dream of an end to two centuries of national recla-
mations mixed with class struggle. What is left of that dream today?

Note

1   I would like to thank Pierre Larrivée for his help in the revision and translation
of this chapter.

3
Federal Language Policy in Canada and the Quebec Challenge

C. Michael MacMillan

> In several ways, linguistic duality is both a blessing and a curse for Canada. ... managing this duality is Canada's greatest challenge, however, and whether or not Canadians like it, the language issue will fuel the Canadian constitutional debate forever.
>
> (Marcel Coté, 'Language and Public Policy')[1]

Introduction

As is widely recognised, language issues are a fundamental element of the Canadian political system. Linguistic accommodation has been a prerequisite to its formation as a nation-state and is central to its continuation. Invariably, the challenges addressed in these areas have been strongly influenced by Quebec's political agenda. That federal language policy, as enacted in the Official Languages Act (1969), and Quebec's language policy, as reflected in the Charter of the French Language, constitute fundamentally different principles for language policy has been widely recognised from the start. Briefly, the federal acceptance of the personality principle for language entitlements, coupled with a recognition of an individual right to language, contrasts sharply with Quebec's territorial model incorporating a collective rights model of language. The question then arises – to what extent is federal policy incompatible with Quebec policy? The issue is succinctly captured in McRae's observation concerning the contrast between 'a federal authority proactive in favour of Anglophones against Quebec governments even more strongly proactive in defending what they saw as vital interests of their linguistically besieged Francophone majority. In this way, divergent language policies became one more item in a growing dossier of Quebec's dissatisfaction with Canadian federalism'.[2] Accordingly, these language policies engage the broader question of Quebec's future in the federation. In this chapter, I review the development of federal language policy in Canada, emphasizing the impact of Quebec concerns on this development and in turn, their consequences for Quebec. From that base I shall address the contemporary status of federal language laws *vis-à-vis* Quebec, maintaining that existing federal policy is largely compatible with Quebec's linguistic agenda and is strongly supported by the Quebec public. Demands for substantial change risk destabilising the existing consensus on language policy.

Background

With its acquisition of the French colonies in North America, Britain encountered the issue of the language of its new subjects. While Britain embraced a policy of informal, gradual linguistic and cultural assimilation, this goal was undermined by a combination of historical events (the American Revolution, the World War of 1812–14), determined resistance from Francophones and even rejection of the policy by some colonial governors. Generally, British policy permitted pragmatic accommodation of the French language, stemming from the fact that they were governing a French language society. The use of French in the courts was officially permitted in the territory of Canada through provisions for Francophone juries for disputes among Francophones and mixed juries for mixed cases (Anglophone versus Francophone). The persistence of the French civil law embodied in the Quebec Act of 1774 reinforced this tendency and strongly implied that French could be used in the courts though this was not explicitly stated. Similarly, the existing political institutions, specifically the appointed legislative council in Lower Canada, adopted practices accommodating the French language, such as maintaining debates and records, and publishing regulations in both languages. To a limited extent, then, governmental institutions prior to Confederation established practices of recognising the legitimacy of the French language for some legislative and judicial activities of government.

The effort to pursue linguistic assimilation reached its high point in 1840, when the colony of Lower Canada (now Quebec) was joined into the single political unit with Upper Canada (now Ontario) in an attempt to create a English-speaking majority. Its rules explicitly established that English was to be the only language of the legislative assembly. Its purpose was immediately foiled when the first French Canadian member to speak in the new legislature addressed the Assembly in French. Accordingly, bilingualism was informally accepted and made official in 1848. Henceforth, linguistic accommodation would become a fundamental feature of Canadian political life.

The formation of the Canadian nation itself required constitutional provisions concerning language, embodied in Section 133 of the British North America Act (BNA Act), the founding constitutional document. Section 133, the sole explicit provision on language, states that:

> Either the English or the French Language may be used by any Person in the Debates of the Houses of the Parliament of Canada and of the Houses of the Legislature of Quebec; and both those Languages shall be used in the respective Records and Journals of those Houses; and either of those Languages may be used by any Person or in any Pleading or Process in or issuing from any Court of Canada established under this Act, and in or from all or any of the Courts of Quebec.
>
> The Acts of the Parliament of Canada and of the Legislature of Quebec shall be printed and published in both those Languages.

These provisions had the effect of embedding pre-existing political practice in the constitution. They did not, however, establish bilingual policies and practices in the national government. Since there were no constitutional requirements governing the provision of government services at any level of government, from federal to municipal, federal government services would remain overwhelmingly English for another century. Similarly, the courts made only modest accommodation of the French language in their operations. While an individual was entitled to present their case in their mother tongue, there was no apparent obligation on such institutions to respond in the same language.[3] While individuals were entitled to the assistance of an interpreter under federal law, it was the judge who decided whether or not it was actually required. If required, the government assumed the cost of such services in criminal cases, but not in civil ones.[4] On balance, it is clear that it did not, as the Royal Commission on Bilingualism and Biculturalism (hereafter the B&B Commission) noted, 'guarantee language rights of citizens in their various contacts with the state'.[5]

The language clause did establish two important features. It officially recognised the equal position of both languages in the national government and in the province of Quebec. Within national institutions, the position of the French language was assured. But, at the same time, the government of Quebec was the only province to be constitutionally required to maintain official bilingualism.[6] The province of New Brunswick, with a substantial Francophone minority, was not included in the clause. The difference in treatment reflected concerns for the fate of an English-speaking minority at the hands of a Francophone majority. In one respect, it embodied a parallel treatment of cultural minorities. It protected the status of the French language from the national English-speaking majority, and the status of the English language from the Quebec French-speaking majority. This allayed misgivings on all sides about the threats posed by the new political arrangements.

Beyond the specific provisions of Section 133, jurisdiction over language matters occupies a 'constitutional vacuum', which leaves both Parliament and the provinces free to enact language legislation within their respective spheres of jurisdiction. Thus, all provinces may develop language legislation covering the broad array of powers they possess. This would be amply illustrated in the 1970s in Quebec, when Bills 22 and 101 had a considerable impact on educational, economic and parapublic institutions.

These modest provisions would suffice for a century, whereupon simmering discontents in Quebec would lead to a more comprehensive language policy being enunciated by the federal government. With the advent of nationalist stirring in Quebec, the federal government made a commitment to develop a comprehensive language policy. It struck a Royal Commission to examine the language question and to propose appropriate policies to redress perceived problems. The Commission discovered profound discontents in Quebec over the language issue, on such a scale as to represent a constitutional crisis. The sources of discontent were multi-faceted, but were centred on the secondary status of the French language in Quebec. The situation was aptly summarized by Jean Marchand, a prominent Quebec union leader, subsequently federal Cabinet Minister, and one of the participants in the Commission's work. He reported

> This is what I learned in the commission when we went around meeting the people. ... I'd say: 'What's wrong?' And the people would say: 'The manager of the mill or whatever it was has been here for ten years – and he has never learned to say "yes" or "no" in French. We all had to learn English.' The population in that area is 99.9 percent French. ... I think that the main source of dispute ... was Quebec itself and the federal institutions where there was surely no equality for all practical purposes.[7]

This remark highlights both the subordinate position of the French language within the Quebec economy and society on the one hand, and within federal institutions on the other. This social reality was fully documented in the federal B&B Commission studies. Within federal institutions, it found that French Canadians were under-represented compared to their share of the national population (22 per cent compared to 28 per cent in the 1961 census) and that they were concentrated in the lower echelons of the departmental public service, such that, the higher the position level, the smaller the percentage of Francophones (i.e. 23.7 per cent of the lowest salary group versus 10.4 per cent of the highest group).[8] Beyond that, only 9 per cent of positions were designated bilingual, a strong indicator of the limited commitment to providing government services in French. In the private sector, Francophones experienced a long history of disadvantages and occasionally outright discrimination concerning their language. A telling incident from previous decades was reported by André Laurendeau, a co-chair of the B&B Commission. An elderly elevator operator at the Chateau Laurier, a respected institution in Ottawa, the nation's capital, and well-known to senior government officials, told him that in the 1920s, they 'were forbidden to speak French'. This policy was changed only after a Francophone Senator who frequently stayed there routinely insisted that the Francophone staff address him in French.[9]

In response to these various problems, the B&B Commission proposed 'a new concept of an officially bilingual country in which the two official languages will have new rights and better guarantees'. The underlying principle was that of an 'equal partnership' between the English- and French-language communities. As a concept, 'Equal partnership' contained several dimensions. One of those was a commitment to language rights for both English- and French-speakers throughout Canada, so that each would be able to use their respective languages in dealing with the state. Another dimension required a more equitable balancing of the costs and benefits of Canadian political life for the two language groups, which required greater political autonomy for Quebec. This latter element received a generally hostile reception and was never adequately developed, with the result that 'equal partnership' disappeared from the debate over official bilingualism.[10]

In justifying their proposals, the B&B Commission indicated that the basis for the privileged position of English and French rested not on their historical claims, but rather on their existence as complete societies (or nearly so) within Canada, meaning that most Canadians were able to live their lives within these language communities.[11] However, this opened an avenue for criticism of the principle, stemming from the fact that the proposition was progressively less true for the Francophone communities the further one travelled from either of Quebec's borders with its neighbouring provinces. Recognising this difficulty, the B&B Commission emphasised that the principle of equality itself was an essential grounding for these rights. Addressing the claims of francophone minorities outside the 'bilingual belt', they averred, 'we believe that these French-speaking minorities have indisputable rights by virtue of the principle of equality, and that provinces consequently have certain immediate obligations to them'.[12]

Thus the feasibility of provision of the services associated with the language rights was the sole question to be determined. The B&B Commission rejected the territorial approach, arguing that 'it would deprive minority groups *en bloc* ... of essential language rights'. The general goal was to ensure that 'wherever similar conditions are found similar services will be offered'.[13] The 'bottom line' was feasibility. So long as there were sufficient numbers of people to warrant the service, then it was imperative that it be provided. On this basis, it urged those provinces with substantial official language minorities (New Brunswick, Ontario and Quebec) to become officially bilingual and the remainder to commit themselves to the provision of bilingual services as they deemed appropriate.

This proposal was expected to have symbolic importance for the future of Canada, by influencing the orientation of Quebec Francophones to the Canadian state as well. In its preliminary report, the B&B Commission observed that

> the people of Quebec have always tended to regard the way these minorities were treated in their respective provinces as one of the tangible indications of refusal or acceptance, by English-language Canadians, of the duality of Canada.[14]

Thus, the treatment of Francophones outside Quebec was expected to reassure Quebec Francophones about their future within Canada. It would simultaneously serve the goals of cultural duality and the purpose of national unity.

Official Languages Act (1969)

The major recommendations of the B&B Commission were embodied in the Official Languages Act of 1969. Section 2 of the OLA (1969) declares that English and French are the official languages of Canada and 'possess and enjoy equality of status and equal rights and privileges as to their use in all the institutions of the Parliament and Government of Canada'.[15] With it, the government recognised a duty to provide services in the both official languages where numbers warrant and in head offices of the federal government. In conjunction with it, the government made a commitment to increase opportunities for individuals to work in the French language in the federal government, and to increase the percentage of Francophones in the ranks of the federal public service to achieve equitable participation. Beyond that, it attempted to develop, with provincial agreement, a plan for the provision of government services in both official languages in designated bilingual districts across the country.[16]

In terms of justifying these policy innovations, the federal rationale was based on principles of equality, pragmatism and considerations of national unity. Three years before the passage of the legislation, Prime Minister Pearson justified the introduction of bilingualism in the public service as 'part of its fundamental objective of promoting and strengthening national unity on the basis of the equality of rights and opportunities for both English speaking and French speaking Canadians'.[17] The goal of national unity was to be achieved by making the federal government more accessible to French-speaking Canadians, by enabling them to 'have a fair and equal opportunity to participate in the national administration and to identify themselves with, and feel at home in, their own national capital'.[18] Eight years later, in the wake of considerable Anglophone hostility to its language legislation, the federal government defended its language policy on the same grounds, in asserting that 'Canada cannot continue to exist as a single country unless the English and French languages are accepted and recognised as the official languages of the country'.[19] The conclusion to be drawn from these various statements on federal language policy is that it was conceived and justified primarily in terms its political necessity for national unity.[20]

With the determined backing of successive Prime Ministers, the federal government moved swiftly to achieve its goals. It was most successful in altering the composition of the federal public service, so that it amply reflected the French fact in its personnel. The creation of a large number of positions designated as requiring bilingual skills created many opportunities to enter and ascend the public service. These achievements are amply documented in the various annual reports of the Commissioner of Official Languages, the officer responsible for monitoring the implementation of official languages policy. For example, the *Annual Report* for 1999–2000 reports that Francophones are 27 per cent of the federal public service overall, compared with their position as

approximately 23 per cent of the national population.[21] This is comple-
mented by a substantial improvement in the presence of Francophones
throughout the various levels of public service, rectifying a key problem
identified in the B&B Commission Report. As of 1990, approximately
75 per cent of management level positions within the federal public
service are designated bilingual or French unilingual. More broadly, the
share of federal public service positions designated bilingual or French
essential has increased from 31 per cent in 1974 to 39 per cent in 1999.[22]
Since Francophones typically fill 75 per cent of bilingual positions, this
has a significant impact on increasing the Francophone share of such
positions and ensures that its overall share of the federal public service
is significantly above its national demographic weight.[23] The requirement that all deputy ministers be fluently bilingual by the year 2001 is
one further indication of the continuing commitment to enhance the
presence of the French language in the senior levels of the federal
administration. It also has firmly established the fact that bilingual
capability is an essential requirement for career advancement in the
upper echelons of the federal public service.

Language of work

The B&B Commission had urged all governments to make concerted
efforts to promote French as a language of work not only in Quebec but
also within national and multinational companies operating in
Canada.[24] Federal language policy largely ignored these suggestions for
the private sector, and thus left untouched central problems underlying
Quebec language grievances. These matters would be core features of
Quebec language policies, notably Bills 22 and 101. However, the federal
government has made repeated efforts to advance the status of French as
a language of work within the federal public service.

This issue was first broached in a statement to the House of Commons
on the government's bilingualism policy by Prime Minister Pearson,
who indicated the government's intention of ensuring that 'a climate
will be created in which public servants from both language groups will
work together toward common goals, using their own language and
applying respective cultural values, but each fully understanding and
appreciating those of the other'.[25] The research of the B&B Commission
found serious frustration among Francophones due to the fact that, as
many witnesses complained, 'I have to hang up my language with my
coat when I go to work.'[26] In its report, the B&B Commission argued
that real equality of opportunity for both language groups required an

equal opportunity to work in their own languages. Accordingly, they proposed that the government establish French Language Units throughout the federal public service wherever feasible wherein the principal if not exclusive language of work would be French, and to ensure that a full range of career opportunities were available to both official language groups. To implement the policy, the federal government experimented with the creation of designated French Language Units, wherein the language of work would be French. However, the lukewarm reaction of francophone public servants, who feared that they would form linguistic ghettoes and career dead ends, lead to its ultimate abandonment.

The problem was emphasised once again in the report of the Task Force on Canadian Unity, which insisted that 'it is not only a matter of equal opportunity to secure employment in the federal administration, for example, but the ability, once hired, for both English and French-speaking Canadians to work in their own language. Too many Francophones still do not enjoy this opportunity';[27] To redress the problem, it recommended that the equality of both official languages as languages of work in the federal government be entrenched in the constitution. However, their proposal was carefully confined to the National Capital Region and head offices of government departments. They proposed that the language of work in federal institutions in the various provinces should be the usual language of work in those provinces. This would mean, for example, that it would be French in Quebec, but English in Ontario and most other provinces.

The 1988 reforms to the OLA actively embraced a qualified concept of a right to work in either official language. The preamble of the Bill asserts that individuals 'should have equal opportunities to use the official language of their choice' within federal institutions, determined by the demographic character of particular regions. In the National Capital Region and prescribed areas of bilingual services, the act specifies that federal institutions must ensure that work environments are conducive to work in both official languages, including support services, supervisory staff and work instruments (Sections 35 and 36). In these areas, employees have a right to work in either official language. In the non-bilingual areas, federal institutions have a responsibility to ensure that the treatment of the minority language for that area is comparable to the treatment of the other official language in the reverse circumstances. For Francophones, this means that the right to work in the language of one's choice applies primarily to the so-called 'bilingual belt' – the National Capital Region, Quebec, and parts of Ontario and New Brunswick. Outside this area, 'the language of internal administration is the official language of the majority of the population of the province in which the office is located'.[28]

These policy developments reflect a formal commitment to equal treatment of the two language groups within the public service, but the practical reality tends to reflect a territorial policy in day-to-day administration. Studies on the use of official languages at work in federal institutions concluded that

> Subtle differences in psychological and psycholinguistic climate and in the working milieu have combined to make English in Ottawa and French in Montreal as the normal, expected and thus dominant language of work in these two cities, and to make innovative use of the minority language in either city abnormal and professionally risky for the individuals involved.[29]

The result is that federal policy on the language of work conforms to Quebec's desire to make French the language of work within the workplaces of Quebec.

Language of service

In response to the B&B proposals, the federal government made unsuccessful efforts to encourage the provinces to co-operate in designating regions within the provinces where the provinces would commit to bilingual services. These failures were strongly related to the determined resistance of most provincial governments, the Quebec government's efforts to limit the scope of the bilingual area within Quebec, and the insurmountable difficulties this created in defining a symmetrical policy design in the rest of the country. The resistance of the other provinces was partly based on the political leaders' perception that these would be controversial policy initiatives with significant political cost for themselves, and partly on the assessment that the expenditures were frequently unjustified in light of the small size of their linguistic minority communities. Since the federal plan proposed more extensive provincial commitments than had even been contemplated by the B&B Commission recommendations, these failures can be seen partly as a byproduct of the federal government's determination to impose its policy vision on the provinces as well. The project was ultimately abandoned and the federal government simply implemented its own policy to provide bilingual federal services as broadly as possible. Subsequently, several provinces would develop less ambitious language policies to serve their Francophone minorities, such as Ontario's Bill 8.[30]

One of former Quebec Premier René Lévesque's more effective quips in support of Quebec independence in the 1960s was to say that whenever he went to Ottawa he felt like he was in a foreign country. Everything – government signs, public services, etc. – was in English. For all intents and purposes, there was nothing to distinguish Ottawa from London or Washington. This message was echoed in the B&B Commission findings, which observed that 'perhaps the strongest impression to emerge from the large volume of attitudinal material concerning the federal capital is that French-speaking Canadians do not feel "at home"' there. They urged the government to adopt a range of policies to ensure that 'any resident of the capital should have the opportunity to live a full and complete life either in French or in English.'[31] This advice was heeded and Ottawa became visually a bilingual capital as part of a national policy to give federal institutions a bilingual face across the country.

The B&B Commission further recommended that government policy should strive as well to provide federal services in either official language at the request of citizens. This has been a progressively expanding commitment since the passage of the Official Languages Act in 1969. The OLA had recognised a duty to provide services in both official languages where numbers warrant and in head offices of the federal government. This did not, however, grant an enforceable right to citizens for access to such services. This further step would be achieved with the passage of the Canadian Charter of Rights and Freedoms in 1982, which embedded such rights in the constitution. Section 20 (1) of the Canadian Charter of Rights and Freedoms grants any member of the Canadian public the right to receive any available government services from head offices of the federal government and other offices where there is a 'significant demand' in either English or French. The definition of significant demand has been the subject of elaborate bureaucratic specification, with the result that service areas have been progressively extended to many small communities.

The commitments regarding language of service were further enhanced in 1988, when Parliament passed Bill C-72, which extended the content of these provisions in the judicial realm.[32] During the 1980s, court decisions in the cases of Société des Acadiens and MacDonald adopted a narrow interpretation of the right of defendants to have a trial in their own language. The question in the former case was whether or not the right to use either official language in judicial proceedings, as stated in Section 19(2) of the Charter, included the right to be understood in that language, meaning that court officers must be fluent in that language. In the MacDonald case, the issue concerned the issuing of a speeding ticket in Quebec in French only, which the plaintiff challenged as a violation of Quebec's obligations under Section 133. In the Société des Acadiens case, the majority reasoned that the absence of particular wording specifying the right to be understood in the official language of one's choice was grounds to conclude that it was not part of this right. Similarly, in the MacDonald case, the majority maintained that while section 133 permitted the use of either official language in court proceedings, it did not require the use of both. Accordingly, governments were empowered to adopt whatever practices they deemed appropriate regarding the language of court proceedings.[33]

Bill C-72 specified that the courts have a duty to use the language chosen by parties to the proceedings conducted before it. Once these choices are made, the court must select judges or presiding officers for particular cases who are at least 'receptive bilinguals' in the chosen language or languages. This provision, it should be noted, applies throughout Canada without qualifications regarding 'significant demand' or linguistic minority concentrations. In addition, at the request of a party to any proceedings, the court must provide simultaneous interpretation of the proceedings, and ensure that any person giving evidence *can be understood* in the official language of their choice.[34] These provisions significantly expand the scope of the meaning of a right to a trial in either official language. In short, the federal government has made a strong commitment to provide services in both official languages wherever remotely feasible resulting in a dramatic improvement in the availability of federal government services in both languages. Though the Commissioner's annual report routinely documents shortcomings for services in a number of provinces and in some areas of federal administration, the pattern is one of gradual improvement in services.[35]

Minority language education

In its analysis of the conditions necessary for equality for the two language communities in Canada, the B&B Commission had strongly emphasised the importance of education in one's own language. 'The school', they insisted, 'is the basic agency for maintaining language and culture, and without this essential resource neither can remain strong'. Accordingly, they recommended that 'the right of Canadian parents to have their children educated in the official language of their choice be recognised in the educational systems'.[36] Any comprehensive system of language rights must include the basic right to an education in one's language.

This point underscores a further feature of federal language policy, namely the extent to which it requires action in provincial jurisdiction. As Leslie Pal has noted,

> One of the less appreciated of Canada's bilingual policy is how much of it must be directed at provincial services like education. This property arises in part because of the dual nature of the policy. The provision of bilingual services by the government throughout the country and the nurturing of linguistic communities ... the latter depends to a great deal on creating a supportive economic, social and linguistic environment at the local level.[37]

There were two notable points of policy development regarding provincial jurisdiction. In the 1970s, the federal government initiated a series of federal–provincial discussions, aimed at establishing a national agreement on access to education in all provinces for official languages minorities, which ultimately culminated in a constitutionally entrenched set of education rights. In addition, the government financed a programme of second-language instruction to be offered by the provinces, including French immersion for English Canadians, and to enhance the capacity for dialogue between the two cultures. The French immersion programme has grown dramatically since it began, from 37,835 students in 237 schools in 1977–8, to 315,351 students in 2,115 schools in 1998–9. However, they constitute a small percentage (approximately 6 per cent) of the elementary and secondary school population in Canada. This involved federal transfers of 192.7 million dollars to support such programmes.[38] The results accomplished from these substantial expenditures have been subject to some criticisms. The French language immersion programme is judged to be vastly superior to the standard French language programme in English schools, but nevertheless produces students 'with restricted vocabulary and simplified grammar'. While these students tend to have more positive orientations to French Canadians, they were noticeably more inclined to use their French language skills. If this programme was intended to demonstrate a positive commitment in English Canada to the 'French fact', the results are even more disappointing. One scholar assesses it as a distinct failure on this score. He observes that 'what was regarded as a major initiative to bridge the two solitudes apparently went virtually unnoticed in the French-speaking community of Quebec'.[39]

The most important development for minority language education occurs in Section 23 of the Canadian Charter of Rights and Freedoms. Section 23 recognises minority language educational rights for English- and French-speaking minorities, where the specified right may be claimed only by those Canadian citizens whose mother tongue is that of the official language minority of the province of residence, or where their children already have such access (subject to the precondition of sufficient demand). This creates a new constitutional obligation on provincial governments to provide such services.

Section 23 makes an important distinction regarding minority language rights between minorities in Quebec versus those in the rest of the country. Outside Quebec, the only requirement concerns mother tongue language; inside Quebec, there is a further requirement that one has received one's primary school instruction in Canada in English (hence, it is generally referred to as 'the Canada clause').[40] Thus individuals in similar circumstances possess different rights depending on their geographic location. A Franco-American immigrant (if French mother tongue) educated in English is permitted to send their children to French language schools outside Quebec; but an English mother tongue American immigrant is not entitled to send their children to English language schools in Quebec. These various distinctions lead McRae to tartly observe that 'the entire text of Section 23 is a contradictory tangle of privileges and exclusions that resonate more of narrow intergovernmental bargaining than of general human rights. It is also a reminder that reliance on the principle of personality – rather than territoriality – in the allocation of rights can lead not to freedom of choice, as is sometimes assumed, but to invidious discrimination between groups that qualify and others that do not'.[41] However, it is worth emphasizing that a major source of such discrimination as does exist stems from the attempt to respond to the particular circumstances of Quebec by granting Quebec a veto on parallel application of its provisions. In practical terms, Section 23 ensures that most Canadian citizens have access to education in their (English or French) mother tongue throughout the country (where numbers warrant). In terms of enhancing the survival prospects of official language minority groups throughout Canada, this is probably the most important innovation of the Charter.

While Section 23 made some accommodation for Quebec, it was also true that it had particularly strong impact upon Quebec language policy. During the 1970s, Quebec had passed two pieces of legislation, Bill 22 in 1974 and Bill 101 in 1977, each of which regulated access to the English-language school system. Since Bill 101 limited access to only those whose parents or siblings were educated in English in Quebec, the Charter had the effect of retroactively overturned an existing provincial law, the only province so effected. This lead to a strong negative reaction from Quebec political leaders about this federal intrusion into Quebec legislative jurisdiction. Once again, Ottawa had enacted language policy which created symmetrical rights and treatment between Francophone minorities outside Quebec and Anglophone minorities within Quebec. This was sharply criticised by those who believed that the federal policy was undermining the strength of the French language in Quebec in order to pursue the hopeless goal of reinforcing Francophone communities outside Quebec. However, this hostile reaction was not shared by the Québécois population, which was strongly supportive of the Charter and federal language policy in general. A major national survey of attitudes toward the Charter language rights in Canada, reported that more than 75 per cent of French Canadians support the right of English Canadians to have their children educated in English in Quebec.[42] More specifically, it must be recognised that the changes imposed upon Quebec policy by Section 23 would have a very modest impact on enrolment in Quebec English-language schools, estimated at 1–2 per cent.[43] This is because it would leave untouched the requirement that all immigrants must attend French-language schools unless they met the 'Canada Clause' exemptions, which very few did. Thus the major policy goals of the Quebec government, to integrate allophones (those whose home language is something other than English, French or an aboriginal language) into the French language community, would be accomplished.

Outside Quebec, almost all provinces were compelled to provide enhanced French-language education to their local minorities where numbers warranted. After 1982, there ensued numerous, lengthy court battles as one Francophone provincial organisation after another took their provincial government to court to force them to meet their constitutional obligations. This has resulted in a dramatic expansion of French-medium schools in Canada, and a substantial increase in their enrolments. At the same time the latest annual report of the Commissioner of Official Languages emphasises the problem that only half of those eligible for French-language schools actually attend them, and the rate has been dropping since 1986. Citing one of its recent studies, it notes that 'more parents are likely to choose a French school if it is associated with a French-speaking community perceived as a vibrant one'.[44] Equally telling, a review of the situation of French-language communities outside Quebec and New Brunswick by one scholar indicates that the beneficial effects of these French-language schools is more than offset by the high rates of shift to English as a home language among French mother tongue individuals, leading him to warn that 'if the growing support for French-medium schools is the expression of a real interest in the survival of francophone linguistic and cultural heritage, then the minorities need to go one step further, and attempt to reverse the English-language shift at home'.[45] The conclusion is that a variety of social factors may well undermine the goals of minority language education.

Beyond these specific policy developments, the other major commitment by the federal government was to provide financial assistance to individuals and groups seeking to defend the rights of official languages minorities, and to local Francophone organisations outside of Quebec. In 1997–8, this financial assistance amounted to 42.6 million dollars.[46] This effectively created publicly funded lobby groups to pressure the federal and provincial governments on behalf of their interests. A particularly important mechanism is the Court Challenges Program (CCP), which was established in 1977 precisely to enable language groups to contest provincial government policies. At the time, the principal target was Quebec's language policy, Bill 101, and it was used successfully by non-governmental groups to overturn a number of its provisions. As Brodie notes, 'the Court Challenges Program had become the legal action branch of the federal government's attacks on the PQ's language legislation'.[47] Between 1984 and 1993, the CCP funded all Charter cases involving language rights heard by the Supreme Court during this time, with the result that 'Canadian courts have steadily expanded entitlements to bilingual services and minority-language education at provincial and local levels. The leading language rights precedents have been set primarily in cases funded by the CCP'.[48] The Supreme Court serves as a mechanism for the federal government to impose its policy priorities upon otherwise reluctant provincial governments without having to bear the political cost of direct intervention itself.

In summary, the federal pattern of the legislative development of language policy follows an expansive trend, with a progressive enhancement of the scope and constitutional status of language rights. This is exemplified in the 1988 amendments to the Official Languages Act, which confers a quasi-constitutional status on the first five sections of the act. Section 82 specifies that all federal legislation and regulations must be interpreted so as to be consistent with the first five sections of this legislation. Furthermore, in assigning the federal Secretary of State the mandate to enhance the vitality of the minority language communities across Canada, the federal government assumes responsibility for the management of language policy across all jurisdictions.[49]

That responsibility it should be emphasised takes the form of encouraging support for linguistic minorities through various kinds of incentives, rather than directly challenging provincial government policy in these areas. At the same time, the federal Court Challenges Program (CCP), which finances third party legal cases on language and equality issues, offers an indirect means for the federal government to prod provincial governments to conform to its policy preferences regarding language.[50]

The Supreme Court has clearly taken notice of the significance of the 1988 amendments to the Official Languages Act. The Supreme Court recognised the constitutional status of this legislation in its reasoning in *R. v Beaulac*, where a Federal Court of Appeal assessment is quoted approvingly to the effect that:

> The 1988 *Official Languages Act* is not an ordinary statute. It reflects both the Constitution of the country and the social and political compromise out of which it arose. To the extent that it is the exact reflection of the recognition of the official languages contained in subsections 16(1) and (3) of the *Canadian Charter of Rights and Freedoms*, it follows the rules of interpretation of that Charter as they have been defined by the Supreme Court of Canada. To the extent also that it is an extension of the rights and guarantees recognized in the Charter, and by virtue of its preamble, its purpose defined in section 2 and its taking precedence over other statutes in accordance with subsection 82(1), it belongs to that privileged category of quasi-constitutional legislation which reflects 'certain basic goals of our society' and must be so interpreted 'as to advance the broad policy considerations underlying it'.[51]

This suggests that the status of language rights are moving to a new plan of existence, as fundamental constitutional principles of Canadian political life. As such, they are progressively less amenable to the asymmetrical, territorial solutions that are being advocated by the critics of the existing policy regime.

Impact of federal policies

If federal language policy was supposed to resolve the national unity issue in Canada, its short-term effects were notably modest – if not counterproductive. Language issues were strikingly intense during the 1970s, both federally and within the province of Quebec. Nationally, negative public reaction to federal implementation of its language legislation gave the government pause. Anglophones were angered by the rapid expansion of bilingual positions and their presumed impact on unilingual English speakers' career prospects, while Francophones were disappointed by the lack of progress in making French a language of work in the federal administration. This was illustrated and exacerbated by 'Les Gens de L'Air' controversy, wherein the federal government, pressured by Anglophone air pilots with significant support in English Canada, rescinded the decision of the federal transportation agency permitting the use of French in cockpit/control tower communications within Quebec – much to the chagrin of Québécois.[52] While these measures were ultimately implemented years later, the fact that the federal government was willing to bow to opposition called into question its willingness to support the enhancement of French. This incident is credited with having aided the election of the Parti Québécois in Quebec in the 1976 provincial election. In Quebec, the development of language legislation assigning priority to the French language and placing various restrictions on the historical position of the English language was a standing contradiction to the federal policy and was greeted with consternation in much of English Canada. More troubling still, the substantial development of federal language policy has coincided with the occurrence of two Quebec referenda aimed at Quebec independence, the most recent of which in 1995 came within a hair's breadth of passing. Insofar as national unity implies acceptance of the status quo, its effects on Quebec have been notably modest, if not counterproductive.

Perhaps this was to be expected. When André Laurendeau submitted the first volume of the B&B Commission's work, he had dejectedly remarked that 'it does nothing for Quebec'.[53] The proposals didn't engage the social and economic grievances of Francophones within Quebec's private sector. Neither did they address questions of immigration and linguistic assimilation within Quebec. As controversial and significant as its innovations would be for Francophones in the rest of Canada, they would have an insignificant impact within Quebec, where federal institutions were already achieving these language policy goals. Instead of reflecting Laurendeau's agenda of constitutional reforms aimed at forging an equal partnership between Anglophone and Francophone communities, the proposals reflected Trudeau's view that 'what French Canadians want are guarantees of their language rights'.[54] One might conclude that Trudeau was mistaken in his assessment of Quebec's concerns. However, he was partly correct, in understanding that Francophone concerns over linguistic security were closely related to their support for Quebec independence. A prominent Québécois commentator maintains that 'when Canada's bilingual image erodes, which happens frequently, a feeling of hurt comes out most often in Quebecers'.[55] A study of support for independence in Quebec reported that attitudes on language issues significantly affected support for independence. When individuals perceived the French language to be currently threatened and its prospects enhanced by independence, they were much more likely to vote 'Yes' in the referendum.[56] It obviously follows that strategies to calm these linguistic anxieties should reduce support for profound political change.

One notable consequence of federal language policy has been a gradual growth of public support for the language rights embedded in the Charter. When the B&B Commission made its initial recommendations in the 1960s, they rightly observed that these proposals for language reform were not generally supported in English Canada and therefore would require determined political leadership to bring to fruition. Twenty years later, the Charter project study would document the existence of a widespread national consensus in support of the Charter language rights shared by Anglophones and Francophones in both the mass public and political élites.

Two findings are particularly instructive. The national Francophone public is much more strongly supportive of the Section 23 English language education rights in Quebec than is the PQ political élite, 81 per cent to 48 per cent. However, the PQ élite is even more strongly supportive of Francophone minority rights outside Quebec than is the Francophone public, 93 per cent to 83 per cent. These findings indicate the continuing importance of Section 23 as a core element of language rights, and also illustrate the way in which the Francophone public has a rather different set of attitudes to the language issue than are reflected in PQ views. Nevertheless, these levels of support are somewhat fragile, and can be readily reduced by political controversies and affected interests. If such rights were seen as imposing significant costs (for Anglophones), or would otherwise threaten the security of the French language in Quebec (for Francophones), for example, support levels plummet.[57]

In addition, Anglophones, and to a lesser extent Francophones, are more supportive of language rights for themselves than they are for the other group. For example, while 97 per cent of Anglophones supported the right to federal government services in English for Anglophones in Quebec, only 64 per cent supported French language services for Francophones outside Quebec. Francophone responses on each question were 91 per cent and 95 per cent respectively.[58] Beyond that, each group is inclined to be more supportive of language rights for others where it perceives a reciprocity of respect for similar rights for itself. The Charter Project study summarised the prevailing logic as follows:

> We are more willing to grant them a right that we ourselves want and believe we are entitled to exercise, and still more willing if our exercising it is contingent on their possessing an equivalent right.[59]

One might further observe that support for language rights declines as the matter moves from being an abstract generality in government policy statements to a specific local case at hand. In that respect, the expanding federal language policy commitments of the past fifteen years have been remarkable for their political invisibility, doubtless a result of the political party consensus in support of these developments. Only the Reform Party (now the Canadian Alliance) challenges this policy, and even this party has become rather muted in its criticisms as it seeks to build support in Quebec. None the less, the development of this political consensus on language rights is quite remarkable. What must be emphasised is that its persistence is strongly dependent on the continued equality of treatment for both official languages. This reality must inform any assessment of alternative policy regimes.

This being the case, the question might then be posed, does federal language policy constitute a significant obstacle to Quebec's drive to enhance the position of the French language?

Policies in conflict?

Some commentators suggest that federal language policy is a barrier to the effectiveness of Quebec policy and thus should be modified to minimise its intrusiveness. They maintain that a language policy of territoriality, which locates decision-making powers regarding language in the group is the only policy consistent with the long-term survival of minority languages. For this reason, a language must be given an exclusive territorial domain in which to operate. Federal bilingualism policy is fundamentally misguided, since it is inadequate to overcome the forces of assimilation for non-Quebec Francophones on the one hand and, on the other, interferes with Quebec's efforts to reinforce the French language within Quebec. On this account, the government of Quebec must have full control over language policy to encourage linguistic assimilation to French. At a minimum, federal language policy should conform to Quebec's policy within Quebec's borders.

This position stems in part from the conviction that 'a language is threatened as soon as it is no longer spoken universally at home, at work, at play, at market, with kin, with friends and fellow workers'.[60] On this basis, the language provisions of the Canadian Charter of Rights and Freedoms are criticised as a mistaken policy which undermines a territorial approach to language policy in Quebec and thereby threatens the survival of the French language. In particular, Laponce sharply criticises Section 23 because, unlike Section 15, the equality rights clause, it 'excludes language from the right to enjoy unequal rights in the form of affirmative action', which, he believes, ultimately reinforces the position of English to the detriment of French.[61]

In response to this argument, one might begin with the empirical question of whether the language rights in the Canadian Charter threaten the French language in Quebec. There is good reason to doubt that they do. The census data, for instance, indicate extremely high rates of language retention among Quebec Francophones, to the extent that language loss is negligible.[62] The major threat to the dominance of French has come from immigrant assimilation to the English language via the English-language education system. The education provisions of Quebec's Bill 101 have effectively eliminated this problem, with the result that the 'Canada Clause' of the Charter has virtually no effect on increasing the strength of the English language in Quebec. Furthermore, Section 23 has been tailored to recognise Quebec's distinctive problems in this area. Section 23 is asymmetrical in that it permits the Quebec government alone exemption from the provisions of Section 23(1)(a). The effect is to allow French mother tongue naturalised immigrants access to French language minority schools outside Quebec, but does not permit their English mother tongue counterparts access to English-language schools in Quebec.

If anything, it is remarkably clear that federal language policy within Quebec is largely irrelevant to the position of the French language. Despite a federal bilingualism policy, the Anglophone population decreased in Quebec by over 79,000 from 1971 to 1981. The Charter protection for minority language education that came into force in 1982 was similarly ineffective. From 1981 to 1991, the Anglophone population declined a further 45,000.[63] The main reason for these declines is the continuing exodus of Anglophones from Quebec. While one could argue that the exodus would be greater in the absence of the Charter protection and federal bilingualism, it cannot be maintained that these figures are consistent with a strong Anglophone language community in Quebec that threatens the francisation of Quebec. Consequently, it is very doubtful that the Charter language rights for the Anglophone minority in Quebec pose a threat to the vitality of the French language in Quebec.

These findings are also relevant to challenging the view that 'a fixed linguistic boundary enclosing a unilingual territory remains the best and probably the only effective way to protect a linguistic minority in the long run'.[64] That it is the best way is almost certainly true. It does not mean, however, that it is necessary for language survival. A recent study of language minorities around the world offered several cases where language minorities manage to survive without this territorial advantage. The same study emphasised the fundamental importance of the use of the language in the home, community and private life as critical foundations to language survival.[65] Quebec Francophones enjoy both sets of linguistic advantages. The Quebec language legislation offers ample testimony that the Quebec government already possesses the main factor in language survival, namely political control over language within its territorial space. In conjunction with its other strengths, the French language exercises control of the education system, and experiences widespread use throughout family, community and economic life. A 1986 Statistics Canada survey on use of mother tongue reported that over 95 per cent of Québécois used their language at home, work, with friends and even watching television.[66] Thus the French language possesses all the major components in the survival of a language within its territory. In such circumstances, the federal language policy may reinforce the Anglophone minority somewhat, without threatening the position of French.

The same conclusion applies to the impact of federal language policy on francophones outside Quebec. Each successive census documents further advances of linguistic assimilation of Francophones, especially in those areas outside 'the bilingual belt'. The linguistic assimilation rate has risen to over 33 per cent for the 1991 census, from 28 per cent in the 1981 census. A major factor in this process is marriage outside the language community, which accounts for roughly half of all Francophone marriages outside Quebec and New Brunswick. In these cases, a high percentage adopt English as their language at home, thus reducing the prospects of their children attaining fluency in French. Such personal factors strongly influence linguistic assimilation and are of course beyond the capacity of legislation to affect.

On the other hand, these Francophone minorities have proved surprisingly resilient. Whereas there were 676,000 French home language individuals outside Quebec in 1971, there were still 636,600 as of the

1991 census. The French mother tongue population continues to rise, from 926,000 in 1971 to 976,000 in 1991. These figures cover a period in which minority language education rights were not generally available. One might expect the Section 23 provisions to significantly improve the prospects for Francophones outside Quebec.[67] Admittedly, this will not overcome the force of other factors in linguistic assimilation, but it may well mitigate them. Despite such modest prospects, it is useful to remember that the rationale for federal policy was not based on its ability to stem linguistic assimilation, but rather to provide institutional support to improve their prospects. In that respect, they are undoubtedly significant. The important impact of federal efforts is strongly endorsed in Joy's observation that 'with present federal support withdrawn, the linguistic minorities would eventually disappear through assimilation or out-migration'.[68]

It is worth emphasising that federal language policy has been well-received in Quebec. Some critics of the national language policy mistakenly assume that Québécois supporters of independence are affronted by national language policy. This is not the case. A CTV poll from the late 1980s reported that 90 per cent of Quebecers favoured a bilingual national government and 61 per cent wanted their provincial government to be officially bilingual as well.[69] More pointedly, the OLA is one of the few federal policies to escape criticism by the Bloc Québécois, the Quebec-based independentist party in the federal Parliament, for the very good reason that it would contradict public opinion in Quebec.[70] A recent analysis of Québécois support for the sovereignty option reports that perceptions of the French language as threatened, coupled with positive expectations about its prospects under sovereignty, significantly increases support for sovereignty. The authors suggest that the best way to increase support for sovereignty is by heightening perceptions of the threatened state of the French language.[71] The corollary of this finding is that a demonstrated commitment by the federal government to promoting the French language will diminish the perceived benefits of independence.

Within Quebec, language issues are once again engaged. At the time of writing, the Estates-general on language policy, a task force established by the PQ government to assess the state of Quebec's language laws, has submitted a series of recommendations for reform which is under government review. While the government has indicated its support for the general direction of its proposals, an official response is not anticipated until late in the Fall, 2001. These proposals address federal policy in a few areas. They call for a constitutional amendment of Section 133 to eliminate the requirement that English be an official language of Quebec. They also propose that Quebec exercise complete authority over immigration to the province, that the federal government enforce more strictly the bilingual labelling requirements on commercial products, and that federal government institutions as well as federally regulated enterprises conform to Quebec's laws on commercial signs.[72] This is a strikingly modest list, of greater symbolic than substantive significance. The proposal to eliminate the official status of English in Quebec is hardly novel. It was proposed by the federal Task Force on Canadian Unity two decades ago, which maintained that 'each province should have the right to determine an official language or official languages for that province, within its sphere of jurisdiction'.[73] While there might be a case for this change on the grounds of equal treatment for each province, such a change is largely irrelevant to the language situation in Quebec. The government of Quebec functions almost completely in French except where it chooses to do otherwise. A brief examination of the debates in the Assemblée Nationale (the provincial legislature of Quebec) suffices to illustrate the point. Such a change would have no impact on the linguistic and cultural integration of immigrants, access to education and the language of work – the traditional central concerns in Quebec. Its significance is principally symbolic, in extending Quebec sovereignty over language matters.

Were the proposal to be taken up this would become part of the problem. The change could be made by legislative resolutions of the Quebec Assemblée Nationale and the federal Parliament. This would have the potential to become a divisive issue in Parliament, where an Anglophone majority would be asked to make a decision which appears to deprive Anglophones in Quebec of their traditional status. One might recall in this context, the reception accorded the 'distinct society' clause in the most recent failed attempts to reform the Canadian constitution – the Meech Lake Agreement and the Charlottetown Accord.[74] These clauses were designed to officially recognise Quebec's distinct character as a French-language society and to have this recognition inform judicial interpretations of the constitution. Both were principal factors in the massive rejection of theses proposals, because they were viewed as a mechanism to permit Quebec governments to deprive its Anglophone minority of their language rights. While this proposal does not directly raise such implications, it is entirely possible that the political debates would revisit these linguistic grievances. However, if such a change were accompanied by a commitment by the Quebec government to recognise an expanded right to government services in English in Quebec, this would undercut the prospect of a divisive debate. At present, rights to health and social services in English are recognised, but a more general right to government services is not. Quebec public servants are permitted, but not required, to provide services in English upon request by individuals – and generally do. Legislation which granted such an entitlement would do much to facilitate success in changing Section 133, and to reinforce an increasingly beleaguered Anglophone minority in Quebec.

Briefly, the other items are similarly modest in their impact on Quebec society. As a result of a bilateral Ottawa–Quebec agreement, Quebec sets its own criteria for selection of the main category of immigrants, which significantly enhances prospects of attracting immigrants to the French language community.[75] This change would enable Quebec to select all immigrants. This is unlikely to have a significant net impact on the composition of Quebec's immigrant population, though once again it extends Quebec's legislative authority. Finally, whether or not the federal government conforms to Quebec's policy on public signs, one might query what effective difference it would make whether a few buildings have bilingual signs where the French characters are significantly larger (Quebec's policy), rather than equal in size to the English characters (federal practice). In short, this list indirectly confirms the point that federal language policy poses no significant obstacles to Quebec's language policy objectives.

In recent years, Québécois public opinion has been less inclined to see the need for action on language policy. A poll in March 1996 reported that a majority of Francophones (59.3 per cent) believe that Bill 101 is severe enough, 25.1 per cent think it not sufficiently severe and 9.7 per cent consider it too severe.[76] A subsequent poll in April 1996 found that Québécois generally report significant improvements in the position of French in the past ten years. Its authors concluded that 'the French language is doing well in Quebec and there is no need to reopen the language laws … .They are saying there is enough space in Quebec for those who want to express themselves in French'.[77] On balance this indicates that existing legislation, both federal and provincial, is broadly acceptable.

In establishing a national regime of language rights, Ottawa has accommodated Quebec's linguistic sensitivities though it has not done what some Québécois (notably language militants within the Parti Québécois) want. Aside from minority language education rights, it has been careful to avoid challenging Quebec language policy directly, and informally conforms to Quebec's priorities in its administrative functions within Quebec. This strategy advances federal purposes without undermining Quebec's legitimate policy goals.

While the present policies in Ottawa and Quebec may well be mutually compatible, can we expect the situation to persist? Some commentators are inclined to think that federal policy must necessarily retrench from its present commitment to French in response to anticipated demographic developments. Barbaud, for example, citing projections of the long-run demographic decline of the Quebec Francophone share of the Canadian population, predicts that 'the notion of equality of languages, represented by official bilingualism, is doomed to disappear, which will inevitably lead to a fundamental redefinition of Canada as a country'.[78] If federal policy were simply a response to demographic patterns, this might well be true. But political factors will significantly reduce the impact of such demographic decline. These elements are strongly conveyed by former Prime Minister Pierre Trudeau, when he defended the national language policy by observing 'We are dealing with straightforward political and social realities. ... If only because of sheer force of numbers, either group has the power to destroy the unity of this country. Those are the facts. ... These facts leave Canada with only one choice, only one realistic policy: to guarantee the language rights of both linguistic communities'.[79] These same realities persist whether Quebec constitutes 28 per cent, or 20 per cent of the Canadian population. Even if such a reduction of commitment were to occur, it would presumably entail a corresponding reduction in federal efforts in support of English in Quebec as well – thus reducing one source of friction between Quebec and Ottawa. Federal language policy, then, treads an uneasy path around a fragile consensus on language matters with limited room for significant change in its fundamental orientation.

Notes

1 Marcel Coté, 'Language and Public Policy', in John Richards, François Vaillancourt and William Watson (eds), *Survival: Official Language Rights in Canada* (Toronto: C. D. Howe Institute, 1992) pp. 7–8.
2 Kenneth D. McRae, 'Official Bilingualism: from the 1960s to the 1990s', in John Edwards (ed.), *Language in Canada* (Cambridge: Cambridge University Press, 1998) p. 81.
3 For an overview of the history of language use policy in the federal administration, see Royal Commission on Bilingualism and Biculturalism, *Report*, Bk 3: *The Work World*, Part 2. My overview of federal language policy draws significantly on my discussion presented in C. Michael MacMillan, *The Practice of Language Rights in Canada* (Toronto: University of Toronto Press, 1998), passim.

4   Royal Commission on Bilingualism and Biculturalism, *Report*, vol. 1, *The Official Languages*, 60.

5   Royal Commission on Bilingualism and Biculturalism, *Report*, vol. 1, *The Official Languages*, 54.

6   Subsequently, the newly-established provinces of Manitoba, Saskatchewan and Alberta would have comparable provisions, which would ultimately be discarded.

7   An abbreviation of the quotation appearing in Kenneth McRoberts, *Misconceiving Canada: the Struggle for National Unity* (Toronto: Oxford University Press, 1997) p. 101. It originally appeared in Peter Stursberg, *Lester Pearson and the Dream of Unity* (Toronto: Doubleday, 1978) p. 146.

8   These figures were reported from studies conducted in 1965. See Report of the Royal Commission on Bilingualism and Biculturalism, Book 3: *The Work World*, Part 2: *The Federal Administration*, pp. 209–14.

9   André Laurendeau, *The Diary of André Laurendeau*, trans. Patricia Smart and Dorothy Howard (Toronto: James Lorimer, 1991) p. 117.

10 For an overview of this concept and its demise, and the impact of the B&B Commission, see Michael Oliver, 'The Impact of the Royal Commission on Bilingualism and Biculturalism on Constitutional Thought and Practice in Canada', *International Journal of Canadian Studies* 7–8, Spring–Fall (1993) pp. 315–32.

11 Noted by Michael Oliver, 'The Impact of the Royal Commission', p. 320. Oliver here reports that the Commission defined 'society' as 'a complex of organisations and institutions sufficiently rich to permit people to lead a full life in their own language'.

12 Royal Commission on Bilingualism and Biculturalism, *Report*, vol. 1, *The Official Languages*, p. 98. The phrase 'bilingual belt' refers to the geographic area of Canada, stretching from Sault Ste. Marie in Ontario, through Quebec to Moncton, New Brunswick, wherein are concentrated the vast majority of Francophone residents. It is identified and discussed in Richard J. Joy, *Languages in Conflict* (Toronto: McClelland and Stewart, 1972) 23–9.

13 Royal Commission on Bilingualism and Biculturalism, *Report*, vol. 1, *The Official Languages*, pp. 73, 74, xliii.

14 Royal Commission on Bilingualism and Biculturalism, *Preliminary Report*, p. 119.

15 Official Languages Act, 1968–9, *Revised Statutes of Canada 1970*, c. O-2, s.2.

16 The ambitious plan to designate bilingual districts foundered on the twin hurdles of provincial intransigence and the peculiarities of the minority language population distribution in the country. For an informative analysis of the failure of this scheme, see Kenneth D. McRae, 'Bilingual Language Districts in Finland and Canada: Adventures in the Transplanting of an Institution', *Canadian Public Policy*, vol. 4, no. 3 (1978), pp. 331–51.

17 Royal Commission on Bilingualism and Biculturalism, *Report*, Book 3: *The Work World*, p. 353. The original statement was presented in the House of Commons (6 April 1966).

18 Rt. Hon. Lester Pearson, 'Statement of Policy Respecting Bilingualism', House of Commons, *Debates*, 1st Session, 27th Parliament (6 April 1966), 3915.

19 Government of Canada, *A National Understanding*, 41.

20   This pattern of government justification also helps explain public perceptions about language rights. The widespread view that language rights are
primarily based on the preservation of national unity is completely consistent with the message presented by the federal government on their behalf.
21   Commissioner of Official Languages, *Annual Report 1999–2000: The Texture of
Canada* (Ottawa: Minister of Public Works and Public Services Canada, 2000),
Figure 8, p. 92. The participation rate is even higher according to the Treasury
Board of Canada statistics, at 30 per cent, up from 25 per cent in 1978. These
figures are reported in Table 12 of the *Annual Report* of the Treasury Board of
Canada Secretariat at <http://www.tbs-sct.gc.ca/report/oflang/olar99-2_e.
html#list> The 1996 census figures for the Mother Tongue populations are
reported at the Statistics Canada website on Population at <http://www.
statcan.ca/english/census96/dec2/mother.htm>
22   These figures are reported in Table 1 of the *Annual Report* of the Treasury Board
of Canada Secretariat at <http://www.tbs-sct.gc.ca/report/oflang/olar99-
2_e.html#list>
23   These figures are drawn from the 1990 *Annual Report* of the Public Service
Commission of Canada. See Table 10.2 and the following text in Stephen
Brooks, *Public Policy in Canada: An Introduction* (Toronto: McClelland and
Stewart, 1993), p. 247.
24   See Royal Commission on Bilingualism and Biculturalism, *Report*, Book 3:
The Work World, Part 4 (Ottawa: Queen's Printer, 1969).
25   Ibid., Appendix B: 'Statement of the Right Hon. Lester B. Pearson Regarding
Policy Respecting Bilingualism in the Public Service' (House of Commons,
6 April 1966), p. 352.
26   Royal Commission on Bilingualism and Biculturalism, *Report*, Book 3: *The
Work World*, p. 3.
27   Task Force on Canadian Unity, *A Future Together*, p. 50.
28   Ibid., 14. The principle does, however, have broader impact across the country. It also means that the federal government is committed to providing
work instruments, such as technical manuals, in both official languages for
unilingual employees working throughout the country. This addresses a standard complaint among Francophones that they were often unable to perform
their work in French, even in Francophone areas.
29   Kenneth McRae, 'Official bilingualism: from the 1960s to the 1990s', p. 71.
30   The Ontario legislation makes both English and French langauges of the legislature and the courts of Ontario, and also commits to providing French language services in designated areas of the province. See Government of
Ontario, *French Language Services Act, Revised Statutes of Ontario 1990*, c.F.31.
31   B&B Commission, *Report*, Book V: *The Federal Capital*, pp. 36, 38.
32   House of Commons, Bill C-72, *An Act respecting the status and use of the official
languages of Canada*, second session, Thirty-third Parliament (first reading,
25 June 1987, passed 7 July 1988).
33   The cases are cited as *Société des Acadiens du Nouveau-Brunswick Inc. et al. v
Association of Parents for Fairness in Education et al.* [1986] 1, *Supreme Court
Reports*, 549, and *MacDonald v City of Montreal et al.* [1986] 1 *Supreme Court
Reports*, 460.
34   See *Official Languages Act*, c.31 (4th Supplement) of the *Revised Statutes of
Canada, 1985*, Part III.

35 Ibid., Chapter 4.
36 Ibid., pp. 122–3.
37 Leslie Pal, 'Official Language Minorities and the State', in William Coleman and Grace Skogstad (eds), *Policy Communities and Public Policies in Canada* (Toronto: Copp Clark Pittman, 1990) p. 178.
38 The enrolment figures are obtained from Commissioner of Official Languages, Annual Report 1998, (Ottawa: Minister of Public Works and Government Services, 1999), Table V.2 on p. 122. The expenditure figures appear in Table III.19 on p. 79.
39 Fred Genesee, 'French Immersion in Canada', in John Edwards (ed.), *Language in Canada* (Cambridge: Cambridge University Press, 1998) p. 322. My summary of the findings are drawn from his discussion.
40 This, of course, is the 'Canada Clause' proposal of the Task Force on Canadian Unity. See Canada, Task Force on Canadian Unity, *A Future Together: Observations and Recommendations* (Ottawa: Minister of Supply and Services, 1979).
41 McRae, 'Official Bilingualism', p. 67.
42 Paul M. Sniderman, Joseph F. Fletcher, Peter H. Russell and Philip E. Tetlock, *The Clash of Rights: Liberty Equality and Legitimacy in Pluralist Democracy* (New Haven: Yale University Press, 1996) Figure 7.3B, 207. Of course, this figure includes both French Canadians outside as well as inside Quebec. But since Quebec French Canadians are the overwhelming majority of the French Canadian population, this figure also indicates strong support in Quebec as well. See the entire Chapter 7, 'The Politics of Language and Group Rights' for a provocative discussion of the factors influencing support for language rights among both language groups.
43 One study indicated that the difference between Bill 101 requirements and a policy allowing all those with English mother tongue into English-language schools by 1886–7 would be 1.6 per cent. This would still constitute a decline from the levels anticipated five years earlier, in 1981–2. For a comparison of various demographic projections for school see Table 7 in Brian Mckee, 'A Socio-Demographic Analysis of Language Groups in Quebec' Working Paper for Center for Research on Ethnic Minorities (Ottawa: Department of Sociology and Anthropology, Carleton University, n.d.), Table 7, 24.
44 Commissioner of Official Languages, *Annual Report*, pp. 36–7.
45 Raymond Mongeon, 'French outside New-Brunswick and Quebec', in John Edwards, *Language in Canada*, p. 248.
46 Ibid.
47 Brodie, 'Interest Group Litigation and the Embedded State: Canada's Court Challenges Program', *Canadian Journal of Political Sciences*, vol. 34 (2, 2001) p. 365.
48 Brodie, 'Interest Group Litigation', pp. 371–2. This program was briefly terminated, then reintroduced in a broader form to cover an expanded range of policy areas.
49 These points are emphasized in Ken McRae, 'Official Bilingualism: from the 1960s to the 1990s', pp. 76–9.
50 For an elaboration of this theme, see Ian Brodie, 'Interest Group Litigation and the Embedded State: Canada's Court Challenges Program', *Canadian Journal of Political Science*, vol. 34 (2, 2001), pp. 357–76.

51   *R. v Beaulac*, at 24. The quotation is drawn from the Federal Court of Appeal decision in Canada (A.G.) V. Viola [1991] 1 F.C. 373, at pp. 386–7.
52   This controversy is examined in considerable detail in Sanford F. Borins, *The Language of the Skies: The Bilingual Air Traffic Control Conflict in Canada* (Montreal: McGill-Queen's University Press, 1983).
53   André Laurendeau, *The Diary*, 8.
54   Ibid., 9.
55   Christian Dufour, *A Canadian Challenge/Le défi québécois* (Halifax: The Institute for Research on Public Policy, 1990) p. 100.
56   See Richard Nadeau and Christopher J. Fleury, 'Gains linguistiques anticipés et appui à la souveraineté du Québec' *Canadian Journal of Political Science*, **28** no. 1, (1995), pp. 35–50.
57   Sniderman *et al.*, *The Clash of Rights*, pp. 210–15.
58   These figures are drawn from Paul M. Sniderman, Joseph F. Fletcher, Peter H. Russell and Philip E. Tetlock, 'Political Culture and the Problem of Double Standards: Mass and Elite Attitudes toward Language Rights in the Canadian Charter of Rights and Freedoms', *Canadian Journal of Political Science*, vol. 22 (2, 1989), pp. 259–84. My critique of their analysis appears in my 'Explaining Support for Language Rights: A Comment on "Political culture and the Problem of Double Standards"' *Canadian Journal of Political Science*, vol. 23 (3, 1990), pp. 531–6. See also their reply in Paul M. Sniderman *et al.*, 'Reply: Strategic Calculation and Political Values – The Dynamics of Language Rights', *Canadian Journal of Political Science*, vol. 23 (3, 1990), pp. 537–44.
59   Paul M. Sniderman *et al.*, *Clash of Rights*, p. 203.
60   Ibid., p. 16.
61   Jean A. Laponce, *Languages and their Territories*, trans. Anthony Martin-Sperry (Toronto: University of Toronto Press, 1987) pp. 163–4.
62   See, for example, Jacques Henripin, 'Two Solitudes in 2001?', *Language and Society*, vol. 4 (1981), pp. 15–19.
63   Ibid., Table 8: 29. The latter figures are drawn from Harrison and Marmen, *Languages in Canada*, Table 1.3, p. 10.
64   Laponce, *Languages and their Territories*, p. 187.
65   See Joshua A. Fishman, *Reversing Language Shift: Theoretical and Empirical Foundations of Assistance to Threatened Languages* (Clevedon, Avon, England: Multilingual Matters, 1991). The most striking example is the case of Ultra-Orthodox Yiddish in the United States. Laponce also recognizes the importance of these other factors. See his *Languages and Their Territories*, p. 159.
66   Reported in Harrison and Marmen, *Languages in Canada*, Chart 4.3, 46. This is not to say that they used French exclusively.
67   See Edmund Aunger, 'The Decline of a French-Speaking Enclave: A Case Study of Social Contact and Language Shift in Alberta', *Canadian Ethnic Studies*, vol. 25, no. 2 (1993), pp. 65–83. Aunger emphasises that the English-language education system has had a significant role in linguistic assimilation. He anticipates that the new French school established in 1990 could have a significant impact on rates of linguistic assimilation.
68   Richard J. Joy, *Canada's Official Languages: The Progress of Bilingualism* (Toronto: University of Toronto Press, 1992) p. 9. At the same time Joy is dubious about the long-term prospects of Francophone communities outside the bilingual belt. He later remarks 'it appears clear that, as Francophones

move away from the Quebec border, they can have little hope of hearing the French language spoken by their grandchildren' (ibid., p. 52).

69 Reported in William Hynes, 'Keep Canada Tuned in to Both Languages', *The Globe and Mail* (3 April 1991) p. A19. The polls were released in the midst of the Meech Lake crisis, when presumably Quebeckers would be relatively upset over Anglophone resistance to the reform package. The poll results are consistent with the findings in Quebec over the past two decades.

70 A point emphasized in Lysiane Gagnon, 'Why Sovereignists Don't Attack the Official Languages Act', *The Globe and Mail* (14 January 1995), D3. She remarks, 'only die-hard separatists do not care about the state of French throughout Canada. All other Quebeckers do, and the last time I looked at a poll, they were a rather strong majority.'

71 See Richard Nadeau and Christopher J. Fleury, 'Gains linguistiques Anticipés et Appui à la Souveraineté du Québec', *Canadian Journal of Political Science*, vol. 28, no. 1 (1995), pp. 35–50.

72 Commission des États Généraux sur la Situation et L'Avenir de la Langue Française au Québec, *L'Avenir du Français au Québec: Une Nouvelle Approche Pour de Nouvelles Réalités*, Forum National, 5 and 6 June 2001, 65.

73 Task Force on Canadian Unity, *A Future Together* (Ottawa: Minister of Supply and Services, 1979) pp. 121–2.

74 For reflections on the significance of the Meech Lake failure, see David E. Smith, Peter Mackinnon and John Courtney (eds), *After Meech Lake: Lessons for the Future* (Saskatoon: Fifth House, 1991).

75 The Cullen–Couture Agreement, adopted in 1978, is a bilateral agreement between Ottawa and Quebec which gives Quebec control over the selection of immigrants to Quebec. Quebec is able to assign greater weight to French language skills, which enhances the prospects of receiving French-speaking immigrants.

76 'Poll backs current law', *The Globe and Mail*, 23 March 1996, A4.

77 The findings were reported by a Léger & Léger poll conducted between 11 and 17 April, 1996. The results are reported in 'French language secure, Quebecers say', *The Globe and Mail*, 20 April 1996, A5. On the matter of commercial signs, 36.9 per cent thought the situation improved over the past ten years, but 25.1 per cent saw it as deteriorated, producing the smallest gap between the two groups for the various areas examined. In regard to customer service in French, for example, 41.5 per cent thought it improved, whereas only 15 per cent thought it deteriorated.

78 Philippe Barbaud, 'French in Quebec', in John Edwards (ed.), *Language in Canada*, p. 179.

79 Canada, House of Commons, *Debates* (31 May 1973) p. 4303.

A Language Policy for a Language in Exile

Marc Chevrier[1]

> This is the way the world ends
> Not with a bang but a whimper
>
> T. S. Eliot, *The Hollow Men*

Introduction

Following the death of Mordecai Richler, the famous Anglo-Montrealer author of *Duddy Kravitz*, a journalist of the Toronto-based newspaper *National Post* commented on the Canadian attitude towards language laws in Quebec: 'Most Canadians, to our shame, looked with benign indifference on the madness of the language laws, hoping they would eventually go away on their own.' In a way, this quotation captures what has been in English Canada a pervasive opinion regarding the appropriateness of language laws in Quebec. Although the Charter of the French Language adopted by the Quebec National Assembly in 1977 has triggered an unending discussion and has been from time to time modified in order to strike a better balance between individual rights and the aspirations of Quebecers to ground the French language on a firm basis, the reasons for this policy are still not understood outside Quebec. In the media throughout English Canada and among some Anglophone interest groups in Quebec, it is often depicted as an unnecessary, illiberal and capricious law that promotes, at the expense of interests viewed as fundamental rights, the rebel language of a minority refusing to jump into the Anglo-American continental mainstream.

This persistent miscomprehension of language laws in Quebec is somewhat surprising, for it is nowadays commonplace for sovereign and non-sovereign states in the world to protect by their laws an official language or the language of a minority. According to a study made in 1993,

75 per cent of the sovereign countries had constitutional provisions protecting or enhancing a language. But making French the common language of a daily use in a society which represents about 2 per cent of the combined population of Canada and the United States is in itself a paradox. As Fernand Dumont, Quebec sociologist, puts it, French is a language in 'exile' in North America. Being the natural language of France and the language of important national minorities in Belgium and Switzerland, adopted as an official language by many African states, French is spoken in Canadian homes by less than 6.5 million people. Contrary to English, Spanish and Portuguese in the Americas, it cannot assert itself as the language of the majority behind the shield of a national state. As Jean Laponce, political scientist, noted in his book *Languages and their Territories*, Quebec is one of the few minorities in the world that are encapsulated by a foreign language. Linguistic minorities are usually stretches of population living alongside the borders of a state whose dominant language is theirs. The French-speaking and the Italian-speaking citizens of Switzerland offer good examples of this situation. In the case of Quebec, we see a large cluster of Francophones being encircled or contained in two ways. Most of the population of Quebec lives in the southern part of the province bordering upon four American states. Furthermore, Quebec cuts English Canada in two parts. In the northern part of Quebec live Aboriginal peoples whose main language is English. This dimension adds to the sense that French is in North America an isolated language, a splendid island where remembrance of the past is the only way to escape the fate of geography.

In the following pages, we will give an overview of Quebec's history and political status, and give some figures on the French fact in Canada. We will also describe the development and content of the two competing linguistic policies applying to Quebec, and finally conclude with some general remarks on the future of French in a multicultural state.

Quebec's status in the Canadian political regime

A province in a dominion

The final ceding of New France to the British Crown in 1763 put an end to two and a half centuries of French settlement in North America. Seventy thousand French colonists suddenly found themselves a conquered people, subject to a foreign language, religion and legal system. After the Seven Years' War between France and Great Britain, it could have been expected that New France would melt away, as had the former Dutch and Swedish colonies on the American east coast.

After the conquest, British subjects came by the thousands to settle in the new colony called the *Province of Quebec*. In 1791, London divided the colony in two, reserving one part, Upper Canada, for some 10,000 of its colonists, and the other, Lower Canada, for the 150,000 *Canadiens* living in the St Lawrence valley. Although they were granted a legislative assembly with limited powers, the *Canadiens* were still in a position of economic and social inferiority. The predictions of foreign observers, like Benjamin Franklin, on their chances for cultural survival were not very optimistic. While visiting Lower Canada in 1831, Alexis de Tocqueville, the acclaimed author of *Democracy in America*, clearly saw that the *Canadiens* were a conquered people dominated by the British. 'The worst thing for a nation is to be conquered', he wrote.

In 1837–8, the injustices and the exactions suffered by *Canadiens* under British rule in Lower Canada led many of them to embrace the modern idea of forming a republican government. The Patriot Party of Louis-Joseph Papineau, a coalition of *Canadiens* and of British democrats, headed a protest movement against the hold London had on its colony's affairs. London's refusal to bring in a truly responsible government gave rise to an insurrection in both Lower and Upper Canada that was quickly put down. Inspired by the famous report written by Lord Durham after the uprising, London concluded that it should force the assimilation of *Canadiens* of French extraction by uniting the two colonies. In 1840, it decreed this union and imposed equality of representation for the former Upper Canada and the former Lower Canada in the single parliament, even though the *Canadiens*, who numbered 650,000, were the majority, Upper Canada's population being 450,000. Because of massive immigration by colonists from the British Isles, the population of British extraction outnumbered the French Canadians.

In 1867, an alliance of Tory loyalists and French Canadian royalists won out over the opposition of the liberal republicans of the time and succeeded in establishing what became on July 1867 the so-called *Dominion of Canada*, a new British colony created out of the union of three provinces, New Brunswick, Nova Scotia and Canada (at that time made up of the union of Upper and Lower Canada). This new political entity was a unique combination of empire and colony, monarchy and democracy, federation and unitary state. The Dominion was composed of four provinces. French Canadians, who comprised only one-third of the new state, would be a majority only in the reborn Province of Quebec. Although the Dominion wasn't a true federation similar in principle to the regime the Americans, in 1787, and the Swiss, in 1848, had founded, some federalism was incorporated in the working of the new colony to accommodate the French Canadians' desire to preserve their language, culture and civil institutions.

The new regime dealt in many ways with language. The Constitution of 1867 made Quebec and the federal government subject to certain obligations regarding bilingualism: they must adopt their laws in French and in English and guarantee parliamentarians, judges, litigants and parties to a legal proceeding the right to use both languages. Nevertheless, this requirement of bilingualism only confirmed what had developed as a common usage under British rule in Quebec, especially before the courts. It was not intended to erect bilingualism or biculturalism as governing principles of the Dominion. Moreover, the Constitution guaranteed that Quebec must maintain confessional schools, both Catholic and Protestant, a system that has given Anglo-Quebecers great control over their schools. These provisions were also extended to the other provinces. In 1867, it was solely by the means of the guarantees provided to Roman Catholic Schools that the 75,000 French Canadians in Ontario and the 85,000 Acadians in New Brunswick could expect some constitutional protection for their language and culture. These confessional privileges were abolished in 1997 by a constitutional amendment applied only to Quebec.

Following the foundation of the Dominion, which many politicians labelled confusingly a 'confederation', many French Canadians were convinced that they had acceded to the status of a founding people, equal as of right to English Canada. Instead of a simple colonial act enacted by the imperial parliament of London, the British North America Act of 1867 was viewed as a 'confederative pact', concluded freely between two founding nations. This conception of what had been the 'spirit of 1867' enticed with romantic dreams many French Canadian leaders and intellectuals, but was systematically rejected or ignored by many politicians and constitutional lawyers in English Canada. It should be added that the creation of the Dominion had not been submitted to popular approval either by referendum or by general elections.

History has shown that Quebec was the sole province to bear the burden of bilingualism until 1982. The new provinces of Manitoba, Alberta and Saskatchewan were also subject to the bilingualism of legislation and the courts, but they soon stopped complying with it. Created as a province in 1870, Manitoba declared English the province's sole official language in 1890 even though its constituent law had prescribed bilingualism for legislation and the courts and guaranteed Franco-Catholic schools provincial government support. In 1896, the Manitoba government had to concede to its Francophone minority the right to instruction in French; this was withdrawn in 1916, and French disappeared from Manitoba schools. After having adopted its laws in English only for a long time, Manitoba was brought to order by the Supreme Court in 1985 when it ruled that the province could not overstep the bounds of the Constitution and must translate into French all its legislation.

In 1897, Ontario made English the only language of the justice system. In 1913, it severely reduced the teaching of French in Catholic confessional schools (Regulation 17); Franco-Ontarians saw this as the sign of a deliberate policy of assimilation. Alberta and Saskatchewan did not comply with the bilingualism of legislation and the courts after their creation in 1905. The Supreme Court ruled in 1988, however, that this violation was without consequence, because the assemblies of these provinces were at liberty to abolish bilingualism which had no constitutional value according to their constituent law. The two provinces simply discharged themselves from the obligation, making French at the most an optional language for parliamentary debates, legal proceedings and legislation.

Quebec in the post-Charter Canada

The Dominion of Canada became a sovereign country only in 1931, with the conclusion of the Statute of Westminster. But Canada didn't free itself totally from the bonds of the imperial parliament of London. The latter kept many powers over its North American Dominion, the most important of which was the power to enact statutes extending to Canada respecting its constitutional laws. From this partial emancipation until 1982, much of the constitutional reform in Canada was absorbed by one issue called the 'patriation' of the constitution. It meant the acquiring by Canada of the power to amend by its own means all of its constitutional laws, originally adopted by Westminster. Finally, after many unfruitful attempts, Canada proceeded in 1982 to the so-desired reform making it fully sovereign. But this reform left Quebec out in the cold, since the nine other provinces and the federal government concluded an agreement without Quebec's participation and consent and managed to make Westminster adopt it by a final statute in April 1982. As a result, Quebec, which had yielded a veto over attempts at constitutional reform, suffered a loss of status and jurisdictions that affected the continuity of its institutions.

The reform of 1982 gave Canada an amending formula for its constitution and incorporated to the latter a Charter of Rights and Freedoms, left to the interpretation and sanction of the courts. The entrenchment of this Charter, modelled on the American Bill of Rights, would have a major impact on linguistic laws in Quebec. With the advent of the Charter, any citizen may directly challenge before the courts, in the name of its liberties guaranteed by the Constitution, the validity of the laws adopted by all parliaments in Canada. The Charter included specific provisions for language rights. One of these provisions vests the so-called official-language minorities in a province with the rights to have their children instructed in their language in public schools financed by the province. When numbers so warranted, the minorities also obtained the right to manage their schools. The Charter also declares that English and French are the official languages of Canada. Such a declaration doesn't transform Canada into a bilingual country; it governs only the federal government and its institutions. Through the Charter, the province of New Brunswick also proclaims French and English official languages and grants them equal status.

The reform of 1982 didn't replace the principle of parliamentary sovereignty that had governed Canada since 1867 by the supremacy of the Constitution and the courts. The new Canadian Charter includes an override clause called the 'notwithstanding' clause, which kept the power of parliaments in Canada to restore their sovereignty for a maximum renewable period of five years. By adopting this special clause, a parliament can exempt a law or all of its legislation for this period from any challenge to its validity with regard to certain rights protected by the Charter. Through this power, a parliament may express its disagreement with the interpretation given by the courts to constitutional liberties or to the impugned law and restore its validity despite the fact it was struck down by judicial nullification. As we will see, the 'notwithstanding' clause was used once to protect Quebec linguistic laws.

Much of the politics following 1982 coped with the necessity to compensate Quebec fairly for its loss of status and jurisdictions over education and language. Projects of constitutional reforms were concluded in 1987 and in 1992 to try to satisfy the conditions the Quebec government of Robert Bourassa made for adhering to the 1982 reform. One condition was the recognition of Quebec as a distinct society by a specific provision in the Constitution. It was thought that such a provision would ease the proof of Quebec's cultural and linguistic specificity before the courts and help buttress the validity of language laws in Quebec and the legitimacy of the Quebec government's role in preserving and promoting such specificity. Besides this recognition, the constitutional accords of 1987 and of 1992 provided for the entrenchment of linguistic duality as a fundamental characteristic of Canada. But both agreements failed to be ratified by parliaments or approved by the population. On October 1992, two referendums, one federal, held outside Quebec, the other held in Quebec under the authority of Quebec laws, decided the fate of the accord concluded in August 1992 by the eleven Prime Ministers and Aboriginal representatives in Charlottetown, Prince Edward Island. Overall, 55 per cent of the Canadian population and nearly 57 per cent of the Quebec population rejected it.

The reform of 1982 marked the triumph of Pierre-Elliot Trudeau, whose thought as a vocal intellectual in the 1950s and the 1960s and political action as Prime Minister deeply shaped the country's face. One of his main concerns was to integrate Quebec Francophones into a new Canadian state and to undermine nationalism in Quebec. It is why when he was first elected as the head of the federal government in 1968, one of his central goals was to place French on an equal footing with English in federal institutions. None the less, this objective had a strategic importance: bilingualism at the federal level was to be fostered in the hope of making Quebec Francophones see the federal government as their primary government. Furthermore, Trudeau rejected the idea that Quebec was the territorial basis of a national community. Advocating a strict individualistic liberalism, Trudeau thought that the only legitimate way to enhance the Francophones' status in Canada was to grant them rights portable throughout the country. These rights were enforceable against provincial governments. Trudeau hoped that such a strategy would make Francophones feel at home from British Columbia to Newfoundland and extend French outside of Quebec. Again, Trudeau was obsessed with defeating Quebec nationalism. As Kenneth McRoberts, political scientist, pointed out: 'If all of Canada, rather than just Quebec, was to become home to French language, he [Trudeau] kept insisting, then the very basis of Quebec nationalism would be undermined.' After retiring from politics in 1984, Trudeau jealously defended his reform, seen as the foundation of a new Canada dedicated to individual rights, official bilingualism and multiculturalism. He strongly disagreed with the attempts made in 1987 and in 1992 to accommodate Quebec demands for compensation. His disagreement helped the mounting of a powerful and decisive opposition against the two agreements, notably in English Canada.

Some figures on the French fact in Canada

It is now useful to look more closely at demographic and linguistic data to have a broader and more precise picture. Since the creation of the

Dominion of Canada in 1867, French has become a marginal language outside Quebec and lost its total weight within the Canadian population. Although the inadequacy of legal and constitutional provisions could not stop or slow down the assimilation of Francophones outside Quebec, the population of French extraction succeeded in maintaining its weight until the end of the nineteenth century and the first half of the twentieth century, thanks to a birth rate unparalleled in the West. History belied Franklin's and de Tocqueville's pessimistic predictions. Between 1881 and 1961, the population of French origin remained at approximately 30 per cent of the country's total population, despite the creation and addition of new provinces and the colonisation of new territories by immigrants from around the world.

The proportion was maintained, but at a price. The federal government pursued a policy of massive immigration at the turn of the century in order to develop the country's economy and settle its vast territories. Between 1896 and 1914, Canada welcomed more than three million British, American and Eastern European immigrants. A large number settled in Western Canada. Since the poor and unschooled French Canadians received little encouragement to locate in the west, about 450,000 crossed south over the Canadian–American border between 1890 and 1920.

Figures show a constant decline in both the relative importance and the number of Francophones outside Quebec. In 1931, 7.2 per cent of the population of Canada outside Quebec had French as a mother tongue. This proportion dropped to less than 5.0 per cent in 1991, and to 4.5 per cent in 1996. If we look at the language of use rather than the mother tongue, the decrease is even more striking. Francophones outside Quebec were 675,925 in 1971, and only 618,522 in 1996, their share of the total population declining from 4.4 per cent to 2.9 per cent in this period. Rapid assimilation seems to be running unabated in some provinces. The proportion of Ontarians for whom French is the everyday language fell from 4.6 per cent to 2.9 per cent between 1971 and 1996. In Manitoba, it slipped from 4.0 per cent to 2.1 per cent in the same period, and in Saskatchewan, from 1.7 per cent to 0.6 per cent. Only the Acadians of New Brunswick seem to be resisting assimilation, their share in the province's population having stabilised at about 30.5 per cent in 1996. Except for New Brunswick and Ontario, the number of people using French at home doesn't exceed 25,000 in each of the English provinces and territories, the average number being 9,940.

Ninety per cent of Canada's Francophone population lives in Quebec, but Quebec's population accounts for only less than one-quarter of the

Dominion, or 7,237,479 out of 30,007,094 people as of May 2001. The situation of English and French is thus very dissimilar in Canada. In Ontario and New Brunswick, Francophones form large communities that are sufficiently numerous and concentrated to have a certain French social life in terms of education, health services and culture. In 1996, Francophones (of French mother tongue) comprised 33.2 per cent of the population of New Brunswick, or 242,413 Acadians, and 4.7 per cent of the population of Ontario, or 500,073 Franco-Ontarians. Elsewhere in Canada, social and economic life is almost exclusively in English except in some communities. It appears that 60 per cent of Francophones outside Quebec live in districts in which they represent 10 per cent or more of the population. There is some bilingualism in federal institutions across the country – government services, postal services, airports, etc. – but only 30 per cent of federal public servants are bilingual and most of them work in the Ottawa region, the federal capital.

The French language seems to have had more stability in Quebec. The percentage of Quebecers with French as their mother tongue remained constant from 1951 to 1991, decreasing from 82.5 per cent to 80.7 per cent from 1951 to 1971, increasing to 82.1 per cent in 1991, and diminishing to 81.5 per cent in 1996. In the same period, the percentage of Anglophones decreased from 13.8 per cent to 8.8 per cent and the percentage of allophones – whose mother tongue is neither French nor English – increased from 3.7 per cent to 9.7 per cent. Most Anglophones and allophones live in the region of Montreal. In 1999, they accounted for respectively 18.1 per cent and 12.1 per cent of the region's population. Some demographers predict that, should the demographic trends keep up, Francophones will become a minority in the island of Montreal between 2016 and 2021 and the allophones will outnumber the Anglophones. (Montreal is a huge archipelago; the island of Montreal is the largest and most populated.)

If these statistics show the vitality of French language in Quebec, they should not let us forget the immediate reasons for its precariousness. Quebec's demographic weight within Canada has declined progressively since 1931, from 27.7 per cent to 25.8 per cent in 1986 and to 24.1 per cent in May 2001. Between 1875 and 1965, Quebec's fertility rate was higher than those of other North American regions. Beginning in the 1960s, however, Quebecers, setting aside the Catholic Church's support for a high birth rate and espousing more modern mores, began to produce fewer offspring. The outcome was that their birth rate became one of the lowest in the Western world. From 1956 to 1961, French-speaking Quebec women had a fertility rate of 4.2 (4.2 births per woman of childbearing age). The rate dropped to 2.3 for 1966–71 and then to 1.5 for 1981–6 before rising to 1.6 in 1990, which is barely enough to replace the population, a rate of 2.1 being required to ensure it. Quebec Anglophones also experienced a less dramatic decline in their fertility rate which is now roughly on a par with that of Francophones. From the years following the Second World War, Quebec's share of Canadian population has started to show a decline which speeded up after the 1960s. The low fertility rate worries many Quebecers who fear that Quebec's demographic weight is continuing to decline and that the proportion of Francophones in Quebec is being eroded.

On top of this is the fear that immigrants who have settled in Quebec in large numbers since the turn of the century prefer English to French as the language of communication and culture. The proportion of Quebecers of other than French or British extraction was 1.6 per cent in 1871 and 8.6 per cent in 1961. As long as their exceptional fertility compensated for the arrival of immigrants, the Francophone majority did not feel threatened. When their fertility began to decline, however, Quebec's linguistic balance became shaky. This realisation was heightened in the 1960s, a time when immigrants were free to choose their schools and *laissez faire* was the practice for commercial signs. Over 85 per cent of immigrants opted for English-language schools in the late 1960s. Statistics show that more and more ethnic minorities adopted English at the expense of French. While 48 per cent of these minorities in Quebec were drawn to English in 1931, the proportion had risen to 69.6 per cent by 1961.

More than one-third of Quebec Francophones are bilingual; only 7 per cent of Anglo-Canadians outside Quebec say they are. In Montreal, 46 per cent of Francophones and 60 per cent of Anglophones are bilingual, and 15 per cent of the city inhabitants speak three languages or more. Overall, trilingualism is nine times higher in Quebec than in the rest of Canada.

The creation of two competing policies

A multilingual state can enhance the status and the use of a minority language in many ways. One solution is to create in the state internal frontiers that separate the minority from the dominant linguistic group. Within a special territory to which it is attached, the minority can require the use of its language in the public sphere, gain control over the educational system, international immigration and its culture. As Jean Laponce stated, 'Territorial solutions stem from the principle that languages in contact should be separated as much as possible by means of fixed frontiers that give a feeling of security.' In Switzerland, for example, each canton can impose the dominant language within its borders in politics, administration, education and at work, except for federal institutions. A French-speaking Swiss moving to a German canton is not entitled to public services in French and must respect the prevalence of German in the public sphere. The creation of unilingual zones into a multilingual state often implies that bilingualism should be limited to national or federal institutions.

Another solution is to tie the rights to use a language to persons, not to territory. Linguistic rights are then transferable over the whole territory of the state. This means that individuals of a minority may claim to speak their language in political institutions, to use it before courts, to be educated in their mother tongue everywhere in the state, with no regard being paid to their actual number or concentration. In a personal scheme, the portability of linguistic rights is seldom absolute, for the state may restrain it to certain types of rights or attach to them some requirements. Whereas the territorial solution tries to prevent the overlapping of languages, the personal solution tends to mix them. Yet the overlapping of languages has often proved to be to the advantage of the dominant language. It is why, according to Laponce, when two languages live in close geographical and social proximity, the best defence for the weaker language in the long run is the territorial solution.

If we go back to the 1960s in Canada, it is clear that the federal state rejected the territorial solution adopted by countries like Switzerland, India and Finland and opted instead for the personal principle. Its decision was partly due to the recommendations of a federal commission of inquiry, whose mandate was to review the existing 'state of bilingualism and biculturalism in Canada' and to 'recommend what steps should be taken to develop the Canadian Confederation on the basis of an equal partnership between the two founding races'. This royal commission was set up in 1963 by the government of Lester B. Pearson – the Laurendeau–Dunton Commission. After holding hearings across the country, the commissioners concluded in their preliminary report in 1965 that Canada 'without being fully conscious of the fact, is passing through the greatest crisis in its history'. The Commission noted the unacceptable inequalities that were causing Francophones great dissatisfaction. Francophones were not playing a role in the economy that was proportional to their real weight. Anglo-Canadians of British origin dominated the economy; they held the most influential and best paid positions. In Quebec, the French Canadians had an income 35 per cent lower than the Anglo-Quebecers. And even bilingual Quebecers earned less than unilingual Anglo-Quebecers. It is why the commission recommended that 'in the private sector in Quebec, governments and industry adopt the objective that French become the principal language of work at all levels'.

Seeing Quebec as a model of an officially bilingual society, the Commission recommended that French and English become the official languages of Canada and that New Brunswick and Ontario, where the great majority of Francophones outside Quebec lived, adopt bilingualism at the provincial level. As for the seven remaining provinces, the B&B Commission contemplated a lesser form of protection for official-language minorities. It also proposed the creation of 'bilingual districts' where French and English would be used currently in educational and municipal institutions when the minority reached 10 per cent of the population.

Far from suggesting that Quebec should gain full jurisdiction over language and that Francophone minorities in the rest of Canada may obtain some form of territorial protection, especially in Ontario and New Brunswick, the Laurendeau–Dunton Commission insisted that the federal government should recognise the formal equality of Canada's two official languages within its jurisdiction and promote an even English–French bilingualism throughout the Dominion. By these recommendations, the Commission blazed the trail for the Official-Languages legislation enacted by the federal Parliament in 1969. By tying language rights to individuals, not to territories, and by seeing rights as portable across the country, the Commission indicated to Ottawa that the federal linguistic policy should focus on the creation and maintenance of two official-language minorities and on the furtherance of French outside Quebec and of English in the French-speaking province. The findings of the Commission were mostly based on the 1961 census which showed that although the assimilation of Francophones to English had been a steady process, the prolific birth rate of French Canadians gave credence to the prospect of an enduring growth for Francophones in Quebec and in New Brunswick. (Curiously, the Royal Commission of Inquiry was inspired by the example of South Africa, which settled language rights on the principle of personality.)

The report of the Commission ran counter, in its spirit, to what would become later the basis of Quebec's linguistic policy. Since the 1970s, the adequacy of the territorial solution imposed itself on Quebec governments, whatever their ideological allegiance, federalist or sovereigntist. The departure from the personal solution appeared with the creation in

December 1968 of the Gendron Commission, a provincial commission mandated to 'inquire into and report on the status of French as a language of use in Quebec'. Its report was tabled in 1972. Like the Laurendeau–Dunton Commission, the Gendron Commission ascertained how English language dominated Quebec's work world to the disadvantage of Francophones: they earned less in general, held less important positions, benefited little from their bilingualism and often worked in English, in a proportion that did not reflect the high number of Francophone workers. The Commission recommended that measures be adopted to make French the common language of Quebecers. It is worth reading the reasons given by the commissioners for such a remedy:

> In America, French is a fringe language. As such, its use is restricted even in areas where it is spoken by a majority of the population. This situation requires a clear policy: French can survive and flourish on the North American continent only with a maximum of opportunity and protection throughout Quebec; and this can be accomplished only by making it a useful communication instrument for all the people of this area. ...
>
> In the vast economic areas made up of Canada and the United States, French is defenseless in the struggle to impose its utility. This situation is not about to change. Thus in Quebec, the vigor and dynamism of French can be ensured only through government support. Failing this, the odds in the match between French and English will remain too one-sided.
>
> This government action should aim at establishing French as the common language of Quebecers by making it useful and necessary for everyone in work communication.

The Commission recommended that the National Assembly declare French the official language of Quebec, and English and French the national languages. In doing so, it didn't advocate for Quebec an exclusive territorial unilingualism. But it established the necessity and the legitimacy of making French a common language in both social and public fields throughout Quebec, notwithstanding the ethnic origin of Quebecers or their residence in the province. In this sense, French ceased to be the propriety or the concern of old-stock Francophones in Quebec to become the common good of Quebecers of all extractions. Therefore, the Gendron Commission insisted that the government take steps to make French the language of internal communications in Quebec in the work place and the language of communication in the government, professional corporations and parastatal institutions; that the right of the Francophone consumer to be served in his language be recognised and that commercial signs be regulated in order to make the use of French mandatory.

From Bill 63 to the Charter of the French Language

Quebec's first law of a linguistic nature created the *Office de la langue française* in 1961. The Bertrand government adopted Quebec's first language law in November 1969, the *Act to promote the French language in Quebec* (Bill 63). This legislation called on school boards to provide instruction in French; while giving parents free choice in the language of instruction, with school boards having to guarantee children registered in English-language classes a knowledge of the use of the French language. This law also charged the authorities of Quebec's immigration department with seeing that immigrants settled in Quebec learned French. But Bill 63 did not seem able to maintain the delicate linguistic balance in Quebec, especially in Montreal, where English-language schools attracted many immigrants and where the free choice of the language of instruction had set Anglophones, allophones and Francophones against one another.

The Liberal government of Robert Bourassa adopted the first language law affirming the Quebec legislature's will to improve the status of French in social life. It drew its inspiration from some of the Gendron Commission's recommendations and it was convinced that language policy could not be based on incentive alone but should also include coercive measures. Assented to in July 1974 after a 92 to 10 vote in the National Assembly, the *Act respecting the official language* (or Bill 22) made it clear in its preamble that:

> the French language is a national heritage which the body politic is in duty bound to preserve, and it is incumbent upon the government of the province of Quebec to employ every means in its power to ensure the preeminence and to promote its vigour and quality.

For the first time in its history, the National Assembly declared French the official language of Quebec. Henceforth, the French language would be the Quebec government's language of communication; workers would be able to communicate among themselves and with their supervisors in French. The French language should become omnipresent in the business world for company management, corporate names, public signs and contracts. As for instruction, parents continued to have free choice, provided their children had a sufficient knowledge of the language of instruction. The law prescribed language tests to evaluate pupils' knowledge. Test results would determine a pupil's enrolment at an English or French school. Finally, agencies were set up to apply and oversee the law. The law created a *Régie de la langue française* (French language board), responsible, among other things, for the application of the prescribed francisation programme for companies.

With Bill 22, the Quebec legislature showed its will to actively defend French, but it did not succeed in establishing consensus on how to implement policy. Making children take language tests and francisising business firms ran into strong resistance in the Anglophone community and among immigrants. As Gretta Chambers said: 'For Anglophones of Quebec, it has been the greatest shock of their life. To make a law on the use of a language is an ideal totally foreign to the Anglo-Quebecer political culture, and this will probably be always so, no matter whether such an idea is justified or not.' Though Francophones saw the law as a loyal attempt at linguistic reform, many saw it as an inapplicable law that went only half way.

Shortly after its accession to power in November 1976, the Parti Québécois government announced it intended to revise Bill 22. In April 1977, the Minister of State for Cultural Development, Camille Laurin, tabled a White Paper on Quebec's French-language policy in the National Assembly. Language would become a priority in its legislative programme and language legislation would take the form of a Charter.

The White Paper identified several pressing reasons why the Quebec state was justified in taking on the task of redressing the situation of French in Quebec. The White Paper feared that Francophones would be less and less numerous in Canada as well as in Quebec. The great propensity immigrants had to integrate into the minority Anglophone group would hasten this decline. In the corporate world, French would still be the language of lesser jobs and lower incomes and English, the language of business, would still govern communications at work. Nor could Quebecers count on help from the Canadian Dominion or the federal government, which had not been able to keep Francophone assimilation in check. Finally, the White Paper noted that many Quebecers were dissatisfied with the quality of the French language in Quebec and had turned to the Quebec state for improving its status, use and quality.

The White Paper also set out the principles of the language policy. First of all, language is not simply a mode of expression whose uses should be regulated. Granting a language the protection of the law involves seeing to the 'quality of the habitat, of which language is a major component'. Then, though he may take steps to plan for the French language in Quebec, the Quebec legislator intended to respect minorities as well as their languages and cultures. The government recognised that 'an English population and an English culture exist in Quebec' and 'this population and this culture constitute an irreducible component of our society'. The government recognises the valuable contribution of other languages and minority cultures to Quebec society, but insists that these minorities acquire sufficient knowledge of the national language to foster their integration into society. Another principle is that the promotion of French as the national language should not in any way keep Quebecers from learning a second or third language. Finally, enhancing the status of French is a question of social justice, that is, it is important that French no longer be an impediment to employment and wealth. 'What Quebec's French-speaking majority must do', the document states, 'is reassume the power which is its own by right, not in order to dominate, but to regain the status and latitude proper to its size and importance.'

In late April 1977, the government tabled a bill called the *Charter of the French language* (or Bill 101) in the National Assembly. It was adopted on 26 August 1977. The preamble to the Charter sets out the Quebec legislator's principles of action. It states that French, 'the distinctive language of a people that is in the majority French speaking, is the instrument by which that people has articulated its identity'. The National Assembly indicates its resolve 'to make French the language of Government and Law, as well as the normal and everyday language of work, instruction, communication, commerce and business'. It recognises the valuable contribution of the ethnic minorities to the development of Quebec and the right of the Amerindians and the Inuit of Quebec to develop their language and culture of origin. (Since 1983, the preamble has specified that the National Assembly intends to pursue the Charter's objective with all due respect for the Quebec English-speaking community's institutions.) It also points out the 'obligation of every people to contribute in its special way to the international community'.

Like Bill 22, the Charter of 1977 proclaims that French is the official language of Quebec. It then enumerates a series of 'fundamental language rights', such as the rights of workers to carry on their activities in French, and of consumers of goods and services to be informed and served in French. French is recognised as the language of the legislature and the courts in Quebec, although judgements and proceedings may be in another language, if the parties so agree. The French language becomes the language of communication of the government, its departments and affiliated agencies as well as of government-owned firms and the professional corporations. The administration of municipal, school and health bodies may be carried out in both French and another language if these bodies serve a clientele where more than half speak a language other than French.

As for commerce and business, French becomes the mandatory, but not the exclusive, language for labels and the only language for signs and posters and commercial advertising. In making an exception to the principle of unilingual French signs and posters, the 1977 law authorises firms employing not more than four people to display signs and posters in both French and another language, provided that French is at least as prominent as the other language. The same kind of exception applies to the cultural activities of ethnic groups and advertising by non-profit organisations. The law also makes French the only language for firm names, bilingualism being accepted for the legal names of ethnic non-profit associations.

Finally, the Charter of 1977 abolished the eligibility criteria for English schools prescribed by Bill 22. Henceforth, a child whose father or mother received his or her elementary instruction in English in Quebec could receive instruction in English, as could a child whose father or mother, on the date of the coming into force of the law, had received such instruction elsewhere in Canada and those already enrolled at English schools, and their younger brothers and sisters. An appeals committee hears from parents who feel their children should have been found eligible for instruction in English.

In addition to the appeals committee, the Charter of 1977 created four agencies responsible for its implementation. The *Office de la langue française* defines and conducts Quebec policy on linguistic research and terminology, authorises municipal and semi-public agencies serving a population with a majority that speaks a language other than French to operate internally in more than one language, and administers the process of francisising business firms. This programme covers all firms with fifty or more employees, and its aim is to certify that the use of French is generalised at all levels of operation. Firms may challenge an Office decision before an appeals committee. The *Commission de toponymie* deals with the cataloguing, rules of spelling and assignment of place names. The *Commission de surveillance* ensures compliance with the law and inquires into failures to comply brought to their attention by a third party or discovered by commission inspectors.

Lastly, the *Conseil de la langue française* advises the government with regard to the situation of the French language in Quebec and on questions relating to the interpretation and application of the *Charter of the French Language*.

Since its enactment, the Charter of the French Language has undergone a number of changes, many of them having been the result of judicial rulings, as we will see further. Other changes were related to the means to implement the law. Abolished in 1993, the *Commission de surveillance* was reborn in 1997 under the name of the *Commission de protection de la langue française*.

The *Charter of the French Language* may undergo other changes in the near future. In June 2000, the government of Quebec set up a special commission, the commission of the States-General on the situation and future of French language, to inquire on the matter and hold hearings throughout the province. The commission tabled a preliminary report in June 2001 and submitted its final recommendations in August 2001. Among other things, it proposed that a Quebec citizenship be officially instituted, that the basic principles of Quebec's language policy be entrenched in the constitution of the province, and that a new pivotal agency replace the existing different agencies responsible for the implementation of the *Charter of the French Language*.

The federal linguistic policy

As we have already pointed out, Quebec is also governed by another linguistic policy designed by the federal government. This policy took shape by the adoption of the *Official Languages Act* in the summer of 1969. As we have already explained, the report of the Royal Commission of Inquiry on Bilingualism and Biculturalism inspired the conception of this law. It states that 'French and English are the official languages of Canada' for everything involving parliament and the federal government. English and French became equal in principle as languages of federal legislation, administration and the justice system. If laws and regulations continued to be published in both languages, as they had to be in compliance with the Constitution of 1867, many federal court judgments would henceforth have to be in two languages.

The law charged the federal administration with communicating with the public and offering its services in the two official languages in the federal capital, Ottawa, and in bilingual districts determined by the federal government. It extended and spelled out the language rights of the accused and parties in lawsuits before a federal court. Finally, it created the position of Commissioner of Official Languages, to be held by a senior civil servant responsible for the application of the law and investigating violations brought to his attention.

The federal parliament adopted a new version of the law in 1988 in which it extended some rights. Thus, federal courts other than the Supreme Court had to ensure that a presiding judge understands the language of the person being tried without the assistance of an interpreter. The obligation to guarantee the availability of bilingual services was extended, under certain conditions, to federal government offices abroad.

The federal government made the most of the reform of the Constitution in 1982 to enshrine some principles of its language policy in the country's fundamental law. The recognition of French and English as official languages of the government and the federal parliament were also enshrined in the *Canadian Charter of Rights and Freedoms*. The principle of the bilingualism of laws and judicial procedures as well as citizens' rights to communicate in French or in English with the federal administration were also enshrined, the latter right being a function of significant demand and the vocation of administrative services.

Added to these provisions on the federal administration is the provinces' obligation to provide education to their Francophone or Anglophone minority in their own language. This obligation is binding for the elementary and secondary levels, is carried out with the provinces' public funds and is applicable wherever the number of children so warrants. The right to instruction in the language of the minority may go as far as giving members of the minority control over their educational institutions, this right being subject as well to the presence of a sufficient number of children from the minority. Members of one or the other official language minority can bring an independent action for redress and petition a court to order the province to guarantee their rights.

Federal language policy is implemented by legislation, the Constitution and a policy to promote bilingualism in the federal public service. Adopted by the federal cabinet in 1971, the policy was designed to increase the proportion of Francophone public servants at all levels of the federal apparatus, up to the demographic weight of Francophones in the federation (about 25 per cent). Another objective was to translate working documents drafted in English nearly systematically into French and to promote at least a passive knowledge of French among Anglophone public servants. Finally, the federal government set up numerous financial assistance programmes to subsidise the activities of official language minorities. It also took the initiative to associate itself with the provinces to subsidise instruction for students of official language minorities and the learning of French or English as a second language.

The legalisation of linguistic conflicts

Legal challenges have marked the life of the *Charter of the French Language*. Many court rulings have limited its scope or forced the Quebec government to redesign its policy. Several lawsuits were taken as far as the Supreme Court of Canada, thereby helping to politicise the legal process. The militancy of the media, especially in the English Canadian newspapers and broadcasting, whose biases against language laws have been conducive to hyberbolic dramatisation, has contributed to maintain an atmosphere of distrust and fear within the Anglophone community in Quebec. Gérald Leblanc, journalist, neatly described the English Canadian media's attitude towards Quebec: 'When Quebec's language policy is discussed, it is simply described as anti-Anglophone, without any reference to the objective situation and in language unrestrained by concern for accuracy and non-partisanhip.' This process of legalisation was not totally foreign to Canada's political culture, since the country had already used it to send to court many of its political and linguistic conflicts. But the legalisation of politics in Canada has dramatically increased in scope and intensity with the entrenchment of the Canadian Charter of Rights and Liberties in 1982. In contrast, the federal linguistic policy has triggered little litigation as such. This is explainable by the fact that the federal statutory law applies only to federal institutions and cannot force provincial institutions to deliver bilingual services, and that educational rights for official language minorities are immune from any challenge. It is less the legal validity than the effectiveness of the federal policy that has proved problematic, as we will see further.

Bill 101 was challenged by Anglophone groups or claimants soon after its enactment. The Supreme Court of Canada ruled in 1978 that the National Assembly could not declare French the only language of legislation and the courts. The constitution of 1867 bound Quebec to comply with bilingualism in enacting laws and for judicial proceedings, and this obligation extended beyond legislation as such to all normative texts emanating from the government. (Manitoba and New Brunswick must abide by similar requirements.)

The *Canadian Charter of Rights and Freedoms* soon had an impact. In 1984, the Supreme Court ruled that Quebec could not restrict access to

English public schools only to children whose parents had attended elementary school in English in Quebec. The Canadian Charter extended this right to all parents who had received their elementary instruction in English in Canada. In 1988, the Court ruled that the National Assembly of Quebec could no longer require that public signs and commercial advertising be solely in French and that only the firm name in French be legal. In the Court's words, these requirements infringed on the freedom of expression guaranteed by the Canadian Charter, even if the holder was a business corporation. Moreover, they ran counter to the right of equality. On the basis of an analysis of demographic and linguistic trends, the Court recognised as a legitimate legislative aim the project to ensure the quality and advancement of the French language. The Court also recognised that the Quebec legislator could legitimately take steps to make the 'linguistic face' of Quebec reflect the predominance of French, without recognising the prescription of unilingualism in public signs as a necessary measure for achieving Bill 101's objectives. None the less, the Court indicated that making it mandatory that the French language predominate, even markedly, on signs and posters would be compatible with the Quebec and Canadian Charters.

Following this judgment, the Liberal government of Robert Bourassa adopted a law in December 1988 removing the *Charter of the French Language* from judicial control – the Canadian Constitution authorised this kind of override for a period of five years – and amended the rules for public signs. The rule of French unilingualism continued to prevail for public signs and commercial advertising outside establishments. Inside, however, the use of another language was permitted, provided that French was visible in a markedly predominant manner. There were exceptions to this kind of bilingualism, franchise companies employing between five and fifty people and shopping centres being subject to a stricter regime.

On 31 March, 1993, the United Nations Human Rights Committee, a body instituted by the International Covenant on Civil and Political Rights, announced its 'findings' with regard to complaints lodged by Anglophone businessmen from Quebec. The committee recognised that it is legitimate for a state to choose one or several official languages, especially to protect a minority in a vulnerable situation such as Francophones in Canada. However, it saw the rules of Bill 101 prescribing unilingual signs, even amended by Bill 178, as an infringement on the freedom of expression the Covenant sanctioned. None of these rules created discrimination based on language nor did they infringe on the rights of minorities, the Covenant recognised. Anglophone Canadian citizens could not, in fact, be considered a language minority, since they were a majority in Canada.

The government amended the *Charter of the French Language* once again, adopting a law (Bill 86) in June 1993 that reformed the public signs and posters and commercial advertising regime. This law was adopted with no notwithstanding clause. From then on, public signs could be in French and another language, provided French was 'markedly predominant'. The law gave the government power to determine the situations in which public signs and commercial advertising must be in French only, where French has to predominate or where signs, posters and advertising may be in another language only.

After the referendum of October 1995, some Anglophone groups and lawyers, reputed for championing unrestrained individual rights, undertook to challenge other core aspects of Bill 101 or even the substance of the Supreme Court ruling of 1988 on public signs. Even among some Francophones, growing dissatisfaction with the stringency of Bill 101 led some of them to advocate a return to the freedom of choice that preceded the adoption of the Law.

In April 2000, the Superior Court reversed a decision of the Court of Quebec striking down the provisions of Bill 101 requiring that French be markedly predominant in commercial signs. It was a case in which the defendants, charged for having violated these provisions, contested their validity. The Attorney-General of Quebec decided not to adduce evidence justifying the reasonableness of them, for the Supreme Court had already indicated, in a hypothesis, that a law requiring the marked predominance of French in public signs would satisfy constitutional law. The Court of Quebec decided that the Attorney-General could not dispense with such a proof and had not therefore justified the restrictions made to freedom of expression. The Superior Court overturned this ruling, for the reason it was bound to follow, as a matter of *stare decisis*, the Supreme Court's decision of 1988. The Quebec Court of Appeal heard the case in June 2001 and is expected to hand over its ruling soon.

In November 2000, the Superior Court ruled that the provisions of Bill 101 relating to compulsory French schooling, except for categories of children entitled to go to English schools, did not infringe upon the rights protected by both the Canadian Charter and the Quebec *Charter of Human Rights and Freedoms*. These provisions as such don't give to the Anglophone community a general right to choose the language of education, they only establish an exception to a general rule that applies to all Quebec residents. Nor can it be said that the educational rights protected by the Canadian Charter substantiate such a freedom of choice.

Furthermore, Francophone parents could not pretend, according to the judge, that their equality rights were violated on the ground of any of the prohibited discriminatory distinctions contemplated by the Quebec Charter. In writing a long judgment on the history of French in Canada, the Superior Court restated the legitimacy of Quebec's policy of maintaining a French majority in the province and sending young immigrants to the French educational system. Though the plaintiff parents could have legitimate concerns about the quality of the English taught in French schools, this deficiency is a problem to be addressed by the government, not the judiciary. The plaintiffs appealed against this ruling.

The legalisation of linguistic issues in Quebec is not the fruit of a transient or trivial phenomenon. Since 1982, Canada's political culture has changed considerably. The adoption of the Canadian Charter of Rights and Freedoms gave rise to what the historian Michael Ignatieff called a 'rights revolution'. The advent of the Canadian Charter didn't only alter the balance of power between courts and parliaments. It has also transformed the political discourse and the way people think about themselves, as citizens or as individuals with special interests and belongings. For sure, this rights revolution isn't peculiar to Canada and appeared before 1982, as was the case in most industrialised countries since 1960. None the less, in Canada, the discourse of rights reached a climax. It has triggered a culture of individualism and a virulent 'patriotism of rights' that prompted individuals and interest groups to challenge laws before the courts and to cast their demands of power and recognition in the language of rights. The tendency has not confined itself to linguistic issues but has also encompassed social and moral controversies, such as abortion, euthanasia, gay rights, aboriginal claims, tobacco advertising, etc.

Before an international forum held by UNESCO in 1997, the Italian writer Umberto Eco warned our societies of the excesses of political correctness in the United States, which was becoming 'a new kind of fundamentalism that invests in a ritualistic and liturgical manner the language of every day life'. The uncompromising discourse of some unconditional belittlers of Bill 101 was called by some observers of the Quebec political scene a 'fundamentalism of rights'. This fundamentalism translates itself in a zealous defence of individual rights that harks back to old religious passions and in the incapacity to take into account dimensions other than individual interests armoured with rights. It is why so many challenges made to Bill 101 by Anglophone groups looked like a trench battle fought with legal arguments.

Another factor fostering this legalisation was the revival of nationalism in English Canada. Studies on Canada tend to focus on Quebec nationalism, as if nationalism were a phenomenon restricted to the French province. The Anglo-Canadian nationalism was slow to come to the fore. The entrenchment of the Canadian Charter gave to Canadians outside Quebec and to many Anglo-Quebecers a sense of nationhood defined by a strict adhesion to an unitary conception of the nation. To take an image used by Michael Ignatieff, Canadian society was to be seen as a pool table where individuals, holding identical rights, spin across a homogeneous political space limited by the bumpers of the laws. This vision leaves no room for the coexistence in the pool table of different collective entities, of various nations. Claims made by Quebecers and by Aboriginals for recognition of their own nationhood and for real autonomy stumbled over an increasing sympathy in English Canada for symmetrical federalism. Equal and identical rights should then be given for all provinces and all individuals, regardless of the fabric of Canadian society. In any case, French, though an official language, shouldn't be preferred by the State to the right of individuals to speak the language of their choice in business, education and consumption. This new nationalism has pervaded the discourse of English media in Canada since 1982. It went along with what some observers called 'legal papism', that is the tendency of public opinion and politicians to view interpretations given by courts to substantive rights as unquestionable 'oracles', as if the responsibility of applying and defining human rights fell under the exclusive authority of the judiciary.

The legalisation of politics in Canada is also the result of a deliberate policy crafted by the federal government. The Trudeau government soon realised that it couldn't count on provinces to implement its policy of pan-Canadian bilingualism. Apart from New Brunswick, the English provinces were reluctant to help sustain their Francophone minorities, and Quebec was trying to build a linguistic policy based on territorialism. The federal government couldn't use the antiquated power of disallowance to overturn provincial laws contrary to its national unity strategy. It is why it saw in the remittance of linguistic conflicts to courts a way to force provinces to better treat their 'official-language' minorities. Thereby, Canadian society would be reconstructed as a juridical nation based on equal individual rights. In 1978, the federal cabinet agreed on setting up a Court Challenges Program designed to make available to official-language minorities some public funds to finance their actions brought against provincial governments. The programme covered actions brought in order to protect confessional education rights or institutional bilingualism, to which Quebec had submitted since 1867. Many of the challenges made to Bill 101 since 1978 were subsidised by this programme. In 1982, it was extended to actions based on the linguistic provisions of the Canadian Charter, and in 1985, to equality rights. When the programme was abolished in 1992, about one million dollars of federal funds had been used to support actions over linguistic rights. The programme was re-established in 1994.

The importance of the legal profession in Canada and in Quebec also sheds some light on the legalisation of linguistic issues. Lawyers are prominently overrepresented in parliaments, cabinets, federal or provincial, and in public administration. Because of their overrepresentation and their ubiquitous influence, Michael Porter described the legal profession, in his famous sociological analysis of Canadian society, *The Vertical Mosaic*, as the 'high priesthood of the political system'. Some political scientists, such as Rainer Knopff and Frederick L. Morton, argue that what they call a 'jurocracy' has taken advantage of the advent of the Canadian Charter to further its own interests and a special type of governance. This *jurocracy* – made up of bureaucrats, judges, private sector lawyers, law professors, interest groups – believes that society can be remodelled by constitutional rights and that litigation should be preferred to political action within the frame of parliamentary democracy.

The current scope of the Charter of the French Language

The Charter of the French Language regulates the use of languages only in their public aspect. The private use individuals make of a language in their interpersonal relations or to express their opinions through a print, electronic, radio or television medium lies entirely outside the bounds of the law.

It should also be noted that the law covers only areas of activity that fall within the jurisdiction of the National Assembly. Quebec lives in a federal system and therefore has limited legislative jurisdiction circumscribed by the Constitution. The Supreme Court has confirmed the power of Quebec, like all provinces, to legislate on the language of activities that fall under provincial jurisdiction. But this jurisdiction is limited by federal power. It follows that the Charter does not apply to the federal government and the public agencies under its responsibility. Similarly, federal Crown corporations – such as Air Canada, Canada Post, etc. – follow the federal language regime and not those of the provinces. Finally, the Charter does not apply to Indian reserves on Quebec territory. Nor does the Charter govern the use of languages in international organisations located in Quebec. For these reasons, it is inaccurate to say that Quebec enjoys full power over language policy: under the current regime, it has only a fragmented jurisdiction. In its preliminary report of June 2001, the Commission of the States-General on the situation and future of French in Quebec recommended that federal institutions and firms incorporated under federal legislation comply with Quebec regulations pertaining to public signs and firm names.

Public signs

Bill 86 of 1993 amended and relaxed the legislative regime for public signs in Quebec for the third time. The new general principle is that bilingual signs are allowed, whether inside or outside a commercial establishment, provided that French is markedly predominant. However, the new law gives the government the power to determine, by regulation, the cases, conditions or circumstances where public signs, posters and commercial advertising may follow a principle other than the predominance of French. The law also specifies that its rules on posting do not apply to advertising in publications disseminating information in a language other than French, or to messages of a religious, political, ideological or humanitarian nature, provided they are not for profit.

The government's regulations temper the application of the principle of marked predominance when safety or public health come into play, or to avoid disturbing the smooth running of business affairs. It prescribes French unilingualism only for the most visible advertising aids, such as billboards, and for advertising done on or in a public transportation vehicle.

Unless it is done by a Francophone media, advertising to promote a cultural product in a language other than French – a book, theatre, cinema, etc. – may be solely in that language. All indications of the country of origin, names of exotic products and specialities and non-commercial mottoes can remain in their language of origin, without translation. The same is true for registered trade marks and the firm name of a company established exclusively outside Quebec.

As for firm names, the law requires that they be in French, without excluding their being accompanied by a version in another language. In this case, the firm name in French must be as prominent as the other.

For all signs to which the rule of the marked predominance of French applies, the visual impact of the French text must be greater than that of the text in another language. The regulation deems this impact to be greater when the text in French is allotted at least twice as much space as the text in the other language.

The language of instruction

The Charter of the French Language states that French is the mandatory language of instruction in kindergarten, elementary and secondary school classes. This principle holds for both schools run by school boards entirely financed by the Quebec state and for private schools that receive some of their funding from the government.

The Charter nevertheless makes an exception to this principle and gives several categories of pupils the right to instruction in English in public or private schools financed by the state under the same conditions as for French-language schools. In general, children whose parents, if Canadian citizens, received their elementary instruction in English in Canada may receive instruction in English. Children of citizens who received or are receiving their instruction in English in Canada, and their brothers and sisters, also have this right.

The Charter protects some acquired rights. Children who, at the coming into force of the law in 1977, had received their instruction in Quebec or in Canada in English, retained the right to continue their studies in English, subject to conditions prescribed by the law.

The law recognised that the Aboriginal peoples of Quebec could provide instruction in an Amerindian language. The languages of instruction of the Cree and Kativik School Boards are Cree and Inuktitut respectively, although English and French are taught as second languages.

The law provides exceptions for people staying temporarily in Quebec. Employees of a foreign or Canadian business firm assigned to Quebec for a period not exceeding five years have the choice of language of instruction – French or English. Regulations also grant this exemption to researchers and students whose activities in Quebec will not exceed a five-year period. Employees on temporary assignment, researchers and students may, if necessary, extend their five-year exemption by one year. Diplomats and employees of an international organisation enjoy full exemption.

Language of work

With the Charter of the French Language, the freedom to communicate in French in Quebec with public agencies and business firms, professional corporations and labour unions became a fundamental right. The right of all Quebec workers to carry out their activities in French was recognised. The Charter specifies that written communications between an employer and his staff must be in French. Similarly, collective agreements and arbitration awards are written in French, the English translation of these awards not being excluded. The Charter prohibits the dismissal or demotion of an employee for the sole reason that he is exclusively French-speaking.

Rights and privileges of the Anglophone community in Quebec

The Anglophone community has always had its own social institutions – hospitals, school boards, colleges and universities – since well before Bill 101 came into force. The Charter of the French Language did not intend to question the continuity of these institutions. With their own schools, colleges, universities, hospitals, radio and television stations, theatres and motion picture theatres, they can, if they wish, live entirely in English, especially in Montreal.

Bill 101 aimed at making French the language of the administration and intermediary agencies of the State of Quebec. As for the language of services, it is usually French, but the use of English or another language is a question of internal administration that the municipalities, hospitals and school boards determine according to their clientele's needs.

The Charter of the French Language recognises certain privileges for municipalities, school boards and health or social services that serve a clientele who speaks a language other than French in its majority. In the case of municipalities, such privileges are given where more than half of the residents have English as mother tongue. These bodies, which must be duly recognised by the Office de la langue française, have some leeway in their internal operations that allows them to use both French and another language. The object of granting this recognition is not to create bilingual bodies or to authorise them to provide bilingual services, since all public agencies in Quebec are allowed to do so, whatever their official status. The privileges that recognised bodies enjoy entitle them to post signs in French and another language, with French being more prominent; to have a bilingual name; and to use both French and another language in their internal communications and in communications they may have with other recognised bodies. As we have seen, the requirement that French be the language of administration does not prevent other intermediary institutions from offering bilingual services adapted to the needs of their clienteles, as is the case with the City of Montreal or so-called 'Francophone' hospitals which can admit English-speaking patients and serve them in their language.

The Quebec legislator also enshrined in the *Act Respecting Health Services and Social Services* the right of English-speaking people to 'receive health services and social services in the English language'. To ensure implementation of this right, the government created an advisory committee of eleven members representative of the English-speaking population in May 1993 to work with the sixteen regional committees. The regional health boards – the authorities administering health care in Quebec's regions – see that this right is applied by drawing up a programme for access to services in the English language.

The effectiveness of both linguistic policies

Quebec's policy

In a paper submitted to the Commission of the States-General on the situation of the French language, the sociologist Guy Rocher gave a qualified and ambivalent run-down on the effectiveness of the Charter of the French Language. He admitted that the Charter has had some positive effects, like stopping the anglicisation of successive generations of young immigrants in primary and secondary schools, restoring an increasing number of workers to their right to work in French, and making more visible the French 'face' of Quebec, particularly in Montreal. These effects didn't come about by the sole virtue of the law, but also thanks to the energetic efforts of those numerous workers, teachers and other citizens who were convinced of its necessity. Although the ambit of the law has been shrunk by the courts, the law has produced substantial results, said Gérald Larose, president of Commission of the States-General. Let us consider them more closely.

Public signs

The main impact language legislation has had on signs has been to substitute the principle of the predominance of French for the principle of 'two majorities' in people's attitudes. As Marc V. Levine pointed out, ' "French predominance" rather than "two majorities" is the starting point for all serious public debate in Quebec on policies involving the linguistic character of Montréal or the province' (free translation). That French has become the common language of Quebecers, particularly in commercial signs, is now firmly rooted in the minds of a majority of Quebecers, even if some members of the Anglophone community challenge the idea or would like to return to the earlier *laissez faire* system.

Despite the public's attachment to the marked predominance of French, it is not always applied, notably in Montreal. According to a study done in 1996 by the Conseil and the Office de la langue française on the basis of a representative sample of business firms on the island of Montreal, 87 per cent of commercial messages are written in French, with 80 per cent of those being in French only and 7 per cent being bilingual. Moreover, it has been estimated in 1997 that 46 per cent of Montreal business firms have an exclusively French image and 78 per cent have a linguistic image that is largely French. The latest studies made in 1997 and in 1999 showed that the rate of commercial messages written in French only was decreasing.

Language of instruction

Overall, the Charter of the French Language's main impact on the language of instruction has been to send children of immigrants to French-language schools. As Marc V. Levine observed, the most radical impact of Bill 101 on Montreal's French-language schools has been to integrate newcomers into the language and culture of the city's majority. Henceforth, Montreal French-language schools could perform a function that most urban schools in the continent had fulfilled since the mid-nineteenth century. This was also the conclusion reached by a committee of experts and Quebec senior public servants who submitted a report on the situation of the French language in Quebec to the Minister of Culture and Communications in March 1996.

Statistics show that children whose mother tongue is neither French nor English are more and more numerous in French-language schools. In 1971–2, 85 per cent of these children attended an English-language school, 80 per cent in 1976–7, 36 per cent in 1986–7 and 21 per cent in 1994–5. In Montreal, 10 per cent of allophone pupils were enrolled in French-language schools in 1971–2. The proportion rose to 79.4 per cent in 1994–5. According to the latest figures, 90.2 per cent of young immigrants were enrolled in French schools in the year 2000–1.

Working language

Figures show a constant increase in the number of business firms that have obtained their francisation certificate: 32.7 per cent of large companies (100 people or more) were certified in 1984 and 68.3 per cent in 1994. The level for small and medium-sized business firms (50 to 99 people) rose from 40.8 per cent in 1984 to 84 per cent in 1994. It seems that since 1996 the rate of certification has levelled off.

In 1971, 52 per cent of Francophones were working in their language. This proportion rose to 62 per cent in 1979 and kept going up until 1993. But French has not yet become the working language. For many people in Montreal, the most striking change was the replacement of 'English only' work fields by a bilingualism giving French some predominance. None the less, English, being the language of business and high technology in

North America, constantly competes with French in offices, premises and laboratories of the Montreal region.

Another notable change has been the language used for communicating with customers in Montreal businesses. A survey made in 1995 by the Conseil de la langue française showed that almost all French-speaking clients were served in their language in Montreal.

The strengthening of French as a common working language has gone hand in hand with the narrowing of the wage gap between Anglophones and Francophones. In 1970, the average earnings of unilingual male Anglophones were 59 per cent higher than those of unilingual male Francophones. In 1995, the gap was only 17 per cent, and unilingual Anglophones earned 12 per cent less than bilingual Francophones.

French as a common language

It appears that Bill 101 has mostly achieved one of its goals: to make French the main language in public settings such as businesses, hospitals, professional associations, etc. Overall, 87 per cent of Quebecers speak solely or mostly French in public. In the Montreal region, this proportion is 78 per cent. Furthermore, in the same region, 97 per cent of Francophones speak mostly French in public, whereas 77 per cent of Anglophones use English. A greater proportion of allophones use French (54 per cent) instead of English (39 per cent) in public. In such a situation where French is increasingly becoming the common language, more Anglophones and allophones are becoming bilingual or trilingual. More than 60 per cent of them say they are able to hold a conversation in French. A significant proportion of young immigrants live in a trilingual environment; they speak their mother tongue at home, learn French at school and English through television and pop culture. Although these figures seem encouraging for the prospect of French in Montreal, many experts doubt they capture the complex reality of the linguistic competition between French and English in the city.

With the decreasing presence of Francophones in the island of Montreal due partly to their moving to the suburbs, many wonder if French will still stand as the main language of public use in the central area of the metropolis.

Immigration policy

It should be noted that Quebec displays many efforts to foster the integration of immigrants into its society and to encourage them to learn

French. Having the power to select independent immigrants – other than refugees and relatives – under the constitution and administrative arrangements with the federal government, Quebec tries to recruit candidates who, by their qualifications and profiles, are most likely to integrate into Quebec society. Quebec has a limited jurisdiction over immigration, for independent immigrants represent only less than half of all immigrants landing in Quebec, the others being admitted under legal categories defined by federal law. Like many modern democratic societies, Quebec has tried to reconcile cultural pluralism and individual freedoms with the sense of a shared public culture. It has done so by promoting a policy of *interculturalism*, as opposed to the multiculturalism of the federal state.

The federal official-languages policy

The federal official-languages policy contributed unquestionably to enhancing the status of French in Canada, and its use also increased appreciably in the federal public service. Francophones who comprised 21 per cent of the federal public service in 1969 saw this proportion rise to 27 per cent in 2000. It helped Francophone minorities to better assert their rights, reinforce the cohesiveness and vitality of some of their communities and acquire a self-consciousness and confidence, since they had thought for a long time they were doomed to disappear in the Anglo-Canadian maelstrom.

But the *Official Languages Act* is far from having satisfactorily met its objectives. In her first *Annual Report* tabled to the federal parliament in 2000, Dyane Adam, Commissioner of Official Languages, found the track record of the law disturbing. She gave out a bleak picture: 'There is insufficient commitment and a flagrant lack of leadership by the federal government with respect to the full implementation of the Act.' Among these deficiencies were the lack of sufficient services in French given by federal agencies in many communities outside Quebec and the inability or unwillingness of federal and provincial governments to allow Francophone minorities to have full access to French-language schools. Although the Supreme Court of Canada has confirmed and clarified to the advantage of Francophone minorities their language rights guaranteed by the Canadian Charter, close to half the pupils entitled to minority-language instruction under the Charter are not enrolled in French-language schools.

It is also crystal clear that the federal policy has failed to halt the rapid assimilation of Francophones to the English-speaking majority. The rate of assimilation is usually understood as the ratio of persons of French mother tongue who ceased to use their language versus the total number of French mother tongue populations. Between 1971 and 1996, this rate increased from 27 per cent to 36 per cent. In provinces such as Newfoundland, Alberta and British Columbia, this rate was as high as 58 per cent, 68 per cent and 71 per cent respectively. This trend means that 352,000 Francophones living outside Quebec have switched to English in 1996.

The ineffectiveness of the federal policy may be explained by the lack of support it has received in the Canadian population. This policy has met with growing opposition in the past few years, notably in English Canada. This opposition was led, as David J. Rovinsky of the Johns Hopkins University Center for Canadian Studies in Washington pointed out, by the emergence of a new Canadian nationalism, hostile to linguistic duality and the recognition of special rights for minorities. This nationalism sees official bilingualism as a costly and inefficient policy contrary to the idea of equality among individuals. In Rovinsky's words, 'bilingualism now faces a difficult climate marked by hostility to government spending on behalf of special groups'.

It should be remembered that the federal policy pursued an eminently political aim in that it was conceived as an instrument of national unity for the federal government. As political scientist Kenneth McRoberts observed:

> Clearly, during the 1960s language policy was not developed simply in response to the demands of the Francophone minorities. ... The real stimulus lay in the surge of nationalist agitation in Quebec. Canada's new language regime was formulated as the centerpiece within a much larger project: the restoration of Canada's national unity. It was part of a new pan-Canadian nationalism, designed to counter the Québécois variant.

It is also important to grasp the ideological framework underlying the federal policy: culture and language are to be dissociated. Language is seen as a simple tool of communication, freely chosen by the individual, not in itself the bearer of a culture nor borne by it. As the federal government clearly indicated in a 1977 policy statement: 'language is a system of communication that is indispensable for government, politics, administration, law, education, business and so on. If Canada has two official languages, Canadian culture is distinguished by its emphasis on diversification and its rejection of any countrywide uniformity. In short,

Canada has no official cultures.' The federal language policy sees Canada as a multicultural mosaic composed of 'linguistic communities' to which 'ethnic groups' of origins other than British or French integrate partially, encouraged as they are to 'maintain their cultures' and 'to retain a knowledge of their mother tongue'. It avowedly sets aside the existence in Quebec of a distinct national community. The policy on bilingualism thus works in conjunction with a policy on multiculturalism – it, too, enshrined in the Constitution of 1982 – that puts Canada's linguistic and ethnic groups on an equal footing. By adopting multiculturalism as a nation-building principle, the federal government discarded the conception of biculturalism which in the view of the Laurendeau–Dunton commission was the necessary counterpart of bilingualism.

Another result of the official-languages policy is the creation of a legal symmetry blind to the asymmetry of the situation of Anglophones and Francophones. In recognising equal status for French and English and giving itself the mandate of supporting 'two official-language minorities', the federal policy gives credence to the idea that English and French are equally at risk in Canada and thus justifies the federal government governing language use throughout Canada. This formal equality presents English as an endangered language in Quebec while it has maintained its assimilating power among both Francophones and allophones. But for the federal language policy, demographic asymmetries between French and English matter less than ideology and abstract principle.

A policy based on legal symmetry can produce unequal results. A study commissioned by the Commission nationale des parents francophones showed that Quebec Anglophones received 47.7 per cent of the $2.32 billion the federal government granted from 1970 to 1987, the Francophone minorities outside Quebec having received only 28.5 per cent.

It was also contended that the federal policy avoided attacking Canada's real language problems. According to sociologist Hubert Guindon, it has supported Francophone minorities outside Quebec in terms of an utopian bureaucratic ideal and increased the influence of French in the federal public service rather than rearranging the rules of the language game in Quebec more fairly for Francophones. Moreover, Guindon thinks that this policy, by maintaining the idea of free choice in schools in Quebec, helped create 'a climate of ambiguity in Quebec for immigrants and uncertainty for big private companies'.

According to Linda Cardinal, political scientist, by refusing to recognise the national and territorial dimensions to the status of French in

Canada, the federal government has reduced its language policy to supporting minorities across the country only 'where numbers warrant'. This policy ignored the existence in Quebec of a political community and succeeded in transforming the 'national unity' question into one of an individual's linguistic choice. But this political success was made at the expense of Francophones outside Quebec themselves, since they now cast their demands in the 'narrow perspective of rights', says Cardinal. And they even show a growing antipathy towards Francophones in Quebec. As a result, the Francophones in Quebec and in the rest of the Dominion feel little solidarity with each other. Under the federal regime, Francophone minorities have been placed in 'an unhealthy state of dependency on government and the courts'. She adds:

> The quid pro quo for this federal generosity toward official-language minorities has been that they accept being used – especially when Liberals have been in office – as accomplices in campaigns designed to undermine Quebec's demands on language and other matters.

In face of the disquieting figures showing a rapid decline of the French-language minorities in English Canada, one can wonder if the 'personality principle' approach to official bilingualism will suffice to ensure a future for French in Canada. So far, it seems that a policy based on 'sustainable assimilation' for French-speaking citizens outside Quebec is a cosmetic makeshift that dodges the real issue.

Should languages be viewed as rights?

There has been an ongoing debate in Canada as to whether the entrenchment of linguistic rights in the Constitution was a good policy or not. In the opinion of André Burelle, former senior public servant in the federal government, the metamorphosis of language issues into individual rights had a number of perverse effects. The federal policy of entrenching symmetrical linguistic rights resulted in uprooting 'linguistic and cultural rights from their community medium' and in 'discrediting the very idea of a host society with a common culture into which new immigrants could integrate'. By cutting Canada off from its community roots, this policy runs the risk of atomising Canadian society, Burelle argues, and of ignoring 'the need for communities as instruments for conveying language and culture'.

Gérald Larose, president of the States-General on the situation and future of French language in Quebec, suggested in June 2001 that linguistic protection for French, Anglophone community and Aboriginal languages should be raised to the status of fundamental rights incorporated in Quebec's *Charter of Human Rights and Freedoms* or in a formal Constitution of Quebec still to be written. (Quebec, as is the case in most Westminster-type parliamentary democracies, doesn't have a written constitution, contrary to all American States and many of the federated entities in the World.) Commenting on the idea, Burelle wrote that this suggestion is bad policy, for linguistic rights cannot be viewed as fundamental rights such as freedoms of expression and of assembly. According to Burelle, linguistic rights are essentially contingent and historical in the sense that they cannot be universalised from one society to another. These rights are usually the result of a political agreement between at least two communities, each community being unique and unequal in terms of wealth, population and geographical extension. Therefore, these rights shouldn't be granted by courts as though they were absolute entitlements but be determined through political bargaining and deliberation. In a reply to Burelle's opinion, Jacques-Yvan Morin said that it is not so unusual to see linguistic rights being entrenched in a Charter or in a Constitution. For instance, the linguistic rights of the Finnish, the Swedish minority and the Aboriginals were guaranteed among the 'fundamental rights and freedoms' of the last Constitution of Finland, amended in March 2000. If the Charter of the French Language had been given the primacy of a constitutional Charter in Quebec's public law, its provisions would have been less exposed to judicial nullification, according to Morin, professor of law.

The debate on linguistic rights in Quebec often opposes the collective rights of Quebecers to individual rights. Many jurists and philosophers in Canada think that the Canadian constitution already protects a blend of individual and collective rights or of what Will Kymlicka called 'community rights'. The problem with the concept of 'collective rights' is that it is difficult to articulate in legal terms and that it obscures the nature of language. If the protection of language belongs to a collectivity, then which is it? In the case of Quebec, is it the group of Francophone Quebecers, the population of Quebec as a whole or the State of Quebec represented by its Attorney-General? Advocates of collective rights often say that collective rights represent the will of the majority. Should then the content of these rights be decided by the majority of the day? Furthermore, a language, by nature, belongs neither to individuals nor to a collectivity. It is a social fact created by the interaction of individuals within a community and passed down from one generation to another. To oppose individual fundamental rights to a collective right for a language would thus make little sense. One can also argue that the survival of a specific language is less a matter of rights than one of duty, since it cannot flourish without individuals and officials having a duty to defend it. This is not to deny the necessity of protecting languages, but to show the difficulty of translating this protection into sound legal solutions.

The difficulty of finding a good legal solution also lies in the concept of the individual itself. Advocates of an absolute freedom of choice in linguistic matters often portray society as a conglomerate of abstract individuals equally capable of free will who are tied together by contractual bonds. Attractive as it is, this conception of society poorly reflects what human aspirations are made of, the life of everyone in society being closely linked to an intricate net of communities from family to nation. This was the motto of a Christian intellectual movement that was born in France and in Switzerland in the 1930s, the *personalism*, which seemingly had had a marked influence on Quebec intellectuals of the generation of Pierre-Elliot Trudeau, Gérard Pelletier, Jacques Godbout and Fernand Dumont. The founder of the review *Esprit*, Emmanuel Mounier, was one of the leaders of this movement. One of its main concerns was to offer a criticism of both liberalism and fascism and to found a social utopia rejecting materialism.

Personalism was hostile to the absolutising of either collective rights, as was the case in a fascist state, or individual rights, as often claimed by libertarians and supporters of classical liberalism. Central to personalism was the concept of *person*, opposed to that of 'individual'. Personalist intellectuals like Mounier, Jacques Maritain and Denis de Rougemont criticised the liberal and juridical conception of the individual, a disembodied atom of egoism endowed with abstract rights. Denis de Rougemont wrote: 'A person is a human being in action, i.e. a human being consciously and willfully involved in the vital conflict that links and opposes him to his neighbor.' A person develops only in his or her relationship with others within communities through which he or she discovers the spiritual dimensions of existence. Therefore, there are no individuals in the real world, but persons engaged within particular communities. None the less, important as they are, communities are subordinate to persons, and laws should be made for the good of the latter.

The French version of Quebec's *Charter of Human Rights and Freedoms* adopted in 1974 uses the term 'rights of the person' instead of a literal equivalent of 'human rights'. The presence of this concept in a universal charter of rights is probably a tribute to personalism. The irony in the

history of linguistic legislation in Canada is that the fou
competing policies, who have been in their youth great readers ᴏɪ ᵖ⁻
sonalist literature, have diverged in the interpretation of a common
thread. It seems that the juridical liberalism of Trudeau has reversed
some principles of personalism and has concluded from it that laws
should be subordinate to the good of the *individuals*, should the communities perish. In Quebec, the heirs of personalism have tried to solve
a far more complex equation: how to find a just balance between (a) the
sustenance of a distinct political community where French is shared as a
common language and a public good; (b) the protection of Anglophone
and Aboriginal communities; and (c) the rights of all the *persons* in
Quebec.

Conclusion

Many political scientists and linguists agree that the territorial solution
is the best defence for a minority language against a more powerful one.
Under the current Canadian regime, Quebec has achieved only a limited
territorialism, for its language policy has competed so far with the federal official-languages policy, based on the personal principle and conceived as a means to meeting a nation-building objective. Echoing the
conclusions other experts have reached, David J. Rovinsky thinks that
'the denial ... that language is territorial is what makes official bilingualism either a waste or an irritant'. How then can Quebec expect to have
full jurisdiction over language? Jean Laponce identified some of the
political ways to obtain territorialisation in a democratic society:

> One can impose a single state language, as France did in law first,
> then constitutionally in its recent anticipation of a more integrated
> federal Europe; or one can seek independence or sovereignty, as did
> the peripheral republics of the Soviet Union and as proposed of
> Quebec by the Parti Québécois. But the goal of security through terri-
> torialization can also be obtained, within a given state, by means of
> rigid internal language boundaries, as first implemented by
> Switzerland, then by Belgium.

It is clear then that a territorial regime for language can be implemented
in Quebec, either through independence or some sovereignty within a
confederal union with Canada, or through devolution of power within
the current Canadian regime. This last possibility was contemplated in
1992 by Stéphane Dion, who wrote at that time as a political scientist on

the aftermath of the failure of constitutional reform in Canada:

> The best solution would be a unilateral devolution of power over lan-
> guage only to the legislature of Quebec and applied only to the
> Quebec territory. Such a policy would be justified by the fact that
> only the French language is in danger and needs protection. The
> rights of English speakers historically have been well respected by
> provincial laws and Quebec's Charter of Rights. The English-speaking
> provinces would not receive the same devolution of powers because
> it is the French language that needs protection, and because nothing
> in the history of those provinces suggests that they will perform such
> a duty.

In other terms, according to Dion's asymetrical scheme, the personal
solution would be applied throughout Canada, except in Quebec, where
territorialism prevails.

One can see, therefore, how closely linked the future of French language in North America is to Quebec's political status. Many efforts in
Quebec have been channelled into attempts at gaining a substantial
change in this status. Yet the referendum held in 1980 and in 1995 on
proposals of political sovereignty have proved inconclusive, and constitutional reform in post-Charter Canada has been unable to compensate
Quebec fairly for the unilateral loss of power and status imposed in
1982. With no solutions in sight, Quebec has reached a kind of political
stalemate, while having to cope with the new Canadian nationalism.

In another article comparing Canada's future and that of Belgium,
Stéphane Dion sketched out the basis of what has been the federal government's strategy towards Quebec nationalism. This strategy has been
mostly one of containment, which consists of resisting claims for autonomy made by Quebec, undermining Quebec nationalism and the role of
the Quebec government as the primary government of Quebecers, and
finally, reinforcing the federal government's role as the trustee of an unified nation. It is clear that this strategy was followed by Jean Chrétien's
liberal government after the referendum of October 1995, which
resulted in the adoption of Bill C-20, whereby the federal parliament
granted itself the power to judge of the appropriateness of the future referendum questions relating to Quebec's sovereignty.

A shrewd observer may also have noticed that a similar strategy of
containment has been adopted by the federal state to treat linguistic
matters. Certainly, the official-languages policy strives to support a
buoyant Canadian *francophonie* from coast to coast, and there is no

doubt that among the officials implementing this policy there are people deeply convinced of the usefulness of their action. Yet this policy has proved ineffective in stopping the rapid decline of Francophone communities outside Quebec and in helping assert French as a fact for the majority in Quebec. It has contributed instead to loosening the solidarity between French-speaking Quebecers and Francophones outside Quebec, to finance legal challenges of Bill 101 and to put Francophone minorities in a state of dependency, close to clientage. Moreover, it has promoted English in Quebec itself, denying the fact that French in Quebec needs the support of both levels of government. In many respects, the French fact in Canada has been more than contained, it has nearly imploded.

The French fact has not only been contained in terms of demography. With the consecration of multiculturalism as an unifying policy, the federal state has refrained from raising the French fact to the status of a principle of civilisation, a path it could have followed by opting for biculturalism. It has chosen instead to reduce French to an optional culture diluted in a cosmopolitan basket of cultures that puts on an equal footing the communitarian mores of newcomers and the culture of a political nation having its own history, shared identity, language and institutions.

If we look at the Americas, it appears that there are three main flourishing civilisations, the Anglo-American, the Hispanic and the Brasilian. What many Quebecers have understood of multiculturalism in Canada, is that there shall be only one main civilisation in Canada, the Anglo-American, universalising itself through adherence to a patriotism of rights and a random commitment to public services. Within this framework, French is allowed to exist, but only as an innocuous culture, in the sense that the French-speaking descendants may still have preferences for reading books and newspapers in their language, for seeing dramas and movies equally in French, for being schooled in their mother tongue and for leading a particular way of life. By conceiving French as an ethnic fact, the federal multicultural policy disregards what has been going on in Quebec, that is the formation of a multi-ethnic society having its own sense of citizenship under the umbrella of a common language. As Will Kymlicka puts it: 'Far from trying to preserve some sort of racial purity, Quebec nationalists are actively seeking people of other races, cultures, and faiths to join them, and jointly help build a modern, pluralist, distinct French-speaking society in Quebec.' A good example of this blind insistence on the ethnic content of the French fact by the federal state is the celebration of 24 June, the national holiday of Quebec. For a long time, St John the Baptist was celebrated as the patron saint of Catholics. In the 1970s, the National Assembly of Quebec made Saint John's day a national holiday for all Quebecers and regardless of their creeds. None the less, the federal government kept celebrating it as the day of French-speaking Canadians. Opposed to a so-called ethnic nationalism depicted as a scarecrow, the new Canadian nationalism takes pride in being a quintessential example of civic nationalism, free of any ethnic content, as if Canada were a prism that filters social life without refraction. This is, however, pure nonsense. Canada has so far been a soft melting pot evolving under the auspices of a dominating core of British descendants.

It is why we may say that in a sense, the federal linguistic policy is not truly a linguistic policy. It is a political scheme purporting the unification of national communities within the country by using language and rights as means. The promotion of a linguistic minority matters so long as it fits within the threshold of a unified and monolithic identity and allegiance.

While the federal state pretends to be neutral when dealing with culture and ways of living, it promotes actively, especially towards Americans, a distinct Canadian culture. It has built, over time, an interventionist policy for the development of a Canadian culture by subsidising arts and publications, by imposing a minimal content of Canadian-made products for broadcast and print, and by restricting the foreign property of Canadian cultural enterprises. As Richard Gwyn, journalist and author of *Nationalism without Walls*, writes, English Canada sees the country as a state-constructed nation: 'The characteristics that really distinguish Canada from all the UN members is that we aren't really a nation-state at all. ... Rather than a nation-state, though, we are really a state-nation. Our state has formed us and has shaped our character in a way that is true for no other people in the world.'

Liberal multiculturalism defended by the federal Canadian state as a means of containing the French fact is all the more ironical since this policy undermines its own legitimacy as the protector of a Canadian culture different from the American. Since the conclusion of the free-trade treaty with the United States, Canada has dramatically increased its dependency on its neighbour for exports and investments. By affirming itself as a liberal and multicultural state relying on a strict juridical citizenship that relegates culture, language and identity to the choice of individuals, Canada is becoming a twin society, akin to the American. According to political scientist Denis Stairs, with the increasing cultural convergence we now witness between the two societies, Canada hardly distinguishes itself from its giant neighbour. Differences between the first and the second are now primarily those of governmental processes, not of substance. As Ray Conlogue, journalist, notices 'the English-language media frequently invoke Freud's notion of the narcissism of minor differences to make fun of francophones pretensions to a distinct culture'. One wonders if the notion of the narcissism of minor differences applies more aptly instead to English Canada's attitude towards the United States.

The hardening of the media's attitude in English Canada towards a distinct French Quebec, which has been most visible after the 1995 referendum, may be interpreted as a sign of the Americanisation of politics in this part of the post-modern Dominion. Ray Conlogue writes: 'But at a deeper level it may also seem that English Canada, after a brief interlude of Trudeau-inspired tolerance, is reverting to the assimilationism of the 19th century.' This new assimilationism, clothed in the noble garment of Charter rights, has fuelled many of the legal challenges made against Bill 101. There are many pundits in English Canada who forcefully argue that there should be an absolute freedom of choice for the language of schooling and public signs throughout Canada. It seems they wouldn't give up their crusade until the Supreme Court of Canada has its final say or reverses its own rulings. Let's imagine similar claims in the context of the European Union. Would it mean that French or German residents in the United Kingdom should be allowed, as a matter of right, to send their children to French or German schools fully subsidised by British taxpayers?

Many intellectuals in Quebec viewed this hardening of the new Canadian nationalism as a remnant of colonialism or paternalism. Christian Dufour writes: 'The fact that the Canadian institutional system pushes for the bilingualization of Quebec is an unacceptable colonial aftermath that will speed up the process of assimilation of francophones in the country.' It may be added that this unitarian discourse reflects also English Canada's own fragility. So far, it has been easier for English Canadians to define themselves against the Americans or the Quebecers. Kenneth McRoberts diagnosed their difficulty to see themselves as a nation: 'Now, within the Trudeau vision, in which there can be no distinct entities of any kind, the notion of a "English-Canadian" nation is totally beyond comprehension.' One can postulate that the more Canada integrates into the United States, the stronger the resentment against Quebec distinctiveness and language laws will be.

This being said, the fate of French in North America does not depend solely on English Canada's attitude towards Quebec. It is only one part of the issue. In a faltering federal state that has striven to contain the

French fact, the future of the language rests ultimately on the shoulders of Quebecers, whether they are of French stock or newcomers enthralled by the idea of experiencing America in a French environment. Bill 101 has succeeded in giving Quebec a predominantly French face in public and economic life, but a law alone cannot maintain a distinct language and nationality. French can flourish in North America as long as Quebecers still believe they have a common heritage to build upon and to share with newcomers, and this for every aspect of social life. Some intellectuals of the generation following the baby-boomers criticised the reformers of the educational system in Quebec for having abandoned the classical colleges where humanities were taught. The teaching of French was entrusted to professionals trained in modern pedagogy who failed, they argue, to inculcate the generations schooled since the 1960s with the basics of French grammar and literature. There is also an ongoing disagreement over the quality of French spoken in Quebec. Some believe that Quebec has made real progress with respect to literacy and access to post-secondary education. Others point out that the French spoken in Quebec has departed too much from what is spoken in France, and that French literature and culture themselves are now seen as foreign, to such an extent that the great works of French literature have virtually vanished from teaching programmes in Quebec's schools. Yet such a debate can go on as long as there is a faithfulness to a common heritage, a past deserving some gratitude.

'We are all Quebecers', wrote the French philosopher Alain Finkielkraut. By these words he meant that in our contemporary world, individuals are tempted to see themselves as fare-dodgers, armed with rights, and at liberty to do without the heritage handed down by society or culture. Either, like many Quebecers, they respond to the call to be grateful, or they leave these legacies aside, doomed to shrivel up in whimpers of solitude.

Notes

1   The author wishes to thank Jean-Philippe Trottier, translator, for his valuable help in reviewing this text.

References

Main studies and articles consulted

Burelle, André (1995) *Le Mal canadien: Essai de diagnostic et esquisse d'une thérapie* (Montreal: Fides).

Cardinal, Linda (1999) 'Linguistic Rights, Minority Rights and National Rights: Some Clarifications', *Inroads*, no. 8, pp. 77–85.

Cardinal, Linda (2000) 'Le pouvoir exécutif et la judiciarisation de la politique au Canada: Une étude du programme de contestation judiciaire', *Politique & Sociétés*, vol. 9, no. 2–3, pp. 43–64.

Castonguay, Charles (1999) 'French is on the Ropes: Why Won't Ottawa Admit it?', *Policy Options*.

Chevrier, Marc (1997) *Laws and Languages in Québec: The Principles and Means of Québec's Language Policy* (Quebec: Ministère des Relations internationales).

Chevrier, Marc (1999) 'Le papisme légal', *Argument*, vol. 1, no. 2, pp. 73–92.

Conlogue, Ray (1999) 'English-Canadian Culture and the Absent French Canadian', *Inroads*, no. 8. pp. 87–98.

Dion, Stéphane (1992) 'Explaining Quebec Nationalism', in R. Kent Weaver (ed.), *The Collapse of Canada* (Washington: Brookings Institution).

Dion, Stéphane (1997) 'Belgique et Canada: une comparaison de leurs chances de survie', in Serge Jaumain (ed.), *La réforme de l'État ... et après?* (Bruxelles: Éditions de l'Université libre de Bruxelles) pp. 131–59.

Dufour, Christian (2000) 'La prédominance du français', paper submitted to the Commission des États généraux sur la situation et l'avenir de la langue française au Québec, December.

Finkielkraut, Alain (1999) *L'ingratitude: Conversation sur notre temps* (Montreal: Éditions Québec Amérique).

Guindon, Hubert (1990) *Tradition, Modernité et Aspiration Nationale de la Société Québécoise* (Montreal: Éditions Saint-Martin).

Gwyn, Richard (1996) *Nationalism without Walls* (Toronto: McClelland & Stewart).

Ignatieff, Michael (2000) *The Rights Revolution* (Toronto: Anansi).

Kymlicka, Will (1998) 'American Multiculturalism in the International Arena', *Dissent*, pp. 73–9.

Laponce, Jean (1987) *Languages and their Territories* (Toronto: Toronto University Press).

Laponce, Jean (2001) 'Politics and the Law of Babel', *Social Science Information*, vol. 40, no. 2, pp. 179–94.

Lavoie, Yolande (1973) 'Les mouvements migratoires des Canadiens entre leur pays et les États-Unis aux XIXe et XXe siècles: étude quantitative', in Hubert Charbonneau (ed.), *La population du Québec* (Montreal: Boréal Express).

Lebland, Gérald (1998) 'The English Canadian Media and Quebec', *Inroads*, no. 7, pp. 23–30.

Levine, Marc V. (1990) *The Reconquest of Montreal: Language Policy and Social Change in a Bilingual City* (Philadelphia: Temple University Press).

McRoberts, Kenneth (1989) 'Making Canada Bilingual: Illusions and Delusions of Federal Language Policy', in David P. Shugarman and Reg Whitaker (eds), *Federalism and Political Community* (Peterborough, Ont.: Broadview Press).

McRoberts, Kenneth (1997) *Misconceiving Canada: The Struggle for National Unity* (Don Mills, Ont.: Oxford University Press).

Morton, F. L. and Rainer Knopff (2000) *The Charter Revolution and the Court Party* (Peterborough, Ont.: Broadview Press).

O'Keefe, Michael (2001) *Francophone Minorities: Assimilation and Community Vitality* (Ottawa: Department of Canadian Heritage).

Pal, Leslie A. (1995) 'Language, Policy and Rights in Canada: Pragmatism v. Politics', *International Issues*, vol. 38, no. 6, pp. 38–55.

Plourde, Michel *et al.* (eds) (2000) *Le français au Québec: 400 ans d'histoire et de vie* (Montreal: Fides and Les publications du Québec).

Rocher, Guy (2000) 'Les origines et les aléas de la Charte de la langue française', paper submitted to the Commission des États généraux sur la situation et l'avenir de la langue française au Québec, December.

Stairs, Denis (2000) 'Liberalism and the Triumph of Efficiency in Canada–US Relations', *ISUMA* (Canadian Journal of Policy Research), vol. 1, no. 1, pp. 11–16.

Venne, Michel (ed.) (2001) *Vive Quebec! New Thinking and New Approaches to the Quebec Nation* (Toronto: James Lorimer).

Press articles

Burelle, André (2000) 'À Brent Tyler et ses disciples qui rêvent d'en finir avec la loi 101', *Le Devoir*, 12 July.

Burelle, André (2001) 'Commission sur la situation et l'avenir du français: le chartisme mal avisé de Gérald Larose', *Le Devoir*, 12 June.

Castonguay, Charles (1996) 'Chrétien, Durham, même combat', *Le Devoir*, 22 August.

Eco, Umberto (1997) 'Le défi du rejet sauvage', *Le Figaro*, 28 March.

Fulford, Robert (2001) 'Seventy years of glorious trouble', *National Post*, 4 July.

Morin, Jacques-Yvan (2001) 'À la défense du "chartisme" de Gérald Larose', *Le Devoir*, 28 June.

Morin, Jacques-Yvan (2001) 'Les droits fondamentaux ne sont pas absolus', *Le Devoir*, 29 June.

Official documents

(Canada) (1967) Report of the Royal Commission on Bilingualism and Biculturalism, *General Introduction: The Official Languages*, Book 1 (Ottawa: Queen's Printer).

(Canada) (1977) *National Understanding: The Official Languages of Canada – Statement of the Government of Canada on the Official Languages Policy* (Ottawa: Minister of Supply and Services Canada).

(Quebec) (1972) Report of the Commission of Inquiry on the position of the French language and language rights in Québec, *The Language of Work*, Book 1 (Quebec: L'éditeur officiel du Québec).

(Quebec) (1996) Report of the interdepartmental committee on the situation of the French language, *Le français langue commune, Enjeu de la société québécoise* (Quebec: Ministère de la Culture et des Communications).

(Quebec) (2001) Gérald Larose, Notes pour une allocution (Quebec: Commission des États généraux sur la situation et l'avenir de la langue française au Québec).

(Quebec) (2001) *Le Français, une langue pour tous, Final report* (Quebec: Commission des États généraux sur la situation et l'avenir de la langue française au Québec).

(Canada) (2001) Commissioner of Official Languages, *Annual Report* (Ottawa: Minister of Supply and Services Canada).

5
Anglophones and Allophones in Quebec[1]

Pierre Larrivée

Introduction

At the core of Quebec questions lies the relation between the Anglophone and the Francophone communities. Brought together by the accidents of eighteenth-century colonial pursuits, the two groups spent two long centuries living side by side, with as little contact as possible. This mutual ignorance was, however, increasingly difficult with, among other factors, the emergence of a democratic political system through the nineteenth century, the social diversification of the British community from the 1900s and the gradual emergence of the Francophone economy after the Second World War. The closer interaction of the two groups since then in a context of rapid social change has forced them to redefine their respective places. A prime example of this redefinition can be found in the language laws enacted in the last quarter of the twentieth century to promote the French language and the interests of the Francophone community through them.

The reaction of Anglophone Quebecers to these linguistic measures was initially quite negative; although the legislative actions have come to be generally accepted, some radical views are still being held in some quarters of the Anglophone community about the laws, where they are decried as draconian measures suppressing the individual liberties of English speakers. Yet, the basis of these claims calls for some explanations, given the exceptional range of legal, economic and social guarantees that this linguistic minority enjoys.

It is the reasons behind the various reactions of the Anglo-québécois to language laws that this chapter explores. The first section provides a historical overview of the relation between Anglophones and Francophones in Quebec, with special attention to material determinants such as the demographic, geographical and economic position of each group. The second section focuses on the period of status renegotiation in which language laws were developed, introducing the ideological perspectives behind the interplay of actions and reactions. The argumentative plans underlying the contemporary radical English discourses are discussed in the final section on the basis of a corpus of press articles. In conclusion, it is suggested that not only self-interest but also intercultural differences may explain the nature of public discourses about Quebec language laws.

The Anglophone community in Quebec

Until the *entente cordiale* at the beginning of the twentieth century, Britain and France had a remarkably long tradition of waging war against each other. These bellicose relations ran through the seventeenth and eighteenth centuries, when the two colonial powers were at odds for the control of lucrative colonial possessions. The conflicts were on many occasions set in the colonies themselves. At the end of the seventeenth century, the British armies had already attempted naval attacks on Quebec City and incited their Iroquois allies to attack French settlers in the Montreal area. In 1713, the British succeeded in taking the Atlantic coastal region of Acadia, where they soon pursued an aggressive colonisation policy. A large British and Irish, and also Dutch and German, immigration was soon to be welcomed, and later, in 1755, over 12,000 French settlers were exiled by force. These Acadians were dispersed all over North America, with a significant number shipped to Louisiana, where they would become known as Cajuns. The deportation of the Acadians also deprived potential support from the other continental French colony, at a time where the British were stepping up the military pressure on *Nouvelle-France*. In the summer of 1759, Quebec City was besieged by the troops of General James Wolfe, which, on 18 September of that year, defeated the French armies of the Marquis de Montcalm on the Plains of Abraham. From there, the British could march upon Montreal, where the French decided to capitulate in 1760, in an attempt to salvage the integrity of the city and to avoid the vast destruction which had defaced Quebec City.

The French colonial administration immediately left the colony for the mother country. This in effect ended a conflict famously condemned by French philosopher Voltaire as a useless quarrel over 'a few acres of snow'. It was officially settled in 1763, with the signature of the Paris treaty. By this agreement, the French Monarchy abandoned all its claims over a majority of its North American colonies to England, with the exception of the tiny fishing post of Saint-Pierre-et-Miquelon and the sunny islands of Martinique and Guadeloupe.

A group of 500 British administrators, soldiers, merchants and artisans took the place of the French ruling élite. The Anglophone population established itself mainly in urban contexts, while the population of more than 65,000 Francophones was spread over a large territory of often small, isolated, rural communities along the St Lawrence River. In the absence of any foreseeable influx of English settlers, the demographic situation of the Anglophones made any assimilationist policy difficult to pursue. The new colonial administration therefore had to take a different approach to the Quebec question than it had in Acadia, especially in the context of the growing unrest in the other American colonies.

Because of the fear that the French-speaking population might lend support to the Revolutionary movement, the British conqueror enacted the 1774 Quebec Act. The Act recognised the rights to practise the Catholic religion and installed an oath of loyalty that allowed Catholics to hold public office. This oath then replaced the Test Act, by which the person taking it was denying the authority of the pope and the virginity of Mary, and that had been used extensively against the French, Catholic population of Acadia. The situation of the Catholic Church and that of the seigniorial system were thus maintained in Quebec, along with the use of French civil law.

These measures reassured the remaining religious and temporal Francophone élites, who opposed any request of support from the Revolutionary movement, to which the settlers remained largely indifferent. The Quebec Act angered the Protestant Puritans of New England. It infuriated the American Revolutionaries and the Montreal Anglophone merchant class. The maintenance of old French institutions was incompatible in their view with the liberal capitalism these groups wanted to pursue, and with the creation of some form of representative assembly that they had been asking for.

Apart from the elaboration of the Act, the American Revolution had another important impact on Quebec, by providing it with its first important influx of English-speaking immigrants. A significant number of Anglican clergy, Crown officers, soldiers and merchants had, by their very position, an attachment to the British government. They soon sought to leave the American colonies, and were joined in time by farmers and members of different religious and ethnic minorities who had variously suffered from the fight for Independence. They crossed the border into British territory to settle in the Maritime Provinces, in the

Gaspé peninsula, in the Ottawa Valley and in the Eastern Townships, around the main areas of French settlement of the St Lawrence valley. Handsome rewards, notably in the form of large stretches of land, were offered by the colonial administration to the newcomers. By 1815, the Anglophone population of Canada totalled 50,000 people, constituting a fifth of the Canadian population, as compared to less than 1 per cent fifty years before.

A second period of important immigration from the British Isles was to follow. The beginnings of industrialisation made urban life difficult; the agricultural crises leading to the Irish 1845 Great Famine made rural life untenable. These conditions led thousands of Irish and Scottish to defy the dire sea-travel conditions in the hope of reaching North America. Many never reached their destination; many more died from cholera on the quarantine island of Grosse Isle, some fifty kilometres from Quebec City. A great number none the less did survive the voyage to settle in Canada: it is estimated that 750,000 English-speaking migrants entered Quebec City. Although most newcomers moved on to other parts of Canada, a significant portion remained in urban Quebec, making Montreal, for the first and only time, a city with a majority of English speakers.

At the time of the 1867 Confederation, when the British North America Act brought together four provinces to form the Dominion of Canada, both Canada and Quebec were peopled by two national groups divided along linguistic, religious and ethnic lines. The Anglophone group was almost entirely from the British Isles; the Francophone one was Catholic of French origin. Swelled by the different waves of immigration, the Anglophone population was mainly established in Montreal, the Eastern Townships, the Ottawa Valley and Gaspésie; most of the French population was living in the Saint-Lawrence river valley, where, in the absence of any contact with other Francophone groups, it maintained its demographic weight by a remarkably high birth rate. Most Francophones lived from subsistence agriculture or unskilled manual work in the natural resources industry or in factories; the few existing French businesses had essentially local markets, and were hindered in their expansion by a limited access capital, which was predominantly controlled by the English community. It was Anglophones who held the large majority of liberal professions, managerial positions and businesses opportunities. As the heart of the Anglophone community, Montreal was the financial centre of Canada, where corporate headquarters were established, where capital could be accessed, where Anglo-Saxon world markets could be reached. From the beginning of the nineteenth century, the Montreal merchants were handling the lucrative market of beaver fur. They developed the exploitation of natural resources like timber, brought about the construction of the coast-to-coast railway system and were responsible for the gradual implantation of the industrial base of Quebec.

This sharp separation between the two groups made difficult the assimilation relentlessly called for by the Montreal business class since the Conquest, a position epitomised in Lord George Durham's report alleging the urgency of bringing into civilisation 'a people with no history and no literature'. Instead, a complex process of accommodation between the powerful Anglophone business élite and the Francophone religious and political leaders was developed. The accommodation was an implicit pact between an Anglophone group that could not directly impose its ways, given the increasing democratic nature of the political institutions that favoured Francophones, and a provincial government which in an age of capitalist *laissez-faire* was careful not to upset the wealthiest of its citizens. Merchants could have unrestricted access to natural resources and unregulated cheap labour, while the Francophone population could continue to practise its language and religion. In effect then, in 1867, Quebec could have appeared to the uninformed observer to be just another British colony that simply happened to have a large French-speaking population. The social fabric of the English-speaking group was, however, to be modified profoundly by two waves of twentieth-century European immigration.

From 1901 to 1931, Canada was presented abroad as a land of opportunities in which new, better lives could be hoped for. These prospects attracted a large number of immigrants fleeing an economically and politically troubled Europe, notably Italians and Eastern Europeans of Jewish confession. The latter mainly established in Montreal, where they worked in commerce and industry (in the garment business in particular). The Italians' presence was also essentially urban, where many took up unskilled work, particularly in the construction of the railway. Both groups would tend to identify with the culture of the dominant group and adopted as their own the language of economic and social promotion.

At the end of the Second World War, the opportunities represented by Canada attracted an even larger number of migrants from a devastated Europe. Germans, Poles, Italians, Greeks and Portuguese generally settled in Montreal, where they ran traditional family firms with which they came to be associated, and integrated into the English language and culture.

Montreal was not only the home of most immigrants in Quebec, it was increasingly becoming that of a majority of Quebec Anglophones, who could benefit there from the demographic support that their birth rate did not allow them. Three-quarters of the Quebec English-speaking population were to be found in Montreal in 1961.

Urbanisation was also marking the development of the Francophone community. The constant expansion of the French Canadian demography led it to leave the countryside, because of increasing scarcity of land impoverished by decades of agriculture. Many sought to find waged work in Montreal factories, or in those of New England. For instance, the Massachusetts city of Lowell, the birthplace of the Franco-American writer Jack Kerouac, was, in the 1930s, a French-speaking city, with its own religious and social institutions. When the United States tightened its immigration laws following the 1929 crash, Quebecers were to turn to develop new regions like the northerly Abitibi, or to settle in the Eastern Townships and Gaspésie, where they slowly assimilated the declining local Anglophone population. They also started to establish themselves in Montreal, where two-fifths of the French-speaking population of Quebec were living in 1961.

Although the urbanisation movement brought the members of the two communities into closer interaction than ever before, there still existed a relatively sharp geographical separation between the two groups that reflected economic distinctions. In Montreal, the division was and still is today marked by the very geography of the city. Anglophones occupy the centre and the west of the Island, the east being inhabited by Francophones, with Saint-Laurent Boulevard setting the symbolic boundary between them.

This separation would become less entrenched as the economic importance of Montreal started to erode after the War. The opening of the Saint-Lawrence Seaway in 1959 meant that more boats could continue their route to the Great Lakes without having to stop in Montreal. The motor car industry established itself mainly in Southern Ontario, near the main American centres of production, after the signature in the 1960s of a free-trade agreement in the automobile sector known as the Auto-Pack. With these industrial evolutions, the movement of capital concentration brought banks and headquarters increasingly to operate from Toronto.

As such, Montreal Anglophones were a slightly less powerful community. Their overall economic situation remained incomparably better than that of Francophones, however. A famous official figure from the Commission on Bilingualism and Biculturalism states that in 1961, the average unilingual Quebec Anglophone earned twice as much as a unilingual Franco-québécois. In fact, almost every other ethnic group inside Quebec, with the exception of Italian immigrants and Native people, were better off than French-speaking Quebecers.

This privileged economic situation of the Anglophones was a central element in the development of the Francophone autonomist movement, as was the alarming demographic situation.

Outside Quebec, the prospects of the French-speaking populations looked grim. French had managed to maintain itself in some communities located near the Quebec borders, in groups of Quebec origin established along the Ottawa valley and in the mining towns in the Ontarian North, as well as in Acadian New Brunswick. This was despite severe laws that restricted rights to French education guaranteed in the Canadian constitution as in Ontario in 1912, or altogether abolishing them, as in Manitoba in 1890. Such assimilationist actions had a dramatic impact on the ever-diminishing French communities in other more remote parts of the country. The rates of assimilation in Atlantic provinces other than New Brunswick, and in those west of Ontario were worryingly high: between 1951 and 1961, over 80 per cent of Newfoundland's small population of French native speakers used English as their main home language; between the 1881 and 1981, the percentage of French speakers in Manitoba to the general population dropped fivefold, from 15.6 to 3.1 per cent. The weight of the Francophones in Canada had dropped from over a third before the Second World War to less than a quarter of the overall population in the 1960s. This was due to the converging effect of assimilation, but also to the demographic situation inside Quebec. With urbanisation and modernisation, the birth rate of Franco-québécois, by which they had maintained their community's weight through 200 years of English rule, simply collapsed to one of the lowest in North America, well below the replacement rate. In these circumstances, it was felt that French culture could be reduced to insignificance in its main American homeland, and be assimilated to what was not only the continental language, but also the first prestigious international language. The fear of disappearing was accentuated by the massive influx of migrants, who tended to become assimilated into the economically favoured English-speaking group. The question of immigration was therefore to become a central issue in the debate over the survival of French in Quebec.

Quebec Francophones were thus gripped by feelings of the urgency of ensuring the cultural survival of their group, feelings of which Anglophones seemed to have remained largely unaware. Indeed, English

Quebecers enjoyed an autonomous life of their own due to geographical, economic, social and linguistic separation, to which could be added the still significant role of the ethnic and religious factors. Indeed, someone could live, shop and work in certain parts of Quebec without speaking or understanding a single word of French. This separation would leave the Anglophone minority quite unprepared for the emergence of Francophone power, and the negotiation of social positions that was to follow.

Renegotiating social positions: 1960–95

The collapse of the Quebec birth rate and the patterns of rapid assimilation in Canada made the question of immigration a central issue for Francophones in Quebec. Immigrants had always tended to integrate into the economically advantaged English-speaking culture, ensuring the maintenance of this group. As this integration trend seemed to be growing stronger in the 1960s, with massive rates of newcomers entering the country, it was the survival of the French-speaking group that was felt to be threatened. This threat was what determined many French-speaking Quebecers to call for action to ensure the integration of immigrants into their community.

The question of immigration was of particular importance in the field of education. From 1951 to 1967, the proportion of children of Italian origin going to French schools went from 49 per cent to a mere 12 per cent. Given free choice between one of the two school systems, immigrant parents increasingly favoured the English one, cutting the Francophone group off from a most needed source of demographic replenishment, while at the same time emphasising the subordinate status of a language in the only state where it was in a majority position in the Americas.

It is in this context that in the Montreal suburb of Saint-Leonard, in November of 1967, the local Catholic School Board decided to replace the bilingual classes that it had created in 1963 by unilingual ones at the primary school level. The measure, which was to take effect at the beginning of the school year 1968, was met with strong opposition from the Allophone parents, mainly of Italian origin, who constituted nearly 30 per cent of the town's population. Its application was therefore delayed for a year, which witnessed the two communities being brought one against the other. The local school elections of May 1968 were one long, bitter debate between the Saint Leonard English Catholic Association of Parents and the *Mouvement pour l'Intégration Scolaire*. Immediately after their victory, the latter declared French the only language of instruction in the elementary schools of Saint-Leonard. The conflict brought legal challenges, political claims about the abrogation of Anglophone rights, civil disobedience in the creation of private English classes, and violent public confrontations during a number of demonstrations.

The Saint-Leonard crisis had polarised Anglophone and Francophone groups not only in that suburb, but also in Montreal and in the whole of Quebec. Inaugurating the overt politicisation of language, it provided clear evidence for the necessity of laws regulating the linguistic situation. In November 1967, Premier Jean-Jacques Bertrand put forward the first full-fledged language legislation of Quebec's history. The Bill officially aimed at promoting French. Among other measures, it created centres known as COFI for teaching French to immigrants. Yet, it rested entirely on incitative measures, and it sanctioned the principle of free choice of language of education. This enraged the Quebec Francophone élites, to the extent that the then Bill 85 had to be withdrawn before it could be reintroduced as Bill 63 in October 1969. While it was debated in the National Assembly, the legislation was severely criticised by a number of lobbying groups, and was the object of staff and student strikes in schools. Although adopted in the end, Bill 63 had failed to solve the issue of the language of education that had made its adoption necessary in the first place.

A different solution to the problem was put forward in 1974 by the Liberal Party of Premier Robert Bourassa in a new piece of legislation. Bill 22 sought to replace the principle of free choice between English and French that had made Bill 63 unacceptable to Francophones by declaring French the official language of Quebec. This declaration was accompanied by a series of provocative measures inviting the use of French in the workplace and in the business world. The measures and the variety of guarantees that they provided to the English minority were well received by the Anglo-québécois, who were, however, outraged by the provisions relating to public education. While free choice of the language of schooling was in theory maintained for all, access to education in English was conditional on a sufficient knowledge of that language. This would bring the future Allophone migrants into the French system, while not limiting the access to English schooling for established Allophone and Anglophone children. However, the required knowledge had to be determined, to which end tests set by the Minister of Education could be administered to pupils. The idea of having young children put through language tests, the prospect of having a family's children placed in different schools, the vagueness of the notion of adequate knowledge which was liable to discretionary interpretations and actions made the application of an already much questioned principle completely unacceptable to English-speaking Quebecers. The Bill was a primary cause of the defeat in the fall of 1976 of the Liberal Party, who by proposing a compromise that sought to appeal to everyone in the end satisfied no one.

The 1976 election was won by the sovereignist Parti Québécois of René Lévesque. The access to power of a party with the central objective of achieving the independence of Quebec from Canada took everybody by surprise, and came as a complete shock to English Canada and English-speaking Quebecers. Its socio-democratic leanings raised eyebrows in Washington, where Quebec was to be referred to for some time as the 'Cuba of the North'.

The party's concerns for social justice and its sovereignist objectives put the language issue at the top of its agenda. Immediately after the elections, the redrafting of Bill 22 was entrusted to an early adherent to the party, Minister Camille Laurin. Laurin presented a first version of the new law, symbolically called Bill 1, which in August 1977 was adopted in an attenuated version as Bill 101. The goal of the Charter of the French Language was to make French the official language of Quebec, and to assert the right to use French in official assemblies, official public services, commerce, the workplace and schools. Anyone had the right to ask to receive education and to work in French, to be served and informed in French in a commercial context, to communicate with government bodies and social services providers in that language. The rights of the majority were thus stated without restricting those of the minority groups: indeed, the preamble of the Charter explicitly recognises the contribution of the linguistic minorities to the Quebec society and the necessity to respect their institutions. Other accommodations were built into the Charter as a sign of openness towards the linguistic minorities, especially the English-speaking groups, as can be seen in the provisions of signs and schooling.

On the signage question, the Charter required that public signage make use of French only, in order to establish the Francophone outlook of Quebec, as the historical prevalence of English signs all over Quebec and in particular in urban centres was felt to be a hallmark of the Anglophone economic and social dominance. The regulations on the language of signs were, however, limited by a series of exceptions that allowed the use of another language. Unilingualism concerned only commercial signage; signs inside a small business of less than four employees could use another language; languages other than French could also be used in cultural activities, and for religious, political, ideological or humanitarian messages from non-profit organisations.

Similar accommodations were proposed to the requirements on the language of education. As a principle, French was to be the language of public education for all children from kindergarten to high school. However, freedom of choice applied to private schools and subsequent education at the university and pre-university collegial level. All children who were in English school at the moment of the enactment of law could along with all their younger siblings continue their education in that language. More generally, primary and secondary schooling was freely accessible in English to any children of a parent educated in English in Quebec. Similar access was proposed by the Quebec government to be extended to the children of parents from any other Canadian provinces agreeing to offer education in French to Francophone parents, but no other provincial government wanted to reciprocate. Finally, children of diplomats and foreign delegates retained freedom of choice.

These measures guaranteed in effect that the Anglophone population could continue to enjoy educational services in their mother tongue, while avoiding the onus of language tests or other similar controls. At the same time, it made sure that immigrants would be brought into the Francophone education system.

The new immigrants did not seem to manifest strong overt reactions, and tended to adopt the conventions of the host nation, although there was some confusion created by the distortion between the official claims and the reality of Quebec's and Canada's languages. An officially bilingual country that really isn't one and a practically bilingual Montreal Island in an officially unilingual province were to cause much surprise to not always well-informed newcomers.

The already established immigrants, however, reacted rather negatively to the new measures. It was felt that the Quebec laws impinged on the continental mobility and economic opportunities of Allophones by forcing their children to learn a local language. It was also perceived that the legislation stemmed from a local historical situation in which few migrants had much interest. The narrative of French identity as displayed, for instance, in the four times *fleur-de-lis*ed Quebec flag had little appeal to established immigrants, who entrusted their loyalty to the federal government that had made their migration possible.

The reaction of the Anglophone community to the French Language Charter was initially extremely negative. English speakers underwent a profound sense of shock in their symbolic passage from being a part of the Canadian majority to having a minority status. Anglophones felt rejected, stripped of their traditional implicit prestige, robbed of their unchallenged position of power. Although these reactions were moderated by the passage of time and with the help of subsequent legislative recognition of the English community through Bill 57 in the fall of 1983 and Bill 142 in 1986, the accommodations built into the French Language Charter were insufficient to completely eliminate the feeling of rejection.

Many Anglophones simply left Quebec. How much of this emigration is related specifically to the Charter is difficult to ascertain. Other factors came into play, such as the deterioration of the Montreal economy, the growth of the economy in other parts of North America, and the traditional mobility of the Anglophone population of Quebec. Important emigration was already manifest from the end of the 1960s, probably due to economic developments in other cities, and in the 1970s, nearly 100,000 Anglophones had already left Quebec before the enactment of Bill 101. In the ten years after the election of the Parti Québécois, there were 100,000 fewer Anglophones in the Montreal area. These were very often unilingual, and presumably unwilling to adapt to a new social organisation: it is often said that learning the language of the majority was the first act of many of the Anglophones who stayed.

After initial tactics of civil disobedience and thinly veiled political and economic threats, some of those who stayed resorted to lobbying groups and legal representations. Although, as was the case with the Quebec city based community group Voice of English Quebec, some associations were founded immediately with the adoption of Bill 101, it took some time for a central organisation to be created, probably because many hoped that the linguistic measures would somehow cease to be. As the stability of Bill 101 became evident to all, more associations were brought into existence, in particular Alliance Quebec. Founded in 1982, this lobby group was to launch a series of legal challenges to the Charter of the French Language, with handsome funds from the Canadian Government.

The most famous case probably remains that against the provisions on the language of signs. A suit was filed by a group including the Brown Shoe stores chain (legally known as the Ford case) and the Montreal stationery-store owner Allan Singer (known as the Devine case). They argued that article 58 of the French Language Charter requiring unilingual signage was unconstitutional. Such a requirement was alleged to violate the right of free speech enshrined in both the Quebec and the Canadian charters of rights. This view was ratified by five judges of the Appeals Court on 23 December 1986. Two years later, the Canadian Supreme Court confirmed the Appeals Court decision. In view of the evidence presented by the Quebec Government lawyers concerning the precarious status of French in Quebec, the federal court, however, conceded that the predominance of French would be a reasonable compromise under the circumstances.

The 1988 judicial decision set the stage for renewed debates on the language question. It gave hopes to many Anglophones that their language could regain its former status, which is exactly what many Francophones feared. Split once again between conflicting interests, the Liberal premier Robert Bourassa, re-elected in 1985, sought a solution that would satisfy everyone. In the short term, one week after the Supreme Court ruling, the government upheld the rejected provisions by invoking the notwithstanding clause, a legal disposition that removes some legislation from legal examination for a period of five years. Before the end of 1988, however, the provincial government introduced Bill 178, which amended the French Language Charter in order to maintain French-only exterior signs and allowed for bilingual interior signage on the condition of French predominance. Some English could be used on signs, without questioning the pre-eminence of French or the French outlook of Quebec cities. Thus, the government believed that it had devised an honourable compromise. While in many difficult questions the politics of compromise served Bourassa, it never brought him much of the anticipated results on the linguistic issue. Many Francophones disliked the weakening of the French Language Charter. Anglophones were most angered by the limited scope of English signage. Three out of the four Anglophone ministers from the Bourassa cabinet were to resign and went on to form a new political party under the leadership of a fourth man, Robert Libman. The Equality Party was to get four MPs in the 1989 election in which the Liberal Party was none the less returned to power.

In order to regain the crucial support of the Anglophone electorate, Bourassa sought to extend the use of English on signs. At the same time, he could not afford to alienate an increasingly nationalist Francophone vote. The difficult task of drafting new amendments acceptable to all was entrusted to senior minister Claude Ryan. One of the central figures of the Liberal government, a former journalist respected for his intellectual honesty, Ryan presented a new legislative piece in 1993, five years after the Supreme Court decision on the French Language Charter. Bill 86 allowed bilingual signage in as much as French remained markedly predominant. French was judged to be predominant on a given sign if the space given to the French text was twice as large as the space given to another language, if the French lettering was twice as big as the lettering in another language, to the exclusion of any characteristic, like colours, that reduced its visual impact. The exclusive use of French was maintained for billboards of 16 square metres or more, on moving vehicles, in the metro and in bus-passenger shelters. In all other cases, other languages could be used.

These regulations allowed for relatively extensive bilingualism while maintaining the importance of French, in line with the Supreme Court ruling that predominance would be legally acceptable. The French Language Charter could be maintained without the protection of the notwithstanding clause, the use of which had been much decried in English Canada. But the proposed compromise rested on a series of regulations that were open to all shapes and forms of criticisms, which were endlessly echoed by polemists like Mordechai Richler. Why did French have to occupy twice the size? Was it legitimate to have English corporate names of stores like *Dunkin' Donuts* or *Canadian Tire* figure on huge signs while French predominance was required of local merchants? Why could an ad in a store use English but not the one in a bus shelter? The regulations were amenable to legal challenges from Anglophone activists. These would bring a multitude of complaints from French activists, following which enquiries had to be conducted. It is probably in order to minimise the number of these enquiries that the Liberal government abolished the *Commission de Protection de la Langue Française*, and devolved its mandate to the understaffed *Office de la Langue Française*.

Litigation had allowed the English community some leverage against the Charter which had established its subsidiary symbolic position. It stirred up stronger Francophone support for the notion of the pre-eminence of French in Quebec that had determined the adoption of Bill 101. The amended Charter of the French Language was to become to Anglophones, Allophones and Francophones alike an acceptable version of a linguistic compromise.

By the end of the century, the Anglophone community of Quebec had undergone dramatic symbolic changes. From the privileged representatives of the colonial power, the Anglophones had become a linguistic minority group. Although Anglophones retained a favourable economic and political situation, their exclusive control over Quebec was a thing of the past. Even with the levels of legal protection and arrays of services unknown to most linguistic minorities around the world, the symbolic transformation took some time before it was accepted. But accepted it is today by a vast proportion of the Anglophones and Allophones. By and large, speakers of English and of other languages accept the necessity to protect French, a language that is spoken fluently by most, especially among younger people. Everyday relations between the linguistic groups are generally very cordial, and show a willingness to accommodate each other. This willingness is a point to be stressed, as it is often overshadowed by extremists' public discourses, which will be discussed in the next section.

Contemporary radical Anglophone discourses on the French Language Charter

At the beginning of the 1990s, the legitimacy of the Quebec language laws was very largely accepted by the Francophone, Allophone and Anglophone communities. Twenty-five years of the Language Charter had made French the common public language of Quebec. With time, and following the compromises proposed by successive Quebec governments, the initial feelings of discontent among Anglophone and immigrant groups gradually eased. Had such discontent persisted, it would have been difficult to express through the traditional channels of economic and political pressures on which intergroup accommodation was previously based. As the large economic gap between Anglophones and Francophones was being closed, economic pressures were unlikely to have the impact that they previously had. The election of a sovereignist government in 1994 made the results of eventual political pressures uncertain. Unlike the Liberal Party which traditionally relied on the English vote and that was to suffer from its disaffection after Bills 22, 178 and 86, the Parti Québécois never enjoyed much support from the Anglophone community, and was therefore not affected by swings in its electoral moods.

In effect, then, protest was to be expressed through public discourses in demonstrations, press conferences and newspaper articles. These public discourses increasingly tended to express radical views, as the moderate perspectives adopted by the majority of Anglophones were by their very nature unlikely to occupy much of the public space. The more critical opinions are associated with a relatively small circle of activist and interest groups: among them, Howard Galganov, head of the Quebec Political Action Committee, Keith Henderson, leader of the Equality Party, William Johnson, president of Alliance Quebec, the lawyers Julius Grey and Brent Tyler, the Cit-Can Foundation and the Chateauguay Valley English Speaking Peoples' Association. These critics of the provincial linguistic legislation were often wealthy people from the Montreal area who refused to accept the legitimacy of some aspect or other of the pre-eminence of French in Quebec.

This radicalisation of the Anglo-québécois discourse was parallel to that of English Canada. The Canadian press has displayed a previously unknown level of aggression at Quebec and Quebecers. This agression is not only displayed in the columns of lesser quality papers like that of Diane Francis in the *National Post* and in other populist dailies owned by the federalist tycoon Conrad Black, but can also be encountered in serious papers like the *Globe and Mail*. As constructive proposals to reconcile both Quebec and the rest of Canada had failed to solve the ongoing constitutional crisis, more space was available for radical attitudes to be expressed. These were adopted not only by marginal reactionary political parties, but by the very mainstream federal Liberal Party elected to power in 1993 under the leadership of Jean Chrétien. Through his premiership as through his political career, Chrétien took a hard-line towards sovereignty movements in Quebec: in 1996, he appointed as Minister for Intergovernmental Affairs Stéphane Dion, an academic known for his standing opposition to Quebec nationalism. In his official capacities, Dion was to play a major role in evoking legal and political obstacles to Quebec independence, by promoting for instance the partitionist discourse during the 1995 Quebec referendum. Several Anglophone activist groups had proposed that if Quebec could secede from Canada, then it could be partitioned between those areas in favour of independence and those mainly Anglophone regions that wanted to remain part of Canada: the Ottawa Valley and the West of Montreal Island were most often mentioned. Although this is obviously a contentious matter, the legal basis for partition both in Canadian and international terms seems weak, as it ignores the difference between cities and regions, which are creations of the provincial government, and provinces, the existence of which does not appear to crucially depend on a larger federal entity. In effect then, the implementation of the partitionist project could only be realised by military actions, a situation liable to have, as history has unfortunately demonstrated, the worst of consequences.

Whether such extreme political projects as partition were meant to be eventually realised is an open question. Their evocation certainly served a political purpose. That such objectives were pursued is evidenced by a declaration by the leader of the Equality Party, Keith Henderson, published on the party's web site, which deserves to be cited at length:

> Broad public acceptance of the case for partitioning a separate Quebec played a major role in Premier Lucien Bouchard's resignation from office yesterday [January 11, 2001] says Equality Leader Keith Henderson, noting the separation movement's sharp descent since partition's merits were widely introduced following Quebec's 1995 separation referendum.

'Anyone who charts public opinion can see this obvious pattern,' Mr Henderson said, noting the consistent 'domino effect' in declining sovereignist support that foreshadowed yesterday's event, and citing Mr Bouchard's same-day lament over French-Quebecers' 'apathy' for the sovereignty option. 'This is a very telling comment coming from the man who dreamed of leading Quebec into nationhood and who has watched that dream fading away in the polls since we introduced partition, which has always been separation's Achilles heel. Mr Bouchard's departure is about as resounding a confirmation of the damage it has done as a Quebec separatist leader could make.'

The claim that the prospect of partition had a major impact on the Francophone vote appears unsubstantiated, as most Quebecers had in fact paid little attention to a project so radical that it seemed to undermine its own credibility. What is certain, however, is the idea that discourses about partition had, in the view of some activists, an effect on the political debate in Quebec. Because traditional economic and social channels by which the Anglophone élites could control the Quebec political agenda were no more accessible, this control could only be achieved from the outside, as it were, through radical public discourses.

The ideological strategies underpinning these discourses can be illustrated by the events following the 1996 crisis on the language of signs. In 1996, Howard Galganov and Alliance Quebec threatened a boycott against major chain stores that did not put up English signs to the extent allowed by Bill 86. Although the amendments permitted languages other than French to be used on commercial signs, in view of the general consensus, some stores had maintained French-only signage. When, following threats by Anglophone activists, the possible use of bilingual signs was evoked by some senior executives, Premier Lucien Bouchard and other senior cabinet ministers intervened and called on the general business community not to disrupt the hard-earned linguistic peace. Yet, this peace was to be threatened by a variety of legal challenges, many of which were conducted by the Montreal lawyer Brent Tyler. Tyler questioned on a number of occasions the disposition of the French Language Charter on the predominance of French on signs, with the support and funding of other advocates of the partitionist discourse, many of which were generously funded by the Canadian Government. His most famous case is no doubt that of the Lyon and Wallrus antique shop. The sign in front of the Kwolton store in the Eastern Townships was in English on one side and in French on the other, with no difference in the height of the lettering. As such, it was in contravention of the French predominance requirements of the amended French Language Charter. After the usual investigations by the *Commission de la Protection de la Langue Française*, the owners were asked to modify the sign, which they refused to do. Their lawyer argued before the Quebec Superior Court that French had made such significant progress that the arguments accepted in 1988 by the Supreme Court of Canada as justifying special measures for its protection were no longer valid. Restrictions on languages other than French were not justified anymore, and they were further claimed to violate equality rights guaranteed in the federal Charter of Rights and Freedoms. In October 1999, the Superior Court judge Danielle Côté rendered a decision in favour of Tyler, invalidating Articles 58 and 205 on predominance of the French Language Charter. Côté wrote that French predominance on commercial signs constituted a violation of the right of freedom of expression guaranteed under Article 2(b) of the federal charter of rights and Article 3 of the provincial charter, as it creates a restriction on the use of other languages. As the case for these restrictions made in 1988 was assumed to prevail and was not presented again by the Quebec Government lawyers, the judge further accepted the view that there was no justification for these restrictions anymore, a view that was soon to be overturned by the Courts of Appeal. When new studies were presented to the Quebec Court of Appeal by Tyler in order to reopen the Lyon and Wallrus case, new procedures were refused to the Montreal lawyer by Quebec's highest court in October 2001, on the grounds that the 1988 Supreme Court decision stood, in view of Quebec's particular situation that justified a rule of predominance.

Before the ideology of rights underlying the courts' challenges on the language of signs be considered, it is instructive to look into similar cases in which Tyler was involved during the same period and their treatment in the Anglophone press, as evidenced from the texts mentioning the lawyer in the Montreal Anglophone newspaper *The Gazette* in the fall of 1999. In February 1998, a Montreal merchant, Clifford Oswald, was condemned to pay a $136 fine because he had refused to make French predominant on the sign outside his shop. Similarly, the owner of a plumbing shop, Vasilios Papoutsis, was condemned to a $664 fine in September 1999 because of his refusal to comply with the predominance of French disposition for the sign on his van. The convicted businessmen are presented not as deliberate law offenders, but rather as victims of 'harassment' (Johnston, 14 October 1999; King, 20 November 1999). This alleged harassment is carried out by what are consistently referred to in the English press as the 'language police'. Yet, unlike a police organisation, the *Commission de la Protection de la Langue française* does not have any executive powers of its own, and it cannot arrest people or close down shops. Its mandate is limited to investigating on the strength of public complaints allegations of language law violations: the offending cases can be referred to the judiciary, although the Commission generally goes out of its way to settle matters through conciliation. In practice, only a small number of offenders who repeatedly refuse to comply with the requests of the Commission are sued and fined if found guilty. These fines can be recouped through the normal judicial process; the following passages describe the strategy that Tyler intends to pursue were this process applied to his clients:

> Tyler said he, Johnson and Henderson will pool resources with fellow Anglo avengers Howard Galganov, head of the Quebec Political Action Committee, and Don Donderi of Cit-Can to buy the Papoutsis van if it's seized for non-payment of the fine. They would, in turn, give it back to the plumber.
>
> Gilles-Louis Racine, spokesman for the Office de la Langue Francaise, said yesterday the OLF doesn't have the power to take possession of vehicles to recoup unpaid fines.   (King, 20 November 1999).
>
> If Oswald again refuses to pay, Vaillant [Quebec Justice Department Spokesperson] said a bailiff could be sent to his shop in Notre Dame de Grace to seize property equal to the $132 he owes.
>
> But Tyler said that threat doesn't faze him because he has another plan up his sleeve: 'We are going to invite Howard Galganov, Bill Johnson, Keith Henderson and the usual suspects to the bailiff's sale and when the goods are put up for auction, they will be bought by these people and given back to Clifford.'
>
> Tyler said the language police will have to prosecute Oswald again 'because he still won't change his sign, even if his goods are seized.' (Wilton and Authier, 15 October 1999)

It is not what these excerpts say about the language regulatory processes in Quebec that is instructive: the evoked seizures of goods bears little relation to reality, as the *Office de la Langue Française* can take no such actions, and as a relatively small fine is unlikely to justify taking possession of a motor vehicle. What is instructive is how they present the actors of the situation. The *Commission* is portrayed as an oppressing bureaucracy, rather than as an administrative body monitoring the application of a legislation. People who repeatedly refuse to comply with the legislative dispositions are depicted as freedom fighters. The same logic of liberty and rights underlies the reference to activists themselves: Tyler is described as an 'English-rights activist' (King, 23 November 2000, 20 November 1999), and an 'Anglo-rights lawyer' (Gordon, 19 November 1999); Howard Galganov, William Johnson and Keith Henderson are designated as 'Anglo avengers' in the first excerpts above from King.

These perspectives provide a useful background to understand the reaction of William Johnson to the Côté decision against French predominance in signage in the Lyon and the Wallrus case.

> Bill Johnson, president of Alliance Quebec, said: 'The lesson of the court, I believe, is: "Get off your knees. Stand up for your rights and your freedoms." The nervous Nellies and jelly-legged Jacks who kept telling us, "Don't rock the boat; don't go to court, you'll provoke the nationalists" – I think they were proven wrong today.'
>
> (Johnston and Gordon, 21 October 1999)

As Tyler says in his defence of the case, the leader of Alliance Quebec expresses unambiguously that the pre-eminence requirements in signage suppresses the rights of Anglo-québécois; similar claims have been made in connection with the dispositions on the language of education. These rights are presumably established by the Federal Official Languages Act and the Federal and Provincial Charters of Rights that bar discrimination between citizens. The equality of citizens must presumably guarantee the equality of their languages. Of course, not each and every language is concerned here, only official languages. They alone are entitled to institutional diffusion. It is therefore exclusively between English and French that equality is demanded, and no request is ever made concerning the other languages used on the national ground, showing to some extent the contingent basis of the rights claimed. This demand for equality between the official languages has led Alliance Quebec to actively support the practical requests for services and institutions from Francophones outside Quebec, in the hope that their theoretical equality status would be in truth granted to the Quebec Anglophones. It is then in this lack of legislative parity between English and French that must be seen the source of the claims of Anglophone oppression.

The difficulty of parity rests on a simple observation shared not only by a succession of Quebec governments, but also by the federal Supreme Court and by the Canadian diplomatic services in official circles such as UNESCO, for instance. Endowing English with an equal status would endanger the situation of French in Quebec. Equality would make difficult the integration of immigrants to the French group; it would not help to reverse the alarming assimilation rates of French Canadians and the diminishing weight of French speakers in Canada, indeed in North America as a whole. With the continental pre-eminence of English and its international prestige, parity would only constitute an apparent version of equality, which would inevitably play to the disadvantage of French, whose decline could be rapid, as rapid as its enhancement was since its promulgation as the official language of Quebec.

The particular context in which Franco-québécois find themselves is the reason why their common language was promoted through legislative instruments. That these laws put some restrictions on languages other than French is obvious; whether these restrictions violate Anglophone linguistic rights is far from clear. Only public expression is concerned, never private exchanges. In the specific case of signs, only commercial ones are affected. Furthermore, even in the commercial context, the use of other languages is allowed since Bill 86, as long as the French version is markedly prominent. The exact right that is being denied here remains to be defined.

The question of signage and the calls for parity illustrate the more general question of the symbolic place of English in Quebec. It is not the material situation of the community that raises concerns. What is of concern is its symbolic situation. In a few years, from the pre-eminence it had enjoyed, English has been relegated to a subsidiary official position. All of a sudden, the language of a completely autonomous ruling minority was brought under the explicit authority of a majority-controlled democratic government. This subordination was what initially shocked the non-Francophones in 1977; it is instructive that anger was directed neither at the general principle of the necessity to promote French nor at the right of the majority to work in that language, but rather at all the requirements about signs and language tests that reminded Anglophones very concretely of this subordination. It is this obligation to comply with a new social order that people like Brent Tyler and organisations like Alliance Quebec continue to reject. Whether this rejection is shaped by a nostalgic desire to go back to a time when being English in Quebec virtually ensured access to power is a somewhat speculative question; what is certain however is that the refusal of the symbolic loss of official status of English is defining the contemporary radical Anglo-québécois discourses on the Quebec question.

Conclusions

In twenty-five years, the respective places of Anglophones and Francophones inside Quebec changed dramatically: from its subsidiary position, French evolved to be the common public language of all

Quebecers; from an unchallenged symbol of power, English became the language of a minority. This process of symbolic change came as a shock to the Anglo-québécois, a shock, however, from which they have, by and large, recovered. Initial anxieties have been dispelled by the accommodations proposed by the legislator; there now exists a general acceptance of the legitimacy to make the language of the majority the common medium of communication. An attitude of realpolitik is generally adopted in the English-speaking community, as its members can enjoy living in an original culture in which they participate while keeping a direct contact with the rest of North America.

This acceptance has paradoxically left more public space for radical discourses developed in certain sectors of the Anglo-québécois group. By putting forward the notion of parity between English and French, originating from the Anglo-Saxon tradition of individual rights, they seek to promote the interests of their own group, in a continental and historical context that favours them; the same context and the same interests had led the Montreal British merchant class to hold in many respects comparable radical discourses on the Francophone society from their very arrival at the end of the eighteenth century. The contemporary Anglophone critique of the French Language Charter is probably in large part responsible for the perception of the legislation in international circles; this perception is also fuelled by the opinions expressed in English Canadian fora in an effort to discredit the legitimacy of aspirations to sovereignty of many Quebecers.

Apart from these contextual self-interest factors, the reaction to the Quebec language legislation is probably related to moral general cultural values. Such values include, among large sectors of Anglo-Saxon populations, a general distrust of state regulations. State regulations in the economic field are often presented as preventing market forces from following their natural course. A similar perspective seems to be applied to the language domain. Linguistic laws seem largely viewed as a futile attempt to divert linguistic resources from their natural evolution. The French Language Charter is of course a case in point of the possible effectiveness of linguistic legislation. Indeed, if laws had no such effectiveness towards languages, it would pre-empt any claim that they modify their natural evolution. That these modifications are somehow less natural than in unregulated contexts rests on the assumption that an explicit social decision is somehow more constraining than implicit individual choices. However, leaving things up to individual choices means agreeing that some choices will have more weight than others. As with the economy, the invisible hand of linguistic markets is in fact the glove hiding a large number of individual decisions, which reflect more or less arbitrary individual interests and are more difficult to challenge than the visible hand of the legislator. As such, there are no such things as unregulated markets, and the nature of the regulations becomes a matter of choice between two views of the world. One proposes that the state is to intervene to guarantee a greater level of equality between citizens, the other that public forces must refrain from interventions so as not to hinder individual liberties. Such dilemmas are likely to be raised again by current discussions of the Quebec question. With the recent Estate-general on French in Quebec, the linguistic interventions are being increasingly envisaged amongst Francophone intellectual circles in terms of a French Republican model of citizenship, by which a society must ensure the linguistic integration of its members if it is to guarantee their equality and to ensure that they can fully enjoy their civic rights, an innovative development away from the notion of protection in the 1970s and promotion from the mid-1980s. Whether this new perspective will come to sanction the linguistic peace by spelling out the terms of the currently implicit social contract of concerns to Francophones, or whether it would disrupt it by proposing a model perceived by Anglophones to be incompatible with the issue of individual freedom, the emergence of either scenario is to be monitored very closely indeed. That the balance between equality and liberty is a matter of choice by individual nations seems the first principle of tolerance; how different views of the world within the same nation are to be reconciled is one of the challenges raised by the Quebec question.

Note

1 Parts of this chapter were presented at the University of Cambridge in May 2000 before the *Groupe de Recherche et d'Études sur le Canada Français* (GRECF), at the kind invitation of Inès Molinaro. I'm grateful to Inès and to the participants of this forum for their encouraging feedback, as well as to Jorg Matthias. A very special thanks to Lynne Wilcox for her extremely detailed and very useful comments on an earlier version of the chapter.

References

Corpus of press articles

Gathered on 26 November 1999, and covering the previous three months, the following are the texts containing the string 'Brent Tyler' in the online archive of the daily Montreal Anglophone paper *The Gazette*.

Chambers, Gretta, 'The Writing is on the Wall', *The Gazette*, 29 October 1999, http://www.montrealgazette.com/editorial/pages/991029/3066494.html

David, Michel, 'Oil on the Fire: Court Decision on Signs could Revive Sovereignty Movement', *Le Soleil*, 22 October 1999, http://www.montrealgazette.com/editorial/pages/991022/3032991.html

Gordon, Sean, 'Judge Erred on Sign Law, Quebec Says: Province Files Appeal of Ruling', *The Gazette*, 19 November 1999, http://www.montrealgazette.com/news/pages/991119/3171186.html

Gordon, Sean, David Gamble and David Johnston, ' "Provocation or incompetence": Sovereignists would Gain from Crisis', *The Gazette*, 21 October 1999, http://www.montrealgazette.com/news/pages/991021/3027070.html

Johnston, David, 'Sign Law in the Balance Ruling in Quebec Court to Influence Six Other Trials for Infractions of Bill 101', *The Gazette*, 19 October 1999, http://www.montrealgazette.com/news/pages/991019/3015836.html

Johnston, David, 'Fighting for his (Illegal) Sign: Not even a Threat to Lift his Driver's Licence would Make him Pay for Language Violation', *The Gazette*, 14 October 1999, http://www.montrealgazette.com/news/pages/991014/2992235.html

Johnston, David and Sean Gordon, 'Sign Law Quashed Quebec Launches Appeal as Bill 101 Provisions Struck Down', *The Gazette*, 21 October 1999, http://www.montrealgazette.com/news/pages/991021/3026567.html

King, Mike, 'Vandals Target Lawyer and his Sign-law Client', *The Gazette*, 23 November 1999, http://www.montrealgazette.com/news/pages/991123/3188751.html

King, Mike, 'Halt Hunt on Signs: Activists – Alliance Quebec, Equality Party call for Moratorium on Language-law Prosecutions', *The Gazette*, 20 November 1999, http://www.montrealgazette.com/news/pages/991120/3175776.html

Legault, Josee, 'Premier Changes Mind on French: Bouchard Now Says Language is Threatened, but he was Singing Different tune 3 years ago', *The Gazette*, 23 October 1999, http://www.montrealgazette.com/editorial/pages/991023/3038392.html

McPherson, Don, 'Quashing Consensus: When Lawyers, Bureaucrats and Hardliners Prevail, Common sense is Casualty', *The Gazette*, 21 October 1999, http://www.montrealgazette.com/editorial/pages/991021/3026793.html

McPherson, Don, 'Quebec's Hermit Crabs', *The Gazette*, 29 September 1999, http://www.montrealgazette.com/editorial/pages/990929/2925719.html

Wilton Katherine, and Philip Authier, 'Our Mistake: Justice Department Threatened to Suspend Man's Driving Licence over Unpaid Fine for Violating Language Law', *The Gazette*, 15 October 1999, http://www.montrealgazette.com/news/pages/991015/2997488.html

Main studies consulted

Bourhis, Richard Y. (2001) 'French in Quebec', in Joshua A. Fishman, *Can Threatened Languages be Saved?* (Clevendon: Multilingual Matters), pp. 101–41.

Bourhis, Richard Y. (ed.) (1984) *Conflict and Language Planning in Quebec* (Clevedon: Multilingual Matters).

Bredimas-Assimopoulos and Michel Laferière (1980) *Législation et perceptions ethniques: Une étude du contenu de la presse anglaise de Montréal au vote de la Loi 101* (Québec: Office de la langue française).

Caldwell, Gary (1994) *La question du Québec anglais* (Quebec City: Institut Québécois de recherche sur la culture).

Caldwell, Gary and Eric Waddell (1982) *The English of Québec: From Majority to Minority Status* (Quebec City: Institut québécois de recherche sur la culture).

Legault, Josée (1995) *L'invention d'une minorité: les Anglo-Québécois* (Montreal: Boréal).

Levine, Marc V. (1990) *The Reconquest of Montreal: Language Policy and Social Change in a Bilingual City* (Philadelphia: Temple University Press).

Maurais, Jacques (1995) 'L'expérience québécoise d'aménagement linguistique', in Jacques Maurais (ed.), *Politique et aménagement linguistique* (Quebec: Publications du Québec), pp. 359–416.

McLeod Arnopoulos, Sheila and Dominique Clift (1984) *The English Fact in Quebec* (Montreal: McGill-Queen's University Press).

Plourde, Michel et al. (eds) (2000) *Le français au Québec: 400 ans d'histoire et de vie* (Montreal: Fides and Éditions du Québec).

Rudin, Ronald (1985) *The Forgotten Quebecers: A History of English-speaking Quebec, 1759–1980* (Quebec City: Institut québécois de recherche sur la culture).

Scowen, Reed (1991) *A Different Vision: The English in Quebec in the 1990s* (Don Mills: Maxwell Macmillan).

6
A Final Note on Culture, Quebec Native Languages and the Quebec Question

Pierre Larrivée

With Israel and Catalonia, Quebec is considered to be one of the success stories of language planning. These positive results can be explained by the conjunction of three factors, as highlighted by the contributions to this volume. French has always been spoken in Quebec by a significant number of people. These people have always been a majority over the whole of the continuous territory of the province. This territory is managed by a democratically appointed government having some jurisdiction over a wide range of issues. To some degree, these elements presuppose one another. The existence of a government rests on some generally continuous stretch of land – although examples of enclaves are given by Palestine and a few other administrations. The importance of territorial continuity is illustrated in the Canadian context by arguments around the perspective of an independent Quebec: Canadian Federalists refuse the physical separation of Atlantic Provinces from the rest of the country by a sovereign Quebec; Quebec Sovereignists have always opposed the partition of the provincial territory. Territorial distribution influences the cohesion of a linguistic community. The bond between groups speaking the same language in distinct lands tends to loosen (as between French Canadian communities of Quebec origins and Quebecers themselves), and the languages themselves can differentiate to some degree (as with Portuguese in Portugal and Brazil), even where a mere border separates the groups (as with Flemish and Dutch). Especially in those cases where they constitute a majority over a given territory, cohesive groups can in turn determine the agenda of the democratic government that represents them, as illustrated by the Quebec language laws themselves. The governmental, territorial and demographic factors made it possible to transform French from the language of use of a local majority into the official common public language of all Quebecers.

The conditions behind these transformations are not specific to the Quebec question, they also play a key role in other cases of linguistic conflicts. Of particular interest in this regard is the situation of Quebec Native languages. I cannot do justice here to the minute details of often extremely intricate and diverse cases (the interested reader will find a thorough discussion in Maurais (1996), from which I tacitly take much of the information presented below). Much more modestly, my intention is to show how the different political, economic, demographic parameters used in this book to analyse Quebec's language issue can provide insights into other problematic linguistic situations. The discussion will lead to the idea that ultimately, language debates reflect wider cultural considerations relating in particular to collective and personal identity.

The history of the Native populations of the Americas is a long narrative of decline and marginalisation. Aboriginal populations were decimated by epidemics of diseases like smallpox that were brought by the first European waves of explorers. They were further reduced by the wars and conflicts with the ever-expanding colonial settlements. The remaining populations were pushed off their lands, confined to reserves, stripped of political autonomy and restricted to the practice of their traditional economic activities. In every respect, Natives were considered as incapable of determining their own destinies: in Canada, the Federal government was made the sole guarantor of Indians by the 1867 British North America Act.

This marginalisation was continued through a variety of assimilationist measures, notably in schooling. The education of Aboriginal children was entrusted to a number of religious congregations, with the goal of presenting them with elements of the white culture in one of the colonial languages. Although the actions of these congregations might have had a positive influence on the preservation of Native languages through translation of the Scriptures and use in religious ceremonies, religious schooling had a notable negative impact. As elsewhere, the use of the Native languages in school was strictly forbidden and severely punished. In many cases, children were in residential schools away from their communities. Similarly, the adoption of Native children by white people was encouraged for some time; as for adults, until recently, they lost their Indian status if they lived outside reserves, and so did women who married non-Natives.

Attitudes did not start to change until the 1960s. A primary actor in this evolution was the Quebec government. Eager to demonstrate its openness towards culturally threatened communities, the provincial legislator recognised the difficult situation of the First Nations in a series of official declarations: in 1978, it expressed the rights of Native groups to determine the appropriate measures for cultural development and to get the support of the provincial government in this; the preamble of the 1977 *French Language Charter* asserts the linguistic and cultural rights of the Native communities; in 1983, a series of fifteen principles adopted by the Quebec Cabinet recognised Native groups as distinct Nations with the rights to protect and promote their collective identity; these rights along with that of governmental autonomy for the First Nations were reasserted in 1985; a statement towards a general policy in many ways similar to the 1978 declaration was issued in 1989; and the importance of economic development and political self-government was put forward in guidelines for negotiations proposed in 1998.

Much goodwill can be found in these declarations; they do not, however, appear to be guided by a stable set of general principles, have often been put forward without much consultation with Native groups themselves, and have been accompanied by few precise action plans.

To be fair, precise action plans and consultation are difficult in these matters. The Native groups are primarily dependent on the federal government, and have been reluctant to engage in discussions with yet another level of administration: it is not far-fetched to think that pressures on Indian bands have been exerted by federal authorities not to enter into agreements that would have established the credibility of the government of a sovereignist province. Also, a good interlocutor is not always easy to find: with powers limited in the best cases to those of city councils, Native administrations do not necessarily have the prestige to muster the agreement of all; the apparent consensual tradition of decision-taking among First Nations has been claimed to render problematic the settlement of complex issues involving conflicting interests. It must also be mentioned that a uniform policy for all Nations would be highly inappropriate; the situation of the Native groups varies so significantly that applying the same solutions to all could only make matters worse. This variation brought the Quebec government to favour negotiations with specific groups over particular situations, which have produced some tangible results.

The best illustration of a positive agreement is given by the first modern land claim settlement in Canada. In 1973, the courts recognised the territorial rights of Native Nations and called for the suspension of hydroelectric projects in the James Bay on Cree and Inuit territory. This recognition initiated intensive discussions leading to the *James Bay and*

Northern Quebec Agreement. By this convention, the Native communities put themselves under the legal protection of the Government of Quebec, thus renouncing the authority of the federal law on Indians, and agreed to extinguish all territorial claims, following which the building of the dams planned by the government-controlled Hydro-Quebec could legally take place. In exchange, there was not only a confirmation of the rights to pursue traditional activities like fishing, hunting and trapping, but also a large monetary compensation of 225 million Canadian dollars given to the small communities. The compensation was not a simple hand-out; the sums were determined within the frame of detailed plans to establish Cree and Inuit schools, hospitals, and to further the environmental, social and economic situation of these groups. By devolving the administration of health and education to Native authorities, it made the communities responsible for their social development, giving them an opportunity to define their own social interventions and priorities.

A similar *North East Convention* was signed with the Naskapi in 1978. Negotiations with the Attikamekw and the Montagnais led in 1980 to the devolution by the provincial government of the administration of all cultural issues and educational institutions to these groups. Agreements with other Nations on a variety of similar issues were negotiated through the 1980s and 1990s. The cultural and social concerns have extended to such areas as policing, which was in many cases transferred partly or entirely to Native organisations.

In essence, the Quebec government has sought to involve communities in the management of their own affairs at the local level, while retaining the prerogative to set the structures and norms on these matters. Schooling, health and social services as well as policing can and often is provided by the communities themselves; the general framework for education, social and health affairs as well as justice remains that set by the provincial authorities. For instance, although it can be offered in the Native languages, schooling must ensure a working knowledge of French for individuals to be able to contribute to Quebec society and benefit from it if they so wish. The Quebec government is adamant that its authority constitutes the ultimate legal and political frame of reference, as does the integrity of the Quebec territory, and that frame is asserted as a precondition of any negotiations towards political autonomy of Native Nations.

This model is, however, evolving as evidenced by recent developments to the James Bay Agreement. On 23 November, 2001, an agreement aimed at furthering Cree economic autonomy was announced by the Great Chief Ted Moses. By this, the Quebec government guarantees to transfer three and a half billion Canadian dollars over the next fifty years to promote hydroelectric, forest and mining activities on Cree traditional territory. The norms and plans of exploitation of these resources are put under the authority of a joint board. A proportion of all jobs and business opportunities has been agreed to benefit Cree people. At the same time, protected areas where projects are excluded or strictly limited are defined. The provincial government pursued the agreement in order to allow Hydro-Quebec to go ahead with the Eastman-Rupert project; the deal also relieves it from a series of expensive suits that allege its lack of compliance with various aspects of the James Bay Agreement, a claim already accepted by various courts and that had been brought to the attention of the international community by Cree leaders through remarkably efficient and skilful communication campaigns raising sensitive environmental concerns; finally, the proposal of an attractive solution to Native problems establishes the credibility of a sovereignist government, as compared in particular to the inability of the federal administration to free itself from a paternalistic approach to the issue and come up with anything comparable. The Cree representatives were keen to sign such an agreement, as they felt the pressing need to provide a young and growing population – 60 per cent of Crees are under 25 – with economic opportunities that would not only help solve unemployment but also health, education and accommodation crises. Ending long years of judicial and political arguments, what Moses called the 'Peace of the Braves' provides a project of sustainable economic development. What's more, it does so by treating the Native group as a fully-fledged Nation, in its disposition and through the negotiation process led by the highest executive representative of each group. Symbolically, politically and economically, therefore, this agreement constitutes a model which might mark a new, constructive way to further the situation of a minority group.

The increasing autonomy of Aboriginal and Inuit groups has an impact on their overall demographic, political and economic position. Taking into account the variable reliability of census figures, it can be estimated that the Native population of Quebec represents around 1 per cent of the provincial population, with 70,000 people from eleven Nations. The languages associated with the groups found in Quebec belong to three linguistic families, each sharing common characteristics and believed to have evolved from the same original language.

1   The Eskimo-Aleut linguistic family is illustrated by two main varieties of Inuktitut spoken by nearly 9,000 people in fourteen towns and

villages distributed over the large Arctic territory known as New Quebec. Because of the peculiar environment they live in and the original culture that they have developed, the Inuit, as they are now called instead of the apparently derogatory term Eskimo, are generally distinguished from the Aboriginal Nations.

2 The Iroquoian group includes three Mohawk communities of nearly 15,000 people living South of Montreal, at the frontier of Quebec, Ontario and New York State. One Huron community of 2,800 people is also found in a suburb of Quebec city.

3 The Algonquian family is represented by several dialectal varieties of Cree: Eastern Cree comprises 12,500 people in nine reserves on the Quebec coast of James Bay; Naskapi is found in one community of 700 people South of the Ungava Bay; Attikamekw acounts for nearly 5,000 people distributed in three reserves North of the Saint-Maurice river in Central Quebec; Montagnais, now increasingly known as Innus, inhabit ten communities adding up to more than 13,000 people, in the Saguenay area, on the North Shore of the Saint-Lawrence River, and up North near the Naskapi settlement. Belonging to the Ojibwa branch of the Algonquian family, nearly 8,000 Algonquins live in nine reserves in the Abitibi region and in the Ottawa Valley. Micmac, found in three communities in the Gaspé Peninsula of 4,300 Natives, Malecite, represented by less than 500 people in one community near Rivière-du-loup, and Abenaki, with 2,000 members in two communities in the Trois-Rivières area, are also Algonquian groups.

The situation between these groups thus varies enormously in terms of numbers, although none of them is over 15,000 people. Most groups have a relatively high birth rate, with a majority of people under thirty years of age. With the exception of the Mohawk living south of Montreal and of the Huron near Quebec City, most Nations are established far from urban centres, in isolated, small communities that are in a majority of cases not connected by any roads to the outside world. Although all studies demonstrate that the material situation of Quebec Natives is the best in Canada, and therefore presumably in North America, this situation is far from satisfactory, as poverty is still the plight of most Amerindians, and in some communities more than others. While the groups that have signed the James Bay and Northern Quebec Agreement have enjoyed a steady economic development, and other communities closer to urban centres have put together a tourism industry, remote groups have had a hard time to come up with economically attractive projects.

The material setting of these communities has a direct connection with the vitality of their languages. Of particular importance is the mass of speakers and their geographical location. The degree of preservation of Native languages is in direct proportion to their isolation from white population centres, which is parallel to the role of isolation between Anglophone and Francophone communities in the survival of French in Quebec after the Conquest. Inuit, Cree and Montagnais have maintained themselves best, as evidenced by high percentages of knowledge of language and the numbers of monolingual speakers among different age groups. These languages are believed to stand the best chances of surviving as a medium of everyday life, and their promotion is supported by a growing demography, as with the pre-1960s situation of French Quebec. For Natives, this demography ensures that the group can handle their own social and economic development, which is why an agreement like the James Bay one is ideally suited to them. This is not to say that such administrative devolutions are without problems. It is often difficult for local authorities to define plans for their own communities and to find trained Native staff to carry on the mandates. In education, for example, appropriate curricula and teaching staff are difficult to find. The isolation and size of each community and the differences between their needs and expectations makes the sharing of resources and experiences difficult. None the less, the relative vitality of these languages and the promising profiles of the groups that speak them are causes for optimism.

The same optimistic perspective does not apply to all Native groups. When communities have a smaller population, assimilation is liable to occur, especially when they are close to white centres, as is thought to be currently happening with Mohawk communities; where they are isolated or distributed over a large territory as with the Gwich'in language of the North-West Territories, they often do not have the resources to attract sufficient economic development, define their own political agenda and manage their social services. Although these situations have often been conceived as a choice between either retaining one's culture with few if any economic opportunities or abandoning one's identity to enjoy a materially decent life, other options can be elaborated. While it is unlikely that threatened languages can be revived for common everyday use in all spheres of activity by each member of small communities, they may well be preserved in certain specialised domains such as local religious, cultural and social events, on commercial signs, or in some aspects of children's education, from which they can eventually be extended. The support of such languages is not only a matter of imaginative planning by the community,[1] it is also dependent on what prestige it can acquire among other groups. The decision of making Gwich'in one of the official languages of the North-West Territories is a spectacular example of status promotion; another example is the idea that has been proposed to encourage the white population to learn at least some elements of these languages at school or through other means of popular education. This support from outside the community can only encourage its members to reclaim the use of the language in some spheres of activity, with the hope of partially reversing the language shift.

Some other Native groups have lost their languages altogether. This is the case for the Huron community, whose language has been extinct for over a hundred years, due to the group's sustained contacts with whites going back to the French regime, their proximity to French settlements, and the huge demographic losses they suffered through early epidemics and wars with other Native groups. The idea of reviving the Huron language has been considered at different moments, but is faced with a number of difficulties. Linguistically, the structure of the language to be brought back to life must be known through existing texts or otherwise well enough for it to be taught, and for its vocabulary to be adapted to the naming of new contemporary realities. Socially, getting people to learn what is in effect a common foreign language can only happen if the new language serves a strong identiary project with official support, a significant number of speakers and use in several significant spheres of activity without the competition of any existing common language. These factors were behind the successful rebirth of Hebrew in Israel: citizens coming from different parts of the world did not necessarily have one language in common, and the new language was to be used in all spheres of public activities, where it supported the project of building a State based on a religion transmitted in that very language, which was therefore well known and in fact still practised for specific purposes. Unfortunately, few extinct Native languages can benefit from so many favourable conditions. It is true that the Huron community appears to have a strong sense of collective identity, and that this identity was closely associated with the language. However, it is unlikely that reviving Huron would get much official support in a context where there are so many more pressing questions to be addressed; it is not likely that it can serve as a medium of communication in many spheres outside the private domain; even if a sufficient community of speakers could be recreated, they would feel the pressure to revert to the current common language of their community and the surrounding Quebec city area.

The reviving of dead languages, the support of threatened languages and the promotion of living minority languages raise more general questions. In the end, what should motivate language preservation and promotion? Considering the Quebec case, the philosopher Habermas[2] has expressed the view that minority cultures and languages should not be artificially preserved (the key word being 'artificially'). And anyone will agree that whatever the patrimonial loss, groups should not be forced to maintain languages and cultures if they do not wish to do so. This view, however, misses the point that Quebecers were not forced from the outside, as it were, to keep a French culture and language; the language laws and other measures were called for by the bulk of the population, who still strongly support them. This collective will is driven by questions of identity; although the identity of other communities is not necessarily defined in linguistic terms, to be a Quebecer is felt to be strongly tied to the knowledge and everyday practice of French. In those communities where a language is a strong factor of identity, the difficulty of using it in all spheres of public activity provokes insecurity in its speakers, with the self-depreciation of their languages and cultures. The impossibility of using that language results in alienation, the feeling of being submitted to foreign values one is never entirely familiar with. In both cases, the psychological impact on individuals and the community they constitute is shattering. The inability to assert one's identity through culture and language provokes well-documented feelings and attitudes of anguished inhibition. The resulting loss of creativity in all spheres of human activity debases not only the lives of these individuals, but also deprives everyone of their full contribution. It is because low language status and language loss robs everyone of the full contribution of each that languages must be preserved and promoted where individuals and communities for which they constitute a strong identity factor wish to do so. The will of those concerned is thus central as a justification of language planning, but also as its source: in the end, no one can better act on a language than the people who speak it.

Of course, whatever the collective will might be, the promotion of some languages should not be done at the expense of others. The originality of the Quebec linguistic measures lies in great part in their respect towards other groups in the province, as demonstrated by the numerous compromises built into the bills and the conciliatory approach to their application. This attitude is explained by the local democratic tradition, but also by the necessity to accommodate the powerful Anglophone minority group, and the concern for the continental and international image of the State. Having to answer to internal and external interests forces administrations to maintain the delicate balance of rights between the various groups in a multi-lingual environment.

The means of language promotion and preservation also raise questions. Are language preservation and promotion best realised through legislative instruments? It is certainly the case that actions on language can be done without such recourse, but it is equally true that language planning can successfully use legal tools, as eloquently demonstrated by the Quebec case. Could French in Quebec have been supported through means other than legal? Could the objectives of maintaining the demographic status of French speakers in Quebec and of bridging the economic gap with Anglophones be attained by implicit policies, or even no policy at all? After all, it is not unreasonable to think that economic development would have followed the general growth that has characterised the rest of the Western world, from which Francophones would have naturally benefited Quebec Francophones (the key word being 'naturally'), thus enhancing the status of their language. But the linguistic stratification of Quebec before the 1960s leads to the equally rational idea that those speaking French at home might have had to adopt English as the language of work and public life. Although there is a correlation between the economic and the cultural security of a group, the economic progression of a linguistic minority can in no way guarantee the promotion of their culture. Only an explicit official act appears to have been in a position to reverse a well-established and deeply entrenched mode of social interaction into a new social order putting the majority in a better position, from where they can integrate new Quebecers. Only legislative measures appear to have the ability to maintain the prestige of French in Quebec, in view of the national, continental and world predominance of English.

Cultures are not simple adornments any more than languages are mere tools of communication. Both tell individuals what the world is made of, and how to act upon it. Deprived of their reference points, subjects are condemned to a foreign world that they can neither fully understand nor efficiently act upon. As a result, their talent and opportunities are limited, making everybody poorer, not just psychologically, but also in very concrete economic terms. It is in their consideration for the central role of culture in all spheres of human life that the legislative answers proposed to solve the Quebec linguistic question constitute a notable model of language preservation and promotion.

Notes

1 A good example of proposals toward such imaginative planning is provided by André Bourcier (1998), 'Language Planning for Gwich'in and Inuvialuit Communities', MS, Université Laval: http://www.ciral.ulaval.ca/alx/texte.

2   In a conference given at the University of Copenhagen on 23 September 1997, reported by Jacques Caron (1999), 'En marge de *trois essais sur l'insignifiance* de P. Vadeboncoeur', *Tribune*, 10, pp. 17–25.

Reference

Maurais, Jacques (ed.) (1996) *Quebec's Aboriginal Languages: History, Planning and Development* (Clevedon, Avon: Multilingual Matters).

Index